ICC Guide to
Export–Import Basics

The legal, financial and transport aspects of international trade

Guillermo Jiménez

International Chamber of Commerce
The world business organisation

Published in May 1997 by
ICC PUBLISHING S.A. (Paris)

Copyright © 1997
International Chamber of Commerce

Published by arrangement with ICC Publishing S.A.
ICC Publishing, Inc.
156 Fifth Avenue
New York, NY 10010
Telephone: 212-206-1150

ICC Publishing S.A.
38, Cours Albert Ier
75008 Paris, France
E-mail: pub@iccwbo.org
Internet: www.iccwbo.org

ICC Publication No 543
ISBN 92-842-1194-8

Foreword

The diversity and variety of the world's nations are not only a source of delight for humanity, they are also the wellsprings of international commerce. As David Ricardo so memorably observed, the very fact of diversity (hence, the existence of comparative advantage) creates the potential for mutual benefit. The diversity of nations and peoples leads inevitably to the multilateral flows of international trade. Indeed, International trade is the only way for modern societies to satisfy their myriad needs and wants in terms of products and services.

Today exporters and importers do business in a complex marketplace requiring the utmost degree of professionalism, especially when it comes to understanding the interplay of national and international rules, regulations and standards. There is a great need for clear, introductory information, in a format useful for beginners and practitioners alike. The International Chamber of Commerce (ICC), the world business organisation, has sought since 1919 to provide standards and services for exporters and international traders. The ICC also publishes a broad range of books related to international trade. This introductory handbook, therefore, represents a continuation of the ICC effort to provide practical, up-to-date information for the international business community.

Amongst the commercial standards that the ICC has introduced, and which are discussed at length in this handbook, are Incoterms 1990, UCP 500, ICC arbitration, ICC uniform rules for bank and surety guarantees, and ICC model contracts for international transactions. Other basic concepts that exporters and importers need to understand, such as those related to international contracts of sale, are also covered in detail. Indeed, the underlying premise of this text is that trade professionals need a broader understanding of the export transaction. Such an understanding should encompass the procedures of each successive phase of the transaction, from negotiation and contract through shipment and payment. This book attempts to provide that broad overview.

The export-import sector worldwide is massive and growing rapidly. Dynamic companies everywhere are discovering that a key competitive advantage is the firm's ability to master new information. Ignorance and misplaced assumptions can be ruinous in international trade, where legal remedies may in some cases prove costly or unavailable. Knowledge is therefore the best seed capital and the best insurance for international commerce, and it is therefore hoped that the information provided in this book will be of practical use.

Maria Livanos Cattaui
Secretary General
International Chamber of Commerce

Acknowledgements

Over the past few years at the ICC I have had the pleasure of working with leading experts in the law and practice of international trade. Several of them have been kind enough to offer valuable drafting suggestions, and I should like to thank them here: Charles Debattista (to whom I am particularly indebted for his close reading of the manuscript), Ole Lando, Roy Goode, Jan Ramberg, Gary Collyer, Sia Chee Hong, Eric Schwarz, Ben Davis, Gray Sinclair, Alexander Von Ziegler, Jean Guédon, Chaim Shachak, George Effaki, Abdul Latiff Abdul Rahim. I would also like to thank my interns for their invaluable assistance, particularly Emmanuel Jolivet and Karin Gruber, as well as my assistants, Sandra Mackay and Emma Dewar. Pascale Reins of ICC publishing has been the prime mover behind this, as all other, ICC publications, and Anne-Marie Harper has provided invaluable editorial assistance; my other ICC colleagues have also contributed key information and contacts. Finally, I must thank my wife Consuelo and sons Nicolas and Pablo for their forbearance in allowing me to spend too many weekends at the office.

Most of the information in this book was verified as of 1996 and early 1997; however, changes in this rapidly-evolving field are common and the author apologises for any information which may have gone out of date, as well as for any errors or inconsistencies which may remain in the text.

Guillermo Jiménez
Head of Division
International Chamber of Commerce

A Note on Terminology

In general, the terms **exporter** and **importer** will be used to denote the **seller** and **buyer**. However, it should be remembered that especially when intermediaries or brokers are involved, the seller may very well not be the original supplier, nor the buyer the ultimate importer.

The reader should be familiar with at least the following basic terms that may be used to refer to either the exporter or importer in different stages of the export transaction.

Contract of sale
> Exporter – **Seller**
> Importer – **Buyer**

Transport
> Exporter – **Shipper**; **consignor**
> Importer – **Receiver**; **consignee**
> Transport service providers: **carrier**, **shipping line**, **freight forwarder**

Letter of Credit
> Exporter – **Beneficiary**
> Importer – **Opener**; **applicant**; **account party**
> Banks involved –
>> Importer's bank: **issuing bank** (and also, in some cases, **advising bank**, **confirming bank**, **paying bank**)
>> Exporter's bank: **paying bank**, **advising bank**, and/or **confirming bank**

Bill of exchange
> Exporter – **Drawer**
> Importer – **Drawee**

Payment obligations
> Exporter – **Creditor**; **payee**
> Importer – **Debtor**; **payer**

Table of Contents

Chapter One

Beginnings:
an Introduction to Export-Import Practice

"A pocketful of currants, c.i.f. London...."
T.S. Eliot, The Waste Land

The basics: Professional exporters and importers increase profits and reduce risks by relying on time-tested practices and techniques. In particular, the export trade requires a mastery of the relevant contracts and documents. Thus, traders should understand how to construct an effective and complete contract of sale, since this "master" contract will in turn determine the other documents to be procured, such as the transport document (e.g., bill of lading), insurance policy, and payment-related documents (e.g., documentary credit).

1.1 Scope of book

This book is intended as a concise introduction to export-import practice, with a focus on the law, finance, and transport aspects of international trade in goods. It will concentrate on the export sale of *goods*, as opposed to the sale of services or other intangibles, such as intellectual property (i.e., patents, licences, trade-marks, goodwill), or financial products (i.e., securities, funds, stocks, bonds).

Nonetheless, many of the basic concepts of international trade introduced here apply also to more complex, mixed transactions. For example, large infra-structure projects, such as the construction of airports or highways, are often grounded on a system of bank guarantees or performance bonds, discussed in Chapter 8. Moreover, the complexity of major international construction contracts often mandates international commercial arbitration as the only effective way of dealing with disputes. Dispute resolution is discussed in detail in Chapter 3.

1.2 Why export and import? The benefits of international trade

a. **Exporting** – In practice, small firms may begin exporting simply through the receipt of unsolicited orders from abroad, rather than as a result of any formal management decision or export strategy. As the volume of export orders grows, management begins to pay attention to export, and may set up an *export department.* In some cases, small trade ventures have been precursors of mighty export empires. Toyota's exports to Europe in the 1950's started at the initiative of a Danish auto dealer who travelled to Japan and bought a few trial cars.

Sometimes exporting begins after a firm has had a successful showing at a foreign trade show, and starts to receive a volume of export orders. Whatever the initial impetus, it makes sense for companies to invest in export whenever they believe it will maximise their long-term revenues or competitiveness. In the past, many companies exported only after domestic markets had become saturated or when it came to their knowledge that extremely high profit margins could be earned from sales to particular foreign markets. However, in today's increasingly integrated global markets, many companies adopt an export pro- gramme as a necessary part of competitive strategy, i.e., "export or die". If a company's competitors are exporting, it may need to do so as well to avoid being placed at a disadvantage.

One of the main sources of competitive advantage today lies in a company's ability to learn faster than competitors. Export activities, in particular, enhance a company's status as a "learning" organisation. The contact with international cus- tomers and foreign marketing and distribution techniques can teach the firm lessons which may prove useful even in the firm's home market. Economies of scale can be achieved with export training, because once personnel have been trained for international trade with one country, that knowledge can be applied to trade with future markets.

Another attraction of exporting is that selling in more than one country diversifies risk, because the firm is no longer wholly dependant on sales from any single market. Exporting also tends to diminish the impact of a domestic deceleration in sales, because the life cycle in foreign export markets tends to lag behind that of the domestic market. When sales are slow in the domestic market, they are often still strong in the export markets. Transitions can then be made more easily to new products.

Since governments consider strong exports to be essential for a healthy economy, most countries provide a variety of public support services for export- ing firms. This support ranges from publications and expert advice to subsidised export credit insurance and low-cost loans. Local chambers of commerce often provide assistance in terms of training and counsel. Small companies that have not fully investigated possibilities for government support may be unaware of low-cost consulting and finance that would greatly increase their chances of success.

b. Importing – The reverse side of export is import. On the import side, a variety of brokers, sales representatives, agents, wholesale buyers, re-sellers and distributors are occupied with bringing products into the domestic market. Importers are often marketing professionals who work exclusively in the domestic market. Frequently, the only international aspect of their business is the supply contract.

In this text we will focus primarily on the international aspects of the export transaction, and not on the domestic marketing of foreign consumer goods. None- theless, since commercial agency and distributorship are two of the principal frameworks for the importation of goods, we will consider in some detail the mutual interests of the parties as regards international agency and distributorship contracts in Chapter 5.

Particularly in small or rapidly-developing markets, business growth is often focused on the import side. In these markets there may be competition amongst domestic merchants to sign on as agents or distributors for manufacturers of pres- tigious foreign brands. Some very large companies have grown by expanding upon foreign representative status, eventually becoming manufacturers in their own right under license. Thus, Turkey's largest company, Koç Holding A.S., grew in the 1920's and 1930's as an importer of Ford and General Electric products, then became a manufacturer in its own right in the 1940's and 1950's.

One of the advantages of importing is that it provides a relatively low-cost entry into international trade. It is possible to begin to broker import trade transactions even with the most minimal of office facilities. Some very successful import traders started out with nothing more than a table-top and a telephone.

1.3 The need for a professional approach

A professional approach to exporting and importing provides the surest way for companies to manage the risks inherent in international transactions. Ideally, each of the parties involved in an international sale would understand the entire process and its component sub-processes. The exporter and importer, bankers, carriers, insurers, inspectors and customs officials, would understand each others' roles. They would further understand the use of each of the legal, banking and transport documents upon which the transaction is grounded.

In reality, however, one often finds that overall understanding of the export process is insufficient. Traders are often expert, for example, in calculating costs and opportunities, but they may not understand transport logistics, preferring to delegate this to freight forwarders. A trade banker will understand perfectly the documentary credit mechanism, but may not fathom the legal implications of the underlying contract. Likewise, the lawyer may prove ignorant as regards customs clearance; and so on. No one can be expert on everything, but some familiarity with the basics of the entire transaction will help alert traders to those areas where they need to consult specialist colleagues, such as trade bankers, lawyers, insurers or customs agents.

1.4 The risks of exporting and importing

Intelligent risk management is at the heart of international trade. While risk is an element of all commercial transactions, international trade multiplies and adds risks to those encountered in domestic trade:

a. **Transport-related risks** – International transportation tends to involve greater distances, with cargo often changing hands or undergoing prolonged storage, so that there is a greater risk of damage, loss or theft, than in domestic trade. Consequently, importers must understand their legal rights against carriers. If the goods have been damaged through the carrier's fault or negligence, the carrier's liability may depend on the contractual provisions and shipping information contained in the *bill of lading* (a document which evidences the terms of the contract of carriage; examined at length in Chapter 9). Similarly, the importer needs to understand the extent of coverage provided by the insurance policy, because she may need to claim under its provisions if the goods are damaged during transport.

b. Credit risk or non-payment risk – Since it is often difficult for exporters to verify the creditworthiness and reputation of foreign buyers, there is an increased risk of non-payment, late payment, or outright fraud. Consequently, wary exporters frequently insist on payment by *irrevocable documentary credit*, (examined in detail in Chapter 6), or make use of other security devices (see Chapter 8).

c. Quality of goods risk – Importers may find it difficult to physically check the quality of the goods before shipment, and thus it may happen that they do not receive goods of the quality they had expected. One way of avoiding this is for the importer to insist on provision of an *inspection certificate*.

d. Exchange rate risk – If a price has been set in a particular currency in an international contract, subsequent exchange rate fluctuations (between the contract currency and the accounting currencies of the parties) will inevitably benefit one party at the cost of the other. The easiest solution for a party wishing to avoid uncertainty is simply to stipulate contractual prices in one's own currency (note that this simple method does not truly *avoid* currency risk, because the trader still has the risk that her own currency will weaken between the time of contract and the time of payment). Quoting prices in one's own currency is useful for small firms because it standardises the currency of payment, which can facilitate accounting and cash-flow projections. However, in many cases it is commercially necessary to make quotes in various foreign currencies. In such cases, exporters will seek to protect themselves from exchange rate fluctuations, such as by purchasing foreign exchange *forward* or *option* contracts, sometimes referred to as *hedge* contracts.

e. Unforeseen events – A strike, natural disaster or war may render delivery impossible. Unexpected events may also dramatically alter the cost of transport, by raising the price of shipping fuel or by closing off the most economical routes. Well-drafted contractual *force majeure* provisions can help protect the parties; these are dealt with further in Chapter 4.

f. Legal risks – Foreign laws or regulations may change or be applied differently than in the past, impeding or frustrating the transaction. A customs licence may suddenly prove impossible to obtain. Moreover, whenever a contract is subject to the jurisdiction of foreign courts under foreign law, there arises the risk that it may prove impossible for the other party to obtain speedy justice in the event of a dispute. This is one reason why exporters and importers alike often seek to impose *choice of law* and *choice of forum* clauses, which stipulate that disputes will be settled under their own, national law and courts. One way out of the resultant negotiating impasse is to contractually stipulate that dispute-resolution will be by *international commercial arbitration*, such as that supervised by the *ICC International Court of Arbitration* (see chapter 3).

g. Investment risks – The normal commercial risks involved in marketing any product become magnified in the export context because of the additional investments required by an export programme. For example, a market which has been steadily growing for several years may suddenly decline (e.g., due to exchange rate instability), before an exporter can amortise investments in local distribution. Companies should begin by seriously considering whether or not to export at all. Some firms are not quite ready to export, and some may never be able to compete internationally and should concentrate on domestic niches. To launch a proper export effort requires the commitment of resources which can be irretrievably lost in the event of failure. This author is aware of companies which have gone bankrupt after investing heavily and over-optimistically in export operations which subsequently foundered.

1.5 The role of standard documents and systems

International trade is flourishing today because traders have learned to manage and overcome the risks listed above. Export-import risk management is based on documentary systems and customs which translate the rights, costs and responsibilities of the export process into documentary equivalents. Thus, the export process is actually twofold, involving :
    1) the real shipment of physical goods, and
    2) the complementary documentary exchanges.

This documentary system developed centuries ago through transactions referred to as "documentary sales" under the classic "shipment" trade terms, FOB and CIF[1]. Documentary sales have been considered by courts of law to be transactions in *documents* to the same extent that they are transactions in *goods*. It is just as important for the exporter to provide the correct documents as it is for him to provide the correct goods.
The key documents in this scheme can be quickly enumerated:
    1) the contract of sale,
    2) bill of lading (or other transport document),
    3) payment-related documents (particularly the documentary credit and bill of exchange or bank draft), and
    4) insurance document (policy, certificate or note).

A good deal of this book is devoted to a discussion of the relationship between these documents. Other important documents include the inspection or quality certificate and certificate of origin. Inspection and understanding of the above documents must be as painstaking as that related to the goods.
    While there are advantages to this documentary system, there are also inherent risks. Paper documents are particularly susceptible to forgery, alteration or simple misrepresentation. In some cases, an importer may find that the documents presented are apparently conforming, but that the goods delivered contain defects. The unfortunate importer may be unable to stop or avoid payment, despite the exporter's breach of contract. Importers seek to protect themselves from these risks by carefully checking the identity of their counterparties, and in cases of doubt, by calling for verification, such as that provided by an inspection certificate.
    On the exporter's side, the documentary system has a drawback in that the fulfilment of physical delivery does not excuse documentary failures. Thus, it is possible for an exporter to substantially perform a contract and yet find himself unable to receive prompt or complete payment, as a result of a failure to comply with a documentary formality. This is particularly a problem for small exporters

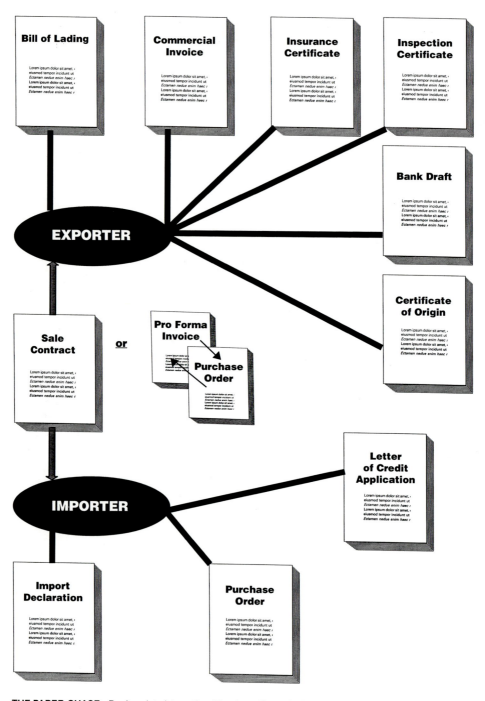

Bill of Lading

Commercial Invoice

Insurance Certificate

Inspection Certificate

Bank Draft

EXPORTER

Certificate of Origin

Sale Contract

or

Pro Forma Invoice

Purchase Order

Letter of Credit Application

IMPORTER

Import Declaration

Purchase Order

THE PAPER CHASE : Don't go into international business if you don't like documents — the export trade is a documentary game. A typical CIF transaction may call for 10 or more important documents.

who have requested payment by documentary credit, but then find that their own faulty record-keeping makes it impossible for them to present conforming documents in time. What was intended to be an irrevocable credit now becomes a credit conditional upon the importer's willingness to waive objections to the documentary discrepancies. The all-too-common result is delayed payment or other payment difficulties.

The only solution, for exporters and importers alike, is to make sure *before* entering into an international contract of sale that they thoroughly understand the documentary obligations that will be required of them.

Example: In a case in which goods were sold on terms "c.i.f. Hong Kong shipment from continental port not later than 31st October", the goods were actually shipped *after* that date, but the bill of lading was forged to indicate shipment on time. The buyers discovered the forgery only after having accepted physical delivery of the goods and did not make any objection to the quality of the goods delivered. The court observed:

> *"[T]here is a right to reject documents, and a right to reject goods, and the two things are quite distinct. A c.i.f. contract puts a number of obligations upon the seller, some of which are in relation to the goods and some of which are in relation to the documents. So far as the goods are concerned, he must put on board at the port of shipment goods in conformity with the contract description, but he must also send forward documents, and those documents must comply with the contract."*

– Kwei Tek Chao v. British Traders & Shippers Ltd. (1954) 2 QB 459

Documentary safeguards, such as those provided by the documentary credit or inspection certificate, can only do part of the overall job of countering international trade risk. Other important services, such as credit investigations, export credit insurance, and factoring, can help complete the risk-reduction plan. Moreover, traders should in general adopt verification procedures for all proposed international transactions – international fraud is a reality and all trade professionals should be aware of the need to verify credentials and deal only with established and well-known partners.

1.6 Cultural and language differences

Misunderstandings in international transactions can arise because the parties come from different cultures and express themselves with differing vocabularies.

Example: An Australian importer of clothing recounts the following story: He had ordered a custom shipment of 5,000 rugby shirts from a foreign supplier. The importer requested a sample shirt to test for cotton content in the fabric. He cut off one of the sleeves of the shirt at the elbow, extracted a few fibres, and tested them. Satisfied, he returned the shirt with the notation: "OK – send shipment as agreed." Several months later he received an irate call from a major clothing distributor, to whom the shipment had been sent directly. The client had received 5,000 rugby shirts – each missing one sleeve!

Not only do cultural and business practices differ across national borders, there are also differing tax systems, regulations, accounting methods, currency controls and customs systems. The same legal term, such as "agent", may have different legal connotations in different jurisdictions. Technical and product standards may differ, as well as consumer tastes. Providing after-sales service to remote markets may be prohibitively expensive, with the result that foreign products can acquire a bad reputation. Also, translating marketing brochures and technical manuals into foreign languages can be unexpectedly time-consuming and costly, especially when the documents must be frequently revised or updated.

1.7 Solutions: examples of risk management for export-import

Well-established professional practices enable traders to manage the above-described risks:

■ **The risk of misunderstanding**, e.g., risk of disagreements over payment terms or quality conditions; risk of having to undertake a legal action in a foreign, biased forum.
Solutions:
– substantial credit checking of counterparties; demanding references
– negotiating firmly for minimum legal protection, or refusing deal
– well-drafted contracts and general terms and conditions, including provisions for choice of law/forum, arbitration
– specify Incoterms 1990
– well-researched and well-prepared contract negotiations

■ **The exporter's risk of non-payment**
Solution:
– suitable payment securities, such as the documentary credit under UCP 500
– alternative: open account terms backed by standby credit

■ **The importer's risk that goods of inadequate quality will be shipped**.
Solution:
– requirement of inspection certificates made out by recognised authorities

■ **The risk that the other party will not go ahead with performance as promised.**
Solution:
– partial advance payment, bank guarantees, standby credits; also, use of performance bonds

■ **The risk that the goods will be damaged in transit, or lost, or that part of the shipment will be stolen.**
Solutions:
– sufficient insurance coverage against all likely contingencies, and attention to stipulations in the bill of lading
– the contract of carriage
– proper packaging and shipment instructions

■ **The exporter's risk that an apparently good customer will manage to receive the goods and then seek to avoid paying; the importer's risk of outright fraud.**

Solutions:
- – thorough credit investigations of prospective partners
- – membership in and/or utilisation of ICC Commercial Crime Services.

1.8 Typical export transactions

International transactions can take an endless variety of forms. The most common categories are summarised below.

1.8.1 The case of a documentary sale

Note: At the risk of some over-simplification, we will now sketch the broad outlines of a "typical" export transaction: *a shipment of consumer goods on CIP Incoterms 1990 in conjunction with payment by confirmed, irrevocable documentary credit*[2]. *This type of transaction will be the focus of much of this book and will be explored in greater detail in Chapters 2 through 9.*

a. **The contract of sale: offer and acceptance – pro forma invoice – general conditions of sale** – Commonly, the *exporter* makes known his range of goods and prices at trade shows or through the direct-mail circulation of catalogues and brochures. Thereafter, he receives an inquiry from an *importer*, requesting a price quote for a certain amount of goods of a specified quality. At that point, the exporter may issue some kind of contractual *offer*, including a price quote. A common technique is for the exporter to send a *pro forma invoice*, a document which specifies the basic terms and conditions of sale, including the price, delivery and payment terms. Since the pro forma invoice is meant to precisely mirror the *commercial invoice* which will be sent to the importer when the transaction is completed, the likelihood of disputes is reduced – the importer can see in the pro forma invoice exactly what she will pay for if she goes through with the deal, in particular as regards transport or insurance costs.

In law, a contract is formed when the seller's offer receives the buyer's unequivocal *acceptance*. The acceptance required to form the contract can be supplied by the buyer's *purchase order*, indicating assent to the prices and conditions contained in the pro forma invoice.

Since a pro forma invoice does not contain many legal stipulations, exporters commonly append *general conditions of sale* to the pro forma invoice, thereby providing a detailed legal framework in support of the brief recitals contained in the pro forma invoice.

This exchange of pro forma invoice and purchase order is just one way to form a contract. It is, of course, also possible (and frequently preferable) to draft a specific *contract of sale* for a particular transaction, to be signed by both parties. A good example is the ICC model contract discussed in detail in chapter 4. In practice, the actual form of international sale contracts varies immensely, ranging from lengthy and precise documents to terse exchanges of telexes or fax communications.

b. **The payment and delivery terms: documentary credits – Incoterms 1990 –** When the exporter does not know the importer or is unable to obtain sufficient credit information about her, the exporter may wish to insist on payment by a

EXPORT DOCUMENTS – PRO FORMA INVOICE

Copyright ©1996 UNZ & CO.

SHIPPER/EXPORTER		PRO FORMA INVOICE NO.	DATE
Glotz Industries 1492 Columbus Blvd. Fort Wayne, IN 12345-6789		TO-06	July/4/96

COUNTRY OF ORIGIN
USA

CONSIGNEE
Widgets by Otto Rudiger Paschold Strasse Baden-Baden, Germany

TERMS
Sale: CIP Hamburg
Payment: Irrevocable L/C calling for "received for shipment" ocean B/Ls

EXPORT REFERENCES
Currency: U.S. Dollars

NOTIFY
Zoll Clearance
6 Haberkamp Strasse
Stuttgart, Germany

Marine Cargo Insurance at 110% CIP value
all risks plus war risk plus strike
and civil commotion risk coverage

FORWARDING AGENT
A. N. Deringer
29320 Goddard Rd.
Romulus, MI 48174

EST. SHIPPING DATE
Within 45 days of receipt of order and L/C

VALIDITY
Thirty days from July 4/96

Terms of sale and terms of payment for this offer are governed by Incoterms 1990 (ICC 460), UCP 500 for letters of credit, and URC 522 for documentary collections.

PKGS.	QUANTITY			DESCRIPTION OF MERCHANDISE	UNIT PRICE	TOTAL VALUE
	6000 ea			Blue widgets (HS# 123456)	$ 4.00	$ 24000.00
				TOTAL EXW FORT WAYNE, IN		$ 24000.00

Approximate gross weight 19,300 kg.
Packing: one 20 foot container

MISC. CHARGES (Packing, Insurance, etc.)

Total Carriage	$ 1900.00
Forwarding	$ 100.00
Marine Cargo Insurance	$ 151.20

CIP HAMBURG	INVOICE TOTAL	$ 26151.20

CERTIFICATIONS
We certify that this proforma invoice is true and correct, and that the origin of these goods is the United States of America.

AUTHORIZED SIGNATURE

Concluding an export contract

Advertising

EXPORTER

1.
Exporters market their products to potential importers. This results in enquiries from prospective customers.

Buyer's enquiry

IMPORTER
2.
The importer's enquiry is generally considered an invitation to negotiate.

Sales offer

3.
The exporter may make a precise sales offer; these are commonly presented in the form of a Pro Forma Invoice.

Purchase order

Negotiation

4.
If the importer's purchase order precisely reflects the terms of the offer, it may constitute an acceptance, concluding a contract. Otherwise, new terms may be treated by the Exporter as a counter-offer.

New proposal

New negotiations

5.
When the exporter is satisfied that the importers purchase order is acceptable, he may wish to confirm this with an acknowledgement of order.

Order

Acknowledgement of order

Contract

confirmed, irrevocable *documentary credit* (commonly referred to as a "letter of credit"), a payment mode which offers certain security features for the exporter. In our case, the exporter quotes a *"CIP" Incoterms 1990* price, which means that the price includes freight to destination, plus insurance. *Incoterms 1990* are a set of 13 standard "trade terms" (such as FOB, CIF or EXW), developed by the ICC. Incoterms define various cost and risk obligations of the parties and are dealt with in detail in chapter 4. In this case, we will assume that the exporter deliberately used CIP Incoterms 1990 rather than CIF Incoterms 1990. CIF stands for "cost, insurance and freight," and was developed in the context of the maritime shipment of general cargo, while CIP stands for "carriage and insurance paid to..." and has replaced CIF as the appropriate Incoterm for containerised and multimodal shipments. We will assume in our example that we are dealing with goods shipped in containers and which will be transferred from one kind of transport conveyance to another ("multimodal" transport).

c. **Transport: the freight forwarder – the bill of lading –** The exporter commonly prepares his shipment with the assistance of a *freight forwarder,* who books space for the cargo and may in addition take care of customs formalities. Under *CIP Incoterms 1990,* the exporter must respect an Incoterms requirement to obtain insurance coverage for 110% of the value of the goods (the extra 10% is meant to cover the minimum profit anticipated by the importer; it is possible to request greater coverage).

The use of CIP enables the exporter to structure the contract on the basis of a multimodal transport document, which can provide payment and transport benefits. In contrast, under CIF (which should be used *exclusively* for maritime shipments) the exporter must provide the importer with *a marine bill of lading,* sometimes called a *"shipped"* bill of lading. A marine bill of lading indicates that the goods have been loaded on board a seagoing vessel. In our example, however, we assume that the goods are delivered to the carrier at an inland terminal, far prior to the loading of the goods on board a seagoing vessel. In such cases, the exporter cannot immediately obtain a marine bill of lading. He can, however, receive from the carrier some form of *multimodal transport document.* When payment is to be by documentary credit, the exporter may be paid more promptly if the documentary credit has specified a multimodal transport document, rather than a marine bill of lading. With the multimodal document, the exporter can obtain an assurance of payment immediately after delivery to the local inland terminal; otherwise he will have to wait until the goods are loaded on board in the distant port.

The exporter must also be aware under CIP sales that he is responsible for export customs formalities, such as obtaining an export license. Import formalities and duties, conversely, are for the importer's account. An experienced export trader understands that there are often disputes about unloading or discharging costs under CIP and CIF, so he may choose to specify in the pro forma invoice or contract of sale that all unloading charges are for importer, in which case this arrangement should also be made clear in the exporter's instructions to his freight forwarder. When the goods are delivered to the carrier, the exporter, as *shipper,* receives from the carrier the *bill of lading.* This central document acts as a receipt indicating that the goods were received in apparent good order and quantity, and also stipulates the contractual rights of the holder of the bill of lading against the carrier.

d. Issuance of the documentary credit– In our example the contract specifies payment by *letter of credit* or *documentary credit* (they mean the same thing). In the bank's terminology, the importer is referred to as the *applicant* or the *account party*. The exporter is referred to as the *beneficiary* of the documentary credit. The letter of credit contains the terms and conditions under which the bank will pay. Generally, this includes a listing of documents which the beneficiary (exporter) must furnish, such as the commercial invoice, insurance certificate, packing list, inspection certificate, bill of lading, etc.

e. Confirmation of the credit – Let us assume in this example that the beneficiary has stipulated that the credit be *confirmed.* By this, the exporter requires the importer to obtain from another bank (usually one located in the exporter's country) a confirmation of the credit, which means that the confirming bank adds its own irrevocable undertaking to pay under the terms and conditions of the credit. This may be considered advantageous by the exporter who prefers to work with a relatively close and reliable paymaster. Let us assume that the confirming bank agrees to confirm the credit. NOTE: not *all* credits are confirmed; confirmation is an additional bank service performed for a fee, and therefore should only be requested when the exporter expects a significant benefit to be derived from confirmation. Generally, confirmation makes sense whenever the exporter does not wish to take the risk that the issuing bank may become unable to pay under the credit (as for example, should the issuing bank become insolvent).

f. Shipment of the goods and presentation of documents for payment– The exporter prepares the shipment and instructs the freight forwarder to obtain the necessary transport document. After shipment of the goods, the exporter goes to the confirming bank and presents the various documents required under the credit. The confirming bank takes up the documents, examines them, and if it finds them *conforming* to the conditions of the credit, gives or promises to give value to the exporter under the credit. There are different ways that the exporter can get paid, depending on the type of credit. He can be paid immediately (sight credit) or at a later time (deferred payment credit), or a draft payable in the future can be discounted for a partial, immediate payment (acceptance or negotiation credit). Documentary credits are explored in detail in Chapter 6.

The confirming bank will transmit the documents to the issuing bank, which, if it finds they are conforming, will in due time reimburse the confirming bank for the funds it has paid out under the credit, and will then turn the documents over to the importer and debit her account for the amount of the credit. The importer will use the transport documents to obtain delivery of the goods from the carrier. This is assuming that everything works out as planned. However, it should be kept in mind that shipping documents frequently contain errors when they are first presented to the bank for payment, and correction and/or waiver of these discrepancies may take time and in some cases even delay or impede payment.

g. Disputes arising out of the transaction– But now let us say that there is a dispute. The market price for the contract goods has fallen very rapidly and the importer wants to escape the contract, the fulfilment of which would be ruinous for her. An unscrupulous or uninformed importer might instruct the issuing bank to "stop payment", claiming the goods were not up to contract quality. Such an importer might claim that an insufficient quantity of goods was delivered, that the insurance coverage was insufficient, or that the carrier damaged some of the goods. However, if the beneficiary is able to present conforming documents, the bank must normally pay or accept drafts against the documents. The only exception is for cases involving manifest *fraud*.

Payment under a letter of credit is not necessarily the end of the story. If it is true that the goods are not of contract quality, then the importer may seek legal redress against the exporter, even though the exporter may have already received payment under the credit. The availability of such a remedy will depend on the law applicable to the transaction, which will in turn depend on provisions in the contract of sale. For example, the parties may have specified that all disputes will be settled under the ICC Rules for Arbitration and Conciliation, in which case arbitration will become the mandatory form of dispute-resolution. Commonly, the exporter's general terms and conditions will include *choice of law* and *choice of forum* clauses, which specify that disputes will be settled under the commercial law, and in the courts, of the exporter's country (see Chapters 2 and 4).

h. **Liability of carriers and coverage of insurance** – If, in fact, the goods are damaged or short-delivered, the ability of the importer to recover from the insurance company will depend on whether or not the damage arises from a cause or circumstance excluded from coverage under the insurance policy. If the damage or loss is a result of the carrier's acts, the importer or her insurer may be able to recover damages from the carrier, but this will depend on the exclusions and limitations on liability contained in the carrier's bill of lading, as well as on the law applicable to the bill.

1.8.2 Common variants on the basic export sale

a. **Ongoing contracts – instalment, supply, output or "line" contracts** – The example of an international sales transaction above was based on the assumption of a "one-off" or "spot" transaction: the one-time sale of a particular cargo under a single contract. In some cases, partial shipments or partial payments can also be encompassed under this basic paradigm. But a different kind of contractual relationship altogether arises when the contract is designed to have a significant duration, as when an importer agrees to purchase the entire output of a particular exporter's factory over a period of years. In these kinds of contracts, it is very important that flexibility be built into the arrangement; for example, by allowing price adaptation according to a particular formula. Particular financing arrangements, such as those of the *revolving credit*, may be called for; these are examined in Chapter 6.

b. **"String" contracts** – In these situations, the "exporter" or "importer" is really only one in a chain of sellers and re-sellers. Transferable and back-to-back credits, dealt with in Chapter 6, are common payment methods in this context.

c. **Different payment mechanism** – Although documentary credits are a very common payment mode in international trade, their expense and complexity are such that they are most advisable in situations of imperfect trust or knowledge between the parties, or when otherwise called for by governmental restrictions. In other situations, such as when both parties are well-established and credit-worthy, *open account* terms are more common – the exporter simply invoices the importer after shipment, granting her a certain credit period. As we will see in Chapters 6 and 8, this kind of arrangement can be risky for the exporter. Another type of payment mode, the *documentary collection*, provides the exporter more protection than open account, though not as much as an irrevocable documentary credit. In a collection process, the exporter forwards shipping documents and a draft, for example, to a bank in the importer's country. To obtain the documents which will allow access to the goods, the importer must pay or accept to pay the draft. With collections, the exporter is at least assured that the importer cannot physically obtain the merchandise without paying or agreeing to pay.

In an increasingly popular payment variant, the exporter agrees to grant the importer favourable open account terms, but only on the condition that the importer issue a *standby credit* or bank guarantee as a payment security. In the contract, the credit or guarantee functions much like a cash deposit, available for the exporter. If the importer fails to pay the invoice, all the exporter has to do is present a copy of the invoice (or other document stipulated under the credit or guarantee) to be assured of payment. Clearly, the importer is exposed to the risk that the exporter will claim the standby credit in bad faith. These types of payment mechanisms are reviewed at length in Chapter 6.

d. **Contracts for the sale of services or other intangibles** – International contracts for the provision of services are beyond the scope of this text. They may, for example, call for an understanding of local employment laws. Similarly, we will not touch upon to any great deal contracts for the cross-border sale of intellectual and industrial property, such as patents and licences. Nonetheless, international franchising contracts – which frequently involve intellectual property rights – will be discussed in Chapter 5. The international sale of securities and financial instruments is a highly-specialised field subject to specific national regulatory regimes, and will not be discussed here.

1.8.3 Other types of international transactions/agreements

a. **Agency and distributorship relationships** – Agency and distributorship are two common modes of export distribution in which the exporter reaches the foreign consumer through the assistance or representation of a foreign intermediary. In the case of agency, the foreign agent merely markets the exporter's products, leaving the contract of sale to be concluded directly between the exporter and the foreign customer. The agent's income is usually derived from a percentage commission on the sales made in his territory. In the case of distributorship, the distributor buys the exporter's products and then re-sells them in the distributorship territory. The distributor's earnings come from the difference between the price at which he buys from the exporter and the re-sale price to the domestic customer.

Both of these types of arrangements are therefore complementary to international contracts of sale. Agency and distributorship will be explored in detail in Chapter 5, with particular reference to the model contracts developed by the International Chamber of Commerce.

b. **International tenders** – In the tendering process an employer or customer issues a public invitation for *bids* (contractual offers) on a particular project. The purpose is to stimulate competition between the various bidders and enable the customer to select the lowest price offered. Common examples of customers using the tendering process are large governmental entities or major corporations. The public tendering process not only provides a mechanism for eliciting competitive prices, it reduces the likelihood of granting contracts on the basis of corruption or inside connections. Although the project which is at the heart of a tendering process may generate a series of "typical" export transactions, we will not examine international tendering processes in themselves at any length. Nonetheless, Chapter 8 on bank guarantees is relevant to international tenders because of the widespread use of tender guarantees, bid guarantees, and other *demand or surety guarantees* in the tendering process and the subsequent project-implementation period.

A related area is that of *project finance,* which covers the array of sophisticated financial devices underlying major construction or infrastructure projects, such as the building of power plants, airports or highways. There are a wide variety of approaches encountered today in project finance, but one increasingly common feature is that lenders are willing to rely to some extent on the revenues generated by the project itself to repay the loan. Although, as noted above, the use of guarantees and bonds is relevant in this context, project finance is not otherwise treated in any detail in this text. It should be noted, nonetheless, that the great complexity of legal questions which can be generated by such projects, with the attendant possibility of *conflict of law* confusion, frequently militates for the selection of *international commercial arbitration*, covered in Chapter 3, as the most appropriate dispute-resolution scheme.

c. **Cross-border finance leasing** – Finance leasing is a form of financing for the acquisition of equipment or supplies which enables the importer, in this case referred to as the *lessee,* to obtain the desired goods without taking on a direct loan. The lessee takes possession of the goods, uses them, pays a monthly instalment on the lease, and at the end of the lease period may acquire full ownership of the goods with the final payment. Under many tax systems, leasing is attractive because the lease payments can be deducted. In a cross-border context, one of the primary legal concerns is the status of the lessor in the event that the lessee becomes insolvent before the end of the lease period. Can the lessor recover the goods, or will they first be subject to the liens of the lessee's other creditors – such as, for example, those of the local tax collector? The answer will depend in particular on the national insolvency law. Finance leasing is a highly specialised field and will not be dealt with in detail in this text. However, note the relevance to finance leasing of our discussion in Chapter 4 on *retention of title*, a contractual device by which the exporter asserts his property rights in the goods until the purchase price has been paid in full.

d. **International Franchising** – Franchising is a form of shared investment in the expansion and replication of successful business systems. Typically, the owner of the successful business format or system, the *franchisor*, sells or leases the right to exploit the system to a local investor, the *franchisee*. Franchising has proven itself to be particularly useful in an international context, because it allows the franchisor to grow rapidly in foreign markets with a minimum of direct capital investment. In the international context, it is useful to distinguish two types of franchise agreement:

■ **Direct (unit) franchise contract** – A direct agreement between the domestic franchisor and the franchisee who operates the foreign franchise.

■ **Master franchise contract** – An agreement between the domestic franchisor and a foreign master franchisor. The master franchisor is authorised to grant sub-franchises (i.e., enter into direct/unit franchise contracts) in the territory. A master franchise structure is particularly suitable for international trade because it allows for flexibility and local supervision.

Franchising contracts can be extremely complex and in some jurisdictions must conform with local laws for the protection of franchisees. The ICC is currently engaged in developing a model set of clauses for international direct/unit franchising contracts, which will be discussed in Chapter 5.

e. **International licensing and transfer of technology** – Many high-technology or engineering firms have found that they can generate substantial revenues in foreign markets by *licensing* the right to use their patents, trademarks, copyrights, trade secrets and or technical processes. As with franchising, licensing provides the exporter with a way of penetrating foreign markets with little or no direct investment. From the importer's side, many companies find that as licences, or purchasers of licences, they may acquire and profitably exploit in their home markets new processes or products. Because of the complex, special rules applying to intellectual property rights, this subject matter is beyond the scope of this text.

f. **Countertrade** – In countertrade transactions an element of barter or an ancillary purchase obligation is attached to the underlying export transaction. Although countertrade transactions adopt myriad forms, it is not uncommon for them to involve governmental entities of developing economies. Typically, the exporter will insist that as part of a particular transaction the importer additionally agree to a purchase of a separate group of goods, which, for example, may be relatively unattractive from a commercial point of view but which the exporting country wishes to convert into ready cash. Countertrade, which is said to account for a considerable portion of world trade (from 5% to 30% according to certain studies), is frowned upon by international trade organisations because it tends to distort international markets.

1.9 International organisations and chambers of commerce

1.9.1 Chambers of Commerce

Local, regional and national chambers of commerce often contain international departments for assisting exporters. Many chambers organise seminars and provide information on export procedures. Commonly, large or well-funded chambers will also organise trade missions, and help new exporters find agents and distributors in foreign markets. The first *chambre de commerce* was established in 1599 in Marseilles. The concept caught on and expanded in the 18th and 19th centuries, with chambers opening in New York (1768), Calcutta (1834) and Paris

(1873). Today, virtually every major city in the world has an active chamber of commerce. The *International Bureau of Chambers of Commerce (IBCC)*, an *ICC* affiliate, acts as the world forum and information-centre on chamber of commerce activities. Currently, the IBCC is involved in several projects aimed at providing electronic network services to international traders through local chambers of commerce. The IBCC oversees an international computer network that provides exporters and importers with a "cyber-market" for posting trade leads and requests.

1.9.2 The International Chamber of Commerce – Supplier of Tools and Standards for International Trade

The International Chamber of Commerce (*ICC*), a world business organisation based in Paris, is of fundamental importance in international trade. Although the ICC's activities are diverse, of primary interest to the exporter and importer is the ICC's role as a developer of international commercial, legal and banking standards. Thus, the ICC developed the rules that govern global documentary credit (letter of credit) practice – *the UCP 500*. On the legal side, the ICC's *International Court of Arbitration* is probably the world's foremost private commercial dispute-resolution forum. The *ICC Incoterms 1990*, standard trade terms such as FOB and CIF, define the legal content of price quotes in international transactions.

Objectives – The ICC serves world business by promoting trade and investment and open markets for goods and services, as well as the free flow of capital. It defends the private enterprise system and encourages self-regulation by business. Founded in 1919, the ICC is a non-governmental organisation of thousands of companies and business associations in more than 140 countries. Approximately 60 ICC National Committees throughout the world present ICC views to their governments and alert Paris headquarters to national business concerns.

Membership and revenues – The ICC is financed partially through revenues received from dues paid by its 7000 member companies and trade associations to ICC National Committees. A further important share of the ICC's revenues is derived from the administrative fees earned by the ICC Court of International Arbitration. Additional income is generated by the marketing of ICC rules and codes, as well as other books (ICC Publishing) and seminars.

Special status – The ICC has Class 1 (top-level) consultative status with the *United Nations (UN)*, where it puts forward the views of business in industrialised and developing countries. It also maintains close working relations with the newly-established *World Trade Organisation (WTO)*, the *Organisation for Economic Co-operation and Development (OECD), the European Commission,* and other intergovernmental and non-governmental bodies. ICC permanent representatives at the UN in New York and Geneva monitor developments affecting business within the UN and its specialised agencies. The ICC ensures that business concerns are brought to the attention of governments, through statements from its international headquarters in Paris, and via the representations of ICC national committees throughout the world.

Business self-regulation – The ICC also draws up voluntary codes for business which set *ethical standards*. Its *Business Charter for Sustainable Development* contains 16 principles governing every aspect of a company's activities in relation to the environment from product design to customer advice. The ICC's *Marketing and Advertising Codes* cover ethical conduct as regards direct marketing, advertising, sales promotion, marketing research, environmental advertising and sponsorship. Recently, the ICC has issued revised rules against corruption, bribery and unethical business practices in international trade.

ICC Commissions and Working Parties – Forums for international business policy – Specialist ICC *Commissions* meet regularly to review issues affecting world business. They cover a wide range of sectors, among them banking, competition, the environment and energy, financial services, insurance, intellectual property, marketing, transportation, taxation, and trade and investment policy. These Policy Commissions are, in effect, international committees of top-level traders, lawyers, carriers, bankers and other professionals. When a particular Commission decides to undertake a project, it creates a sub-committee, known as a *Working Party,* to accomplish the given task.

Many of the ICC's key instruments are products of these high-level Working Parties. For example, the revision of the Incoterms or UCP is initially entrusted to a small Working Party operating as a drafting team. Revised drafts are then circulated broadly and internationally through ICC National Committees, with the resulting comments channelled back to the Working Party. Final drafts, once approved by the Working Party and Commission, are submitted for adoption by the ICC Executive Board. Although the broad international consultation entailed by this procedure is quite time-consuming, it ensures that official ICC products carry a certain authority as representing the true consensus viewpoint of the world business community.

ICC Commercial Crime Services – This is the umbrella organisation of three ICC units dealing with different aspects of crime affecting business. They are the:
– *Commercial Crime Bureau,* set up to combat the increase in commercial frauds worldwide;
– *International Maritime Bureau,* which deals with all types of maritime crime, including fraud, cargo theft, and piracy; and
– *Counterfeiting Intelligence Bureau,* which helps companies to prevent the faking of their products.

The *International Bureau of Chambers of Commerce (IBCC)* works to strengthen world-wide co-operation between local chambers of commerce. It provides technical assistance and training programmes for those in developing countries and central and eastern Europe. The IBCC also manages the *ATA Carnet* system for temporary duty-free imports, which is particularly important for companies which are forced to travel substantially with industrial samples. The IBCC is currently involved in various electronic commerce ventures, including *IBCC Net –* an international electronic network and source of information/contacts between chambers.

ICC Publishing S.A. offers international business people more than 60 practical reference works. New guides, sets of rules, model contracts and handbooks are added to the list every year. Publications may be ordered directly from ICC Publishing in Paris, or from ICC National Committees.

1.9.3 International organisations

There are a variety of other international organisations involved in the field of international trade. International organisations are commonly divided into two categories: *intergovernmental organisations (IGO's),* which are the creation of nation states and are staffed with international civil servants, and *non-governmental organisations (NGO's),* which may be associations or federations representing business, sectoral, professional or consumer interests. Several of the key international organisations are listed below.

a. Inter-governmental organisations (IGOs)

See page 235 for addresses and telecommunications details.

The ***United Nations Commission on International Trade Law (UNCITRAL)*** (Vienna) – The United Nations' international private law body is UNCITRAL. UNCITRAL works primarily on instruments intended to become a part of international or national law, such as treaties, conventions, model and uniform laws. Recently, UNCITRAL has worked on an international convention for independent bank guarantees and a model law for electronic data interchange. Perhaps UNCITRAL's key contribution to international trade has been the Vienna Convention on the International Sale of Goods, the drafting of which was concluded in 1980 and which entered into force in 1988. UNCITRAL Rules for international commercial arbitration provide an alternative to other arbitral and litigation systems.

Unidroit (Institute for the Unification of Private Trade Law) (Rome) – This international organisation was set up under the old League of Nations and continued an independent existence after the founding of the United Nations. In recent years, Unidroit has been active in studying the international private law relating to leasing, agency, franchising and inspection contracts, with a view to proposing international legal conventions where necessary.

World Customs Organisation (Brussels) – A global union of customs organisations, which works together to advance the efficiency of the customs process.

The ***International Trade Centre (ITC)*** UNCTAD/WTO (Geneva) is the central agency of the United Nations' system for export assistance for developing nations. ITC conducts a very wide range of training programmes for exporters and importers as well as local chamber of commerce trainers. The ITC also publishes a full range of export guides focusing on specific areas of trade, such as packaging, marketing or promotion.

b. Non-governmental organisations (NGO's)

International Air Transport Association (IATA) – (Montreal and Geneva) – The trade organisation for the world's airlines, IATA has had an important role in simplifying and standardising air transport documents, such as air waybills.

International Federation of Freight Forwarder's Associations (FIATA) (Zurich) – A world organisation which promotes standards and quality in international freight forwarding. Certain FIATA standard documents, such as the FIATA Bill of Lading, have become important references in international trade. FIATA's customs clearance manual is a professional reference in transport circles.

International Maritime Committee (CMI – for Comité Maritime International) – (Brussels) – An organisation founded in 1897 to promote the unification of maritime and commercial law, maritime customs, usages and practices. Between 1910 and 1971, the CMI's work gave birth to 18 "Brussels" conventions and protocols on maritime law, including those key pieces of international regulation of bills of lading generally referred to as the Hague and Hague-Visby Rules.

International Road Transport Union (IRU) – (Geneva) – An international federation representing commercial operators of road vehicles, the IRU notably administers the *TIR* customs system which allows lorries or trucks sealed by customs officials to cross intervening national borders without having to undergo full customs formalities.

1.10 The Multilateral framework for world trade: the GATT and the WTO

a. **The GATT and free trade** – After World War II there was a strong international consensus in favour of creating an international trade organisation to oversee the progressive liberalisation of international markets. From 1947 until 1995, the supposedly "interim" GATT (General Agreement on Trade and Tariffs) functioned very effectively as the co-ordinator of the multilateral trade system. As a result of the GATT, tariffs which had averaged 40% world-wide from 1945 to 1950 dropped to about 5% by 1990. World exports grew from $61 billion in 1950 to $2 trillion by 1985. With the conclusion of the Uruguay Round in 1994, the GATT came to an end and gave way to the new World Trade Organisation (WTO). The Uruguay Round, which lasted from 1986 through 1993, was the most ambitious and comprehensive trade liberalisation agreement ever attempted. Its content is summarised in the ICC business guide, *"The GATT Negotiations"* (ICC Publication N°533).

b. **The World Trade Organisation** – The World Trade Organisation (WTO) replaces the GATT, and has quite a different character. While the GATT was primarily a set of rules, administered by an interim body, the WTO is a permanent institution with its own secretariat. Although the GATT's scope of application was limited to trade in goods, the WTO also covers trade in services and trade-related aspects of intellectual property. Of great practical significance is the fact that settlement of disputes under the WTO mechanism will be much faster and more automatic than under the GATT system, so that trade blockages will be more rapidly and efficiently overcome.

The long-standing principles enshrined in the original GATT have not disappeared under the WTO – rather, they have simply been subsumed under the new structure. Thus, the original GATT (from 1947) lives on as the so-called "GATT 1994", an amended and updated version of GATT 1947, which forms an integral part of the WTO agreement.

Notes

[1] also spelled f.o.b. or c.i.f.; see generally Chapter 4 on Incoterms 1990.

[2] This Incoterm is chosen simply as example; for a full discussion of the different Incoterms, see Chapter 4.

Chapter Two

The Export–Import Legal Framework

The basics: International trade transactions are composed of an interlocking series of contracts involving exporters, importers, agents/distributors, banks, insurers, transporters and brokers, and inspection agencies. Ideally, these contracts will interact harmoniously. All too often, however, important details are left un-negotiated, or terms in one contract (e.g., the transport or insurance contract) are allowed to conflict with terms in another (e.g., the sale contract), leading to unwanted and even disastrous consequences.

Properly drafted contracts are the first step in managing the risks of international commerce. Since the contract of sale plays the role of "master" contract, it is particularly important that it be drafted carefully and completely. Trade professionals should in addition have a good understanding of the legal principles generally applicable to international transactions.

Traders are well-advised to rely on expert legal counsel, and in any event should go through a checklist of basic legal questions before signing a contract or concluding a deal. In particular, the parties should be clear as to which law and dispute-settlement procedure will apply to the contract. As an alternative to formal court procedures as the means of resolving disputes, traders may wish to stipulate that dispute resolution will be by commercial arbitration, such as that administered according to the ICC Rules for Arbitration and Conciliation.

The key legal difference between international transactions and domestic ones is that in the international context one is faced with the question of *applicable national law*. A court requested to decide a particular case will first have to decide whether or not the case has been brought in the appropriate forum, and if so, which law to apply.

During negotiations, exporters may wish to refer to model contracts (such as the ICC Model Contracts for international sale, agency or distributorship). Even when the model contracts are not used directly, they may be useful for preparation of contract negotiations – one can compare the standard model provisions with the provisions in the contract offered by the counterparty.

2.1 Introduction to legal concepts and terminology

Note: Because national systems of law may differ on significant points relating to commercial matters, the many general statements on legal subjects made in this book should always be understood as mere generalisations. There may be exceptions in particular jurisdictions, and the general contractual principles stated herein may not apply under all systems of law.

2.1.1 The value of a precise, written contract

International traders are not always fully aware of the value of having negotiated a precise, detailed, written contract. Some traders prefer to do business without recourse to lawyers or formal written contracts at all. For them, their word – and perhaps a brief fax or telex confirmation – is enough contract. Indeed, in certain commercial sectors and in certain countries, informal means of contracting may be customary. However, traders should be conscious of the dangers of contracts based on a "handshake" or a "gentlemen's agreement".

Reliability of a "gentleman's agreement"– Too often, traders agree to conclude negotiations informally; they would be well-advised to consider the following humorous definition of a gentleman's agreement: "An unwritten agreement, not a contract, between two parties – neither of which may be a gentleman – under which each party believes the other side is fully bound, while its own performance is strictly optional."

International trade lawyers can attest – through the cases they plead – to the risks of casual optimism. When a dispute arises, reference to the contract is the first recourse of the parties. If the contract is silent or is unclear with respect to the element in dispute, the parties may have to enter into litigation or arbitration. International contracts, especially, should provide clear and detailed stipulations regarding the range of documentary obligations required by the particular transaction, such as, for example, the obligation to open a confirmed letter of credit or tender a negotiable bill of lading.

Traders are notorious for signing contracts without reading them, then waking to the danger when faced with a loss. Consequently, the contracting process should involve more than signing a long standard document produced by the other side or by one's own export department. Traders should not be hasty to assume that they have no negotiating power. Even if the other side is clearly in control of the negotiations, it may still be possible to obtain a single contractual concession, which may resolve an important concern. A failure to insist on minimum contractual precautions, regardless of the severity of the counterparty's negotiating posture, amounts to recklessness.

Contract negotiation should not be seen as mere haggling, or a test of wills between the parties. Contracts should not be thought of as weapons to be wielded in the event of disputes. Rather, contracts should be looked at as the written record of an information-exchange process by which the vast majority of foreseeable disputes can be *completely avoided.*

2.1.2 Written vs. oral contracts

Traders may be uncertain as to whether or not they have any legal recourse for a dispute when there is no written contract underlying a given transaction or part of a transaction, although there may be a verbal agreement or other informal understanding. In many cases, it may indeed be possible to enforce an agreement that was made orally between the parties, even if there is no writing evidencing the agreement. This will depend on the national law governing the contract (in some countries, all commercial agreements must be evidenced in writing), and on the existence of other contractual clauses (some contracts contain clauses specifying that any modifications to the contract must be in writing).

One potentially relevant consideration will be whether the parties have an established *course of dealing* (a habitual or standard way of doing business established in past transactions) or whether there is a *custom of trade* (a standard practice in the particular industry). In any event, any allegation of the existence of an oral promise or contract would have to be proven somehow, such as by acts of the parties consistent with the terms of the alleged oral contract or condition.

2.1.3 The key contracts related to export transactions

a. **Contract of sale** – The central export-import contract is the *contract of sale:* the parties to this contract are the *seller* (exporter) and *buyer* (importer). A *broker* or *agent* may act for seller or buyer in this basic framework. In a contract of sale, the parties generally specify at least the price, quantity, products, delivery and payment terms. If the parties do not specify one of the essential terms, the question arises whether there is a way of "filling the gap", and the answer will depend on the circumstances of the case and the applicable law. In some sectors, standard form sale contracts are prevalent.

If there is no formal written contract of sale, it is quite common for the contract to be formed by an exchange of telexes or faxes comprising, for example, the *buyer's enquiry* (the invitation to negotiate), the seller's *pro forma invoice* (the *offer*), and the buyer's *sales order* or *confirmation* (the *acceptance* of the offer). This exchange of offer and acceptance forms a valid contract in many jurisdictions, even in the absence of a more formal document.

The contract of sale is the "master" contract ruling the export transaction, because the series of contractual arrangements which follow – as regards transport, insurance and payment – should always accord with its provisions. The surest way to put the transaction on solid footing is to negotiate a precise contract of sale which deals unambiguously with all these key elements. Thus, the export contract should stipulate the delivery point and include a trade term under Incoterms 1990, such as FOB or FCA Incoterms 1990. Moreover, if payment is to be by letter of credit, it is helpful if the documentary requirements under the credit are already spelled out. If traders have any doubt about the completeness of their contracts, they are well-advised to compare their contracts with one of the standard form contracts, such as the ICC Model International Contract of Sale (see Chapter 4).

b. **Contract of carriage** – Another basic contract is the *contract of carriage*, which is formed between the *shipper* (seller *or* buyer) and the *carrier (transport company)*. The carrier may act through an agent or broker (e.g., freight forwarder). Legal recourse for damage to the goods during transport may be significantly affected by whether a freight forwarder was contracting as an agent or as a principal. The contractual terms and conditions of transport contracts are generally found in a transport document known as a *bill of lading* (or a similar but non-negotiable transport document, such as a sea waybill, air waybill, data freight receipt, cargo quay receipt, etc.). The bill of lading plays a triple role in the international sales transaction, acting as 1) transport contract, 2) evidence of receipt of goods, and 3) document conferring the right to control delivery of the goods. It is discussed in detail in Chapters 6 and 9.

The export "symphony": harmonizing the contracts

Contract of sale

The Contract of Sale is the "conductor" of the export symphony - all related documents should accord with it.

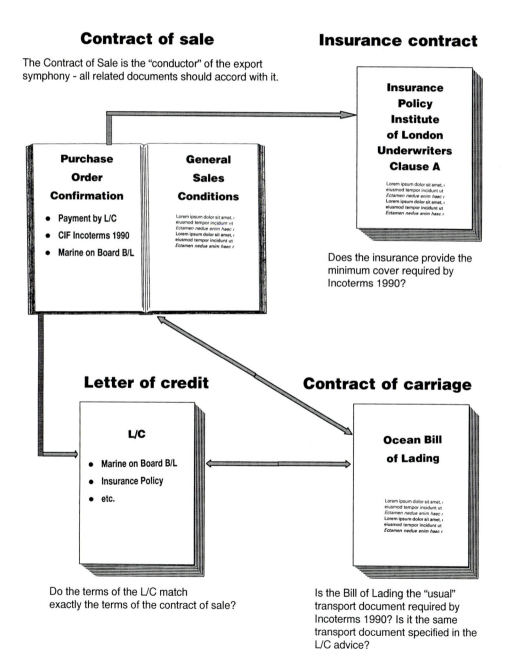

Purchase Order Confirmation

- Payment by L/C
- CIF Incoterms 1990
- Marine on Board B/L

General Sales Conditions

Lorem ipsum dolor sit amet, eiusmod tempor incidunt ut Ectamen nedue enim haec r Lorem ipsum dolor sit amet, eiusmod tempor incidunt ut Ectamen nedue enim haec r

Insurance contract

Insurance Policy Institute of London Underwriters Clause A

Lorem ipsum dolor sit amet, eiusmod tempor incidunt ut Ectamen nedue enim haec r Lorem ipsum dolor sit amet, eiusmod tempor incidunt ut Ectamen nedue enim haec r

Does the insurance provide the minimum cover required by Incoterms 1990?

Letter of credit

L/C

- Marine on Board B/L
- Insurance Policy
- etc.

Contract of carriage

Ocean Bill of Lading

Lorem ipsum dolor sit amet, eiusmod tempor incidunt ut Ectamen nedue enim haec r Lorem ipsum dolor sit amet, eiusmod tempor incidunt ut Ectamen nedue enim haec r

Do the terms of the L/C match exactly the terms of the contract of sale?

Is the Bill of Lading the "usual" transport document required by Incoterms 1990? Is it the same transport document specified in the L/C advice?

c. **Payment-related contracts** – International *payment mechanisms* generate another series of contractual agreements. A letter of credit, for example, is based on an underlying contract of sale, which requires that the buyer then form a contractual agreement with its bank (credit application and issuance), and in the case of a confirmed credit, requires that the confirming bank irrevocably undertake to pay the beneficiary under the credit and that a further contract be formed between the issuing bank and confirming bank.

d. **Insurance contracts** – Almost all international sales are insured in some way, which requires an insurance contract (a policy) between the insurer and the seller or buyer. When the seller is obliged under the sales contract to procure insurance, it is important that the conditions and insured amount under the policy be in accord with the conditions of the contract of sale.

2.1.4 Avoiding conflicts between contracts

It is essential in international transactions that the above-listed contracts do not conflict with each other. Again, the easiest way to ensure this harmony is to begin with the solid foundation of a *detailed contract of sale* covering all the main issues.

a. **Harmonising the contract of sale and the contract of carriage** – Depending upon the Incoterm chosen in the contract of sale, either seller or buyer will incur transport obligations under the contract of sale. For example, the CIF Incoterm requires the export seller to provide a negotiable bill of lading (as contract of carriage) conforming to "usual terms". What is "usual" will vary according to the particular commercial context. Were the seller to furnish a bill of lading on "unusual" terms (e.g., indicating that the goods were not shipped by a common route, or that transhipment of the goods is permitted, or that the goods were shipped on deck, etc.), the buyer in a falling market might be able to escape his contractual obligations.

It is therefore essential that the contractual shipper be aware of the extent of his transport obligations under the given Incoterm. For example, an FOB Incoterms seller should know that the goods must be safely loaded on board a vessel in the port of shipment. For further detail on this issue, see Chapter 4.6 dealing with Incoterms.

b. **Harmonising the contract of sale and the payment mechanism**– If payment is by documentary credit, the credit application should likewise be prepared so as to reflect the terms of the contract of sale. Thus, if the contract of sale specifies delivery on a lorry or railway wagon, the credit application must not require a marine on board bill of lading. If the contract specifies that the letter of credit must be confirmed, then provision by the importer of any other kind of credit will constitute a breach of the contract. The safest practice is to prepare a contract of sale which adequately spells out the characteristics of the letter of credit to be required (e.g., is it to be confirmed, payable at sight/90 days, transferable, require an inspection certificate, etc.). One way of doing this is for the exporter to provide a sample filled-in application for a letter of credit, indicating exactly how the importer must apply for the credit.

There is also a strong link between the documentary credit and the bill of lading in terms of the latter's security for the importer's obligation to repay the bank. The bank will in many cases want to ensure that the bill of lading it receives is a negotiable one; or, if it is not negotiable, that it irrevocably consigns the goods to the bank. By insisting on this security, the bank seeks to protects itself in the event of an eventual default by the importer, because the bank can theoretically seize the goods and sell them. In practice, of course, such a sale would usually recover much less than the market value of the goods, because of its forced nature and the inexperience of the bank as a seller of goods. Thus, banks are generally quite cautious in terms of the credit line they will extend on the security value of a negotiable bill of lading associated with the transaction

c. **Harmonising the contract of sale and the insurance contract** – Certain trade terms generate the requirement that the seller procure an insurance contract. For example, an exporter under CIF Incoterms is required under the sales contract to conclude both transport and insurance contracts. As for the insurance contract, CIF Incoterms requires a minimum level of insurance (specifically: 110% of the contract value under the A, B, or C clauses of the London Institute of Underwriters – see Chapter 9 on Transport).

The parties should have procedures in place which ensure that the sales, transport, insurance, and payment contracts accord and dovetail with each other. As stated above, one common device is for the exporter to furnish, along with the pro forma invoice that represents his offer, a sample letter of credit application, filled in according to the contract of sale he proposes to conclude – thus providing, as it were, a "road map" for the importer to follow.

2.1.5 Jurisdiction and Choice of Law

In international contracts one has a choice (and therefore, potential uncertainty) as to the applicable national law and forum. Because of the great distances which may be involved in international transactions, this can be an important choice. An American company based in Cleveland will prefer not to have to send several key executives to testify in Ulan Bator in the event of a dispute with its Mongolian counterparty. Consequently, a well-drafted international contract of sale will contain clear answers to the following crucial questions:

a. **What law governs this contract of sale?** The parties are free in principle to choose an applicable law, provided it has some reasonable relation to the contract. If the parties make no election, a court or arbitral tribunal called upon to settle a dispute arising under the contract will first examine all elements related to the contract which may help in ascertaining the intention of the parties. The court will then apply the principles of that body of the law known as *conflict of laws*.[1]

Note that in the case of arbitration this question can be broken down further into two sub-parts: 1) procedural law, and 2) substantive law. It is possible to contractually stipulate to the application of one national law to the substance of the contract and a different national law as to the legal procedure in the event of a dispute.[2]

b. **In which court or arbitral forum should a case be brought in the event of a dispute?** – The parties have some freedom to choose the court or arbitral forum. However, certain types of cases, such as labour disputes, must be settled under national law or before specialised courts. If the parties choose arbitration, they should include in their contract an effective arbitration clause, such as the standard clause provided by the ICC (see Chapter 3). Parties choosing arbitration are well-advised to further specify the applicable law, the language of arbitration, and the number of arbitrators (1 or 3).

Thus, a properly drafted contract between a French seller and a New York buyer will contain a clause making the transaction subject either to French law or to New York law, or to the law of a third country which bears some reasonable relationship to the contract (the controlling law is termed the *governing* or *applicable* law). A further clause will very likely specify either the French or New York Courts as the appropriate dispute-resolution forum, or may instead choose a type of commercial arbitration, such as ICC arbitration. These contractual provisions are known as the "*choice of law*", "*choice of forum*", and "*dispute resolution*" or "*arbitration*" clauses.

2.1.6 Performance and remedies for breach of contract

Whether or not a particular act or omission is deemed a breach may depend on which national law applies to the contract. Moreover, in practical terms, whether or not there is anything that an aggrieved party can do about a breach will also depend on the stipulated forum and dispute-resolution method. In some cases, the expense and inconvenience of having to sue in a foreign court will rule out the possibility of fully enforcing a particular contract.

a. **Factors affecting the range of remedies available** – The remedies for a breach of contract will vary according to the:

1) *Terms of the contract* – The contract may itself specify particular remedies, as for example, liquidated damages in the event of a particular default or breach.

2) *Applicable law* – National legal systems have different approaches to particular remedies. Common law courts, for example, have been less receptive to the application of the specific performance remedy (in essence, forcing a party to go through with their contract) than civil law courts.

3) *The nature and gravity of the breach* – In addition to the above factors, the remedies available to an aggrieved party will depend on the characteristics of the breach. In general, most legal systems seek to avoid creating harsh remedies for minor breaches. However, some breaches are so serious or flagrant that the aggrieved party should have access to the full range of possible remedies, such as those of consequential damages. Two of the concepts that may be applied in this regard are:

- *Substantial performance* – if a party (the exporter, for example) has performed the bulk of his obligations, but has failed to perform only to a small degree or in unimportant matters (e.g., short-delivery by a commercially insignificant amount), the aggrieved party may only be allowed the remedy of a price-reduction.

• *Fundamental breach* – if a breach that is so serious that it deprives the aggrieved party of the intended benefits of the contract, the aggrieved party may be allowed to terminate the contract.

b. **Types of remedy available** – Most legal systems make all of the following remedies available to some extent, depending on the circumstances of a particular case:

1) *Money damages* – An aggrieved party may be entitled to receive money in compensation for the contractual breach. The money may be calculated, *inter alia*, as a reduction in the price or as a lump-sum damages payment. If the breach was foreseeably likely to cause further or related damages (such as the lost sales occasioned by the shutting down of the aggrieved party's manufacturing operation), the aggrieved party may be able to obtain *consequential damages* as compensation for the results of the breach. The aggrieved party may have to *mitigate* damages, e.g., make reasonable efforts to reduce the extent of damages (thus, a buyer receiving a shipment of tomatoes of non-contract quality, but which are nonetheless merchantable, must make some efforts to sell the tomatoes rather than let them rot).

2) *Termination* – If the breach is a particularly serious one, it may entitle the other party to *terminate* the contract, and with it any remaining obligations she may have under it.

2) *Specific performance* – A party that has not performed according to her contractual obligations can be required to do so. A court may issue an order requiring that party to pay the contract price, deliver the contract goods or substitute goods, or otherwise fulfil that party's contractual obligations. Under common law legal systems, however, specific performance may be only available when damages are not an adequate remedy. Thus, a buyer who has not received the contract goods is expected to first terminate the contract and seek to buy the goods elsewhere. Specific performance is not often requested in practice.

2.1.7 Practical aspects of performance and breach

It is perhaps safe to say that most international agreements and contracts are successfully performed, uneventfully, to the satisfaction of both sides. Professional business persons only invest in transactions they expect will prove profitable and practicable.

Many minor contractual breaches are *curable* – the problem can be fixed or set right. Thus, if the seller delivers non-conforming goods before the delivery deadlines, and the non-conformity is pointed out, he may still make a second delivery of conforming goods. On other occasions, the aggrieved party will simply *forgive* a particular breach. Thus, if goods arrive a day or two late, and the time of delivery is not crucial, the buyer may simply overlook the breach. However, parties should be aware that by repeatedly forgiving a particular breach they may be taking the risk of establishing a *waiver* of their rights. One solution is to insert a clause in the contract to the effect that all modifications of the parties' rights under the contracts must be in writing signed by both parties (however, such provisions may be enforceable in all cases or in all jursidictions, so they should be checked by experienced legal counsel). Another solution is for the aggrieved party to object in writing to the small breaches, thereby establishing a paper record that that party had no intention of waiving its right to insist on performance.

a. **Lawyer's fees, court and arbitration costs** – Usually, a party will only consult lawyers as regards legal remedies when all other means of obtaining satisfaction have been exhausted (i.e., repeated requests for performance or re-negotiation). At this point the party will be confronted with the practical reality of the cost of enforcing the contract. Legal fees and court or arbitration expenses come into the picture. The choice of law, forum and arbitration clauses become crucial.

Let us say, for example, that the cost to a Bolivian buyer of a particular breach by an American seller is $10,000. Should the buyer sue for damages? If the lawsuit will cost the buyer more than $10,000, it may make no sense to undertake it. While in many countries the winning party can oblige the losing party to pay attorneys' fees and court costs, there is always the possibility of losing in a foreign court – and being forced oneself to pay the other side's attorneys' fees! It may end up costing more to pursue a claim than to walk away from the contract. The aggrieved party must ask, how much would it cost to win this case – and how much to lose it? What are the chances of winning? The costs in lawyer's fees, court and arbitral costs, and lost executive time spent testifying, must be weighed against the potential money award. Depending on the circumstances of each transaction, there will be a threshold of money damages beneath which it will be impractical or dangerous to sue, and this calculation will depend on the convenience and cost of the appropriate forum. Hence, the practical importance of the choice of law and choice of forum clauses in the sales contract.

In order to have some security against small disputes (i.e., those involving damages beneath the threshold for which it becomes practical to sue), traders can only rely on other, extra-legal safeguards, such as: export credit insurance, advance deposits, bank guarantees or performance bonds by the counterparty, and good foreign credit information

An additional practical observation is that it costs money to defend oneself against a lawsuit, regardless of whether or not one is in the wrong. This is simply one of the risks of doing business anywhere: one may be unjustifiably sued by a counterparty. In an international context, the inconvenience can be magnified when the defence must take place in an expensive city across the globe from the defendant's place of business. If a defendant chooses not to appear because of this expense, she runs the risk that a default judgement may be obtained against her, which might eventually result in a money judgement being enforced against her in a jurisdiction in which she has funds. Parties are thus justifiably wary of agreeing to a choice of forum clause specifying that claims must be brought in the counterparty's domestic courts, especially if the two countries are quite distant.

b. Adaptation and Force Majeure Clauses – A common cause for failure to perform in international business transactions is that of sharp market swings during or before the time for performance. A party's business may suddenly decline as a result of turbulence in the national economy in which it operates. Long-term contracts, such as those for agency and distributorship, are especially exposed to these time-based contingencies. Prudent traders are therefore advised to build *adaptation clauses* into contracts likely to be affected by changing economic or commercial circumstances. Adaptation provisions allow for flexibility in prices and supply terms, enabling parties to avoid a total breakdown in their relationship.

It is also generally advisable to include a *force majeure* clause, which excuses non-performance in the event of unforeseeable events, such as earthquakes, wars or "acts of God" (the ICC has developed a *Model Hardship and Force Majeure Clause*, which is described below in Chapter 4).

2.2 Contract formation and pre-contractual liability

2.2.1 Pre-contractual actions

In law, a contract is formed between exporter and importer when one party has made a *sufficiently precise* offer and the other has responded with an *unconditional* acceptance. However, the first contacts between the exporter and importer may arise far earlier, as for example when the importer views a catalogue or advertisement prepared by the exporter, and in response addresses a *purchaser's inquiry* to the exporter, requesting detailed product specifications or prices. Another possibility is that the importer will issue an invitation to submit *tenders* (offers) for a specific project. There are many possible variations, ranging from informal telephone contacts to highly-detailed and binding offers. Initial contacts may lead to prolonged negotiations over prices or specifications, or may lead immediately to contract. Statements made during the course of these initial contacts (*pre-contractual* statements) may or may not have a legally binding nature.

In most cases, statements made during negotiation will *not* be contractually binding (unless they are later incorporated into the contract). Courts have generally allowed parties some freedom to negotiate without the fear of incurring pre-contractual liability. However, there are several exceptions to this rule. If a contract results from the negotiations, and the pre-contractual statements made by one party turn out to have been misleading, the offending party may be held liable for the consequences of its misleading statements. While it is not possible to state a single, common legal principle that will apply in all jurisdictions, traders should apply common-sense notions of good faith to their pre-contractual negotiations and should take care that not to make statements upon which the other party is likely to rely to its detriment.

2.2.2 Offers/Tenders

In the parlance of the export trade, offers (or tenders) are those sufficiently precise communications – generally including product, price, payment and delivery elements – which an export seller specifically addresses to a particular buyer with the *intention* that a binding contract will be formed if the buyer accepts. The question may arise whether a price quotation made by an exporter amounts to a legally binding offer. Generally, the decisive criterion is whether or not the exporter intended to be bound by the offer.

Can an exporter change his mind and *revoke* the offer prior to acceptance? The answer varies widely according to the applicable law. Under certain legal systems the determining factor is whether the offer can be characterised as a *firm offer.* Under these systems, if the exporter specifically states that the offer will remain open for a given period of time, the exporter will be bound by any acceptance made within that time period, regardless of the exporter's attempts to revoke the offer. Different systems of law have different criteria for what constitutes a firm offer so that it is not possible to state a single, universal rule. In some jurisdictions an exporter may be able to preserve the right to revoke by stating in the offer that it will not become binding until a written acknowledgement of order has been sent.

Exporters and importers should also keep in mind that offers, tenders and other commercial proposals have a dual nature: they are not only legal instruments, they are also important sales and informational communications. The ideal tender will be professional-looking, detailed and complete. It will include such important sales information as key selling points, technical specifications, price, service conditions, as well as such legally significant items as general sales conditions, delivery time, and payment terms.

2.2.3 Acceptance

Generally, a buyer's acceptance must be unconditional in order to conclude a binding contract. A *conditional* acceptance may constitute a *rejection and counteroffer*, leaving it up to the exporter whether or not to accept the new condition. However, under some important systems of law (i.e., the Vienna Convention on the International Sale of Goods, or the US uniform commercial code – the UCC), if the new condition concerns a minor or trivial matter, then the conditional acceptance will be valid and conclude a binding contract unless promptly objected to by the exporter.

Many tricky questions of law arise under different legal systems as to when and how an acceptance actually creates a contract, but it is not possible here to go into these in detail. In general, exporters and importers should make sure that both have *expressly* agreed to the same set of terms and conditions. Unfortunately, in the rapid back-and-forth flow of international commerce, many traders do not take the time to be so rigorous.

The role of the exporter's *general conditions of sale* (and the buyer's *general conditions of purchase*) in the formation of contract will be considered below.

2.2.4 Letters of intent and other preliminary agreements

In certain complex transactions, the parties may wish to come to a preliminary agreement, sometimes called "an agreement to agree", which may or may not be enforceable, depending on circumstances and applicable law. Such an agreement may take the form of a "letter of intent," "memorandum of understanding," "heads of agreement," "agreement with open terms," "commitment letter" or "binder". These preliminary agreements may be necessary when a certain major issue (such as obtaining bank approval for a loan, or obtaining a government authorisation) is not yet known or definite. The preliminary agreement itself may be useful in getting a bank officer or government official to grant an approval or authorisation. Another possibility is that the parties will use the preliminary agreement to resolve certain basic issues, while continuing to negotiate on more complicated matters.

One danger of preliminary agreements is that the courts of some countries will interpret them as being legally binding, even though one of the parties had no intention of being bound. One way of avoiding this problem is to include express language in the agreement to the effect that "this document is not intended to constitute a binding contract," or "this document is only intended to indicate the parties' willingness to negotiate and nothing more".[3] However, not all courts will consider such language to be decisive.

In some cases, both parties intend to conclude a contract, but will intentionally leave a term or terms to be agreed upon in further negotiations. Here, the critical issue for courts will be whether, in the event that the further negotiations fail, there is a suitably definite mechanism or "fall-back" standard enabling the court to supply the missing term(s).

It should be clear from the above that an instrument such as the letter of intent should be used with some discretion. If the document is too vague or contains too many disclaimers, banks or government officials may not wish to rely on it. However, if it is highly-detailed and contains no disclaimers, it may be held to bind the parties as a valid contract. Ultimately, parties should generally refrain from signing even a preliminary document unless they are truly ready to conclude a binding agreement on terms which they are reasonably likely to obtain from the other party.

2.3 Model or standard contracts in international trade

2.3.1 The recourse to model or standard form contracts

The use of standard form contracts is quite common in international trade. For example, various commodity and raw materials markets use highly-specific form contracts, which are virtually obligatory for market participants.

a. **FIDIC and ORGALIME Contracts** – A typical contractual standard is found in the FIDIC (Fédération Internationale des Ingénieurs-Conseils) form contracts. These are intended to serve as models for international engineering projects, primarily those based on competitive bidding in developing countries. Perhaps the best known of the FIDIC Contracts is generally known as the Red Book (official name: "Conditions of Contract for Works of Civil Engineering Construction"). The Red Book includes a standard form of tender, a form of agreement, general conditions, and conditions of particular application. It is available in a variety of languages. Orgalime (Liaison group of the European mechanical, electrical, electronic and metalworking industries) also produces a series of model general conditions for the supply of mechanical and electronic products.

Similarly, the United Nations Economic Commission for Europe (UNECE) has developed a series of standard terms and conditions for contracts for the construction of plant and machinery (mixed transactions involving supply of goods and services).

Yet another type of model is to be found in the professional form books published by legal publishers, such as Matthew Bender and Kluwer. These references are primarily intended as drafting guides for international trade lawyers, but they may prove useful in a trader's export library. Most large law firms also find ways to stockpile and classify their contracts and forms over the years, so that lawyers working on repetitive transactions or parts of transactions can make use of detailed contracts which have been previously drafted and tested in actual transactions.

Great care should be used by beginning lawyers and non-specialists in the use of forms. The worst way to use a form is simply to sign it without reading it (although in some markets or sectors this may be common). The better approach is to prepare for negotiations by going through each clause of the various models that are available, seeking to determine whether the clause is favourable or not, and developing negotiating strategies as a function of one's conclusions.

b. **The ICC Model Contracts** (currently available for Sale, Agency and Distributorship Contracts, with model clauses for Franchising in progress) – These ICC model contracts respond to the need of international traders for some kind of uniform framework for their contractual dealings.

As regards the choice of applicable law for a particular contract, the main alternatives available for international traders are to base their contracts on the national law of one or the other parties, or to apply an international treaty or convention. The latter course may well be impossible, because in areas such as agency or distributorship the establishment of a worldwide convention is unlikely, since countries would have to adapt their mandatory laws. Since agency law is related to labour and employment laws, and since distributorship law is related to competition and antitrust law, areas in which many governments wish to maintain domestic control over the law, it is unlikely that governments will soon cede way for the development of a uniform international law.

A common solution is to subject the contract to the national law of one of the contracting parties. Generally, this is satisfactory for the stronger party in the negotiations and undesirable for the other party. The weaker party is forced to adhere to a contract despite its relative ignorance of the substantive and procedural intricacies of the other country's law – a significant practical disadvantage should a dispute arise. The ICC Model Contracts provide a reliable alternative for parties faced with this problem. These ICC Contracts are developed on neutral premises, independent of any specific national legislation. Instead, they are based insofar as possible on prevailing standards of international trade practice.

1) *Balanced contracts* – An essential aspect of the ICC Model Contracts is that they seek to provide balanced instruments which do not give undue advantage to either side. This means that they may not be ideal for parties in extremely strong negotiating positions who are able to impose virtually any conditions. There are many other model contracts available on the marketplace, some of which may provide better protection for one or the other parties under particular circumstances. For example, a national commercial agents' association may publish a model agency contract which gives stronger protection to the agent than

the ICC contract, while a manufacturers' association may publish a contract giving stronger protection to the principal. Seeking the middle way, the ICC contracts attempt to provide a neutral, fair and equitable document. Both sides can sign an ICC contract with a certain peace of mind, knowing that it was specifically designed to provide reasonable protection for both sides without either taking undue advantage.

2) *Application of the Lex Mercatoria in ICC Model Contracts* – The ICC Model Contracts rely to some extent on the principle of "lex mercatoria" as the groundwork for interpretation of the contract. Lex mercatoria is a legal concept that refers to *internationally accepted general trade practices.* In the event of a dispute arising under an ICC Model Contract, the respective rights and obligations of the parties will be determined by reference firstly to the contract itself, and secondly to the lex mercatoria. This solution implies that in some cases an arbitrator trying a case based on the ICC Model Contract will have a certain degree of freedom to decide the case on those commonly accepted legal principles which constitute the lex mercatoria, rather than upon specific, national statutes.

The ICC Model Contracts are sufficiently detailed that the greater part of possible disputes are covered by their provisions. National statutes and jurisprudence are generally more detailed and precise than the combination of ICC contract and lex mercatoria, but this advantage in precision is outweighed by the potential conflicts and misunderstandings that may arise when parties from different countries try to negotiate and perform an international contract. Nonetheless, ICC Model Contracts do provide for the possibility of expressly submitting the contract to a specific national law. In any event, the mandatory laws of particular countries may apply in certain situations regardless of contract provisions.

While it is possible that an ICC Model Contract may conflict with mandatory principles of the national law of one or the other parties (in which case the national law might override the model contract, depending upon whether the national provision is a matter of strong public policy or "ordre public"), this is rather unlikely, given the Contracts' reliance on widely-accepted principles.

3) *The central role of international arbitration* – Like many standard international contracts, ICC Model Contracts prescribe international commercial arbitration as the preferred mode of dispute resolution. Arbitration is especially suitable for truly international projects. Moreover, arbitrators, who come from a neutral background, are more likely to be comfortable with the ICC Model Contracts' reference to lex mercatoria, and feel unhindered by the lack of application of a specific national legislation. It remains to be seen whether an arbitrator would consider reliance on an ICC Model Agency Contract as evidence that the parties were willing to have the dispute resolved with reference to lex mercatoria independently or reference to an applicable national law. National courts might have difficulty in applying the lex mercatoria to a dispute. Certain kinds of disputes, nonetheless, are considered "non-arbitrable" under the New York Convention of 1958.

Notes

[1] As to contractual obligations, please refer to the Rome Convention on the Law Applicable to Contractual Obligations (1980).

[2] Note however, that courts will always apply their own procedural law.

[3] See Fox, International Commercial Agreements, p. 128.

Chapter Three

Resolving International Disputes

The basics: International traders should prepare their dispute-resolution strategy *before* negotiating or concluding a contract. *After* a dispute has arisen, some methods of dispute-resolution may become unavailable.

Discuss dispute-resolution during contract negotiation and drafting – Ideally, parties will have ensured that their contract partners are trustworthy and reliable, thereby avoiding many disputes. The ideal contract will be sufficiently precise so that surprises are unlikely, and sufficiently flexible so that foreseeable contingencies can be handled by adaptation clauses. If the parties desire a long-term commercial relationship, they may wish to specify in their contract that disagreements be initially addressed by renegotiation, mediation or conciliation (sometimes called "alternative dispute resolution" or "*ADR*"). The well-drafted contract will also contain a clear and precise clause specifying the conditions of binding dispute-resolution. For major international transactions, commercial arbitration will generally be preferred to litigation because arbitration is considered to be more neutral and tends also to be faster, cheaper, less adversarial and more confidential than litigation. However, a party in a strong negotiating position may prefer to insist that disputes be settled by litigation under its domestic laws and procedures (somewhat surprisingly, this may not always be to its own benefit).

After dispute arises – Even if the parties have failed to contractually stipulate a form of dispute-resolution, they may still come to an agreement after a dispute has arisen. However, this becomes more difficult when the parties have adopted hostile, defensive postures. It often happens that a party who is conscious of its own guilt or liability will seek to delay justice, and in such cases the absence of prior agreement on applicable law and appropriate forum will multiply the opportunities for dilatory tactics.

3.1 Working it out – contractual foresight and adaptation clauses

Ideally, most possible contractual disputes will have been avoided by sufficient foresight. Parties will have thoroughly investigated their future partners before signing a contract, and will have made sure they have a reputation for reliability, trustworthiness and credit worthiness. By negotiating a precise, detailed contract, parties will elicit, discuss and resolve most potential areas of dispute before concluding the contract.

Especially in the case of contracts that are expected to last for many years or which are expected to begin a continuing commercial partnership, *adaptation clauses* are useful. These have already been discussed above as regards the contract of sale. *Force majeure* and *excusable delays* clauses are what might be termed automatic adaptation clauses, in that certain future events automatically trigger a suspension of contract responsibilities. Under typical force majeure clauses, wars, strikes and natural catastrophes will excuse non-performance by one or both parties.

Price provisions are often linked to an *escalation clause* in the case of long-term contracts. A given price may remain in effect, for example, for six months, and thereafter be pegged to a publicly-available inflation index. Thus, a buyer may be given a "best price" or "most favoured" clause, according to which the buyer is assured that she will never pay a higher price than any other customer. Product specifications may be subject to updating of catalogues or verifiable changes in market conditions. Variation and substitution clauses may allow a party to deliver goods which are functionally as good as the contract goods, but which may differ slightly in composition. Delivery provisions may be made flexible by allowing for excusable delays or time extensions, particularly in the event of unexpected occurrences. Specific clauses are often drafted to excuse non-performance as a result of significant changes in government policy, legislation or tax rules.

3.2 Talking it over – Waiver, Renegotiation, Mediation and conciliation

3.2.1 Waiver

Perhaps the easiest response to a minor contractual breach is for the other party to ignore or forgive the breach. It is quite common for minor breaches to be forgiven, as for example with respect to lateness in delivery under sale contracts, or with failure to reach minimum sales targets in agency and distributorship contracts. Such forgiveness may amount, from a legal point of view, to a "waiver" or abandonment of the aggrieved party's right to object.

The party who decides to forego any objections for the time being should be aware that in some cases its silence or acquiescence may be legally equivalent to a modification of the contract. This is especially so if it is likely that the other party will in some way rely to its detriment on the indications that the breach would be forgiven or ignored. One way of preserving one's rights and avoiding an unwitting waiver is to insert a clause in the contract specifying that all contractual modifications must be in writing. Another possibility, in the event that a party may wish to tolerate a particular breach on a single occasion, but not as a general rule, is to object in writing in response to each event of breach.

3.2.2 Renegotiation

The parties can always *mutually* agree to modify an existing contract. In some cases, the parties may wish to expressly include a clause which requires executives of the two parties to meet for *formal renegotiation* in the event of a disagreement. Under such a clause, the parties commit themselves to a concerted effort to avoid more acrimonious forms of dispute resolution, such as litigation. Boeing is one example of a large company which has been reported to use mandatory renegotiation clauses in its contracts.

⒊2.3 Mediation and conciliation

These terms refer to a relatively amicable way of resolving disputes by resorting to a neutral third party. Mediation/conciliation is theoretically a very cheap, fast and amicable form of dispute resolution. Whether it succeeds or not will depend on such variable factors as the commitment of the two sides to a friendly resolution, and the personal skills and dedication of the mediator. The weakness of mediation is the absence of compulsory or enforcement powers – the procedure is usually not binding. Therefore, the parties can simply walk away from the mediation if they are unhappy with the results.

⒊2.4 ICC Rules for optional conciliation; Docdex system for documentary credit disputes

The ICC provides a procedure for conciliation under the auspices of the Secretariat of the ICC International Court of Arbitration. Either party may begin the process by sending a request for conciliation to the ICC Secretariat. The other party must agree to the conciliation within 15 days, or the process terminates. If agreement is given, the ICC appoints a conciliator, who then requests the parties to submit the details of their respective positions. The conciliator may then call for a meeting, and may request the parties to send representatives empowered to negotiate a settlement, which appears to increase the likelihood of a successful conclusion. The proceedings are informal and confidential. The process will either end with the parties signing a binding settlement of the dispute, or with a withdrawal by one or both of the parties from the conciliation. The costs of the conciliation are shared equally by the parties. In 1997 the ICC approved a specific procedure and set of rules, called Docdex, for resolving documentary credit disputes via non-binding opinions issued by panels of experts.

3.3 Suing the scoundrels: international litigation

3.3.1 Litigation

Dispute resolution via recourse to public courts or tribunals is generally the most costly and confrontational of the various dispute-resolution options. Experienced traders and their counsel often try to avoid the possibility of court actions by negotiating for the inclusion of mediation or arbitration clauses in their contracts.

Considering the limitations of litigation, it may seem surprising that there are still traders and lawyers who appear to work from the assumption that litigation is the principal means of solving commercial disputes, even minor ones. Some companies, and some countries, appear to be more litigious than others. This may be partially due to training, or lack of it (i.e., an ignorance of the benefits of international commercial arbitration or of the benefits of adaptation and re-negotiation clauses).

In some cases practical or economic considerations may play a role in dictating the choice of litigation: the more powerful party can use the threat of costly court procedures to intimidate the weaker party.

International litigation can be slow, complicated, unfriendly, and expensive. It is technically difficult and requires professional counsel (although the same can be said for international commercial arbitration). Advantages of litigation are that it is normally final (after appeals are exhausted) and enforceable in the country in which it takes place. However, in an international context, arbitration can sometimes be even more effective than litigation in terms of enforcement, because arbitral awards are supported by the widely-accepted 1958 New York Convention on the Recognition and Enforcement of Arbitral Awards.

In particular cases, the reputed drawbacks of litigation can be useful to one of the parties. A party which is in the wrong and expects to ultimately lose a case may prefer to stall the case in his national court system and delay judgement as long as possible. Such parties may seek from the outset to challenge the validity or enforceability of arbitration clauses, should a dispute arise – one additional reason to use a reliable, standard arbitration clause such as the one provided by the ICC. The stronger party in a negotiation may be reluctant to include an arbitration clause in the contract, insisting rather on dispute resolution in the courts of his country and under his country's law. By forcing the weaker party to sue him in unfamiliar courts, the stronger party will discourage legal recourse against him. The weaker party may be unable to afford the expense and inconvenience of having to hire foreign legal counsel and travel to testify in legal proceedings in a foreign jurisdiction.

In addition to the foregoing, there are two commonly cited advantages to litigation over arbitration:

1) *The possibility of appeal* – Arbitration is a one-shot opportunity, and in this sense more risky;

2) *Greater predictability* – When the chosen jurisdiction and law are familiar to one of the parties, it is clearly possible to have knowledge of the procedures likely to be followed, the track record of the courts, and even the judges who will hear the cases. With arbitration, all of these factors are more uncertain and may vary from case to case.

3.3.2 Jurisdiction and choice of forum

a. **Introductory** – Law suits must be brought in the proper courts of the proper country. This is referred to as *jurisdiction,* the power or competence of a particular court to hear a case. The first thing an aggrieved party must do in an international dispute is find a court or tribunal (a *"forum"*) which has jurisdiction over the case.

Under the Roman law principle, *actor forum rei sequitur,*[1] the plaintiff was required to bring suit in the defendant's local courts. Such a rule was probably practical in its day. Since recourse to the defendant's local court would have been necessary to enforce any resulting judgement, a lawsuit brought anywhere else would have involved a duplication of effort. However, as modern international trade developed, companies and their assets spread across the globe, fundamentally altering the underlying economic context. It became a matter of practical interest for an aggrieved trader to assert jurisdiction over a foreign defendant in any jurisdiction where that defendant had assets. While under the Roman jurisdictional rule the plaintiff followed the physical defendant, modern plaintiffs sought the freedom to follow the defendant's money or tangible assets. As international centers of commerce, particularly London and New York, grew in the 19th and early 20th centuries, their courts developed legal theories for sustaining this exercise of jurisdiction over foreign defendants.

Today, most courts asked to hear a case arising out of an export-import dispute will look first to the contractual agreements between the parties to see if there is a forum-selection clause (see below), and will then determine in light of circumstances and national law whether it shall assert jurisdiction. In some cases, a court will refuse to exercise its power to hear a case because it would be either inconvenient or unfair to do so: this legal doctrine is referred to a *forum non conveniens* (inconvenient forum).

b. Choice of forum and forum-shopping – If a contract is silent on the country of the proper court, the parties involved in a dispute will commonly try to invoke the jurisdiction of the national courts in which they think they have the highest likelihood of success, or the courts which are most convenient for them. This practice is referred to as *forum-shopping*. The availability of forum-shopping can create problems. For example, a party may try to bring suit in a country only tangentially related to the contract. Another problem is that after a law suit has commenced in one country, the other party may bring a counter-suit in yet another country.

In order to avoid these uncertainties parties to an international contract will frequently include a *forum selection* or *choice of forum* clause. Commonly, the party with the stronger negotiating position will propose a choice of forum clause stipulating that lawsuits must be brought in the stronger party's domestic courts.

Choice of forum clauses are usually subject to a test of *reasonableness*: the chosen forum must bear some logical relation to the subject of the contract. Thus, in a lawsuit arising under a distribution contract between a large German manufacturer and a small Puerto Rico distributor, it was held that a choice of forum clause specifying Mexico as the appropriate forum was unreasonable. The tacit effect of such a provision was, the court held, to render it difficult for the Puerto Rico distributor to undertake any legal action. However, even where the choice is reasonable, choice of forum clauses may not be respected in all countries or in all situations.

c. Types of jurisdiction – the competence of a forum to receive a case

1) *Subject matter jurisdiction* – this term refers to the power of a particular court to hear a particular *type* of case. In some countries, for example, only special commercial courts are empowered to decide commercial cases. This scope for receiving cases is sometimes also referred as the *competence* of the particular court.

2) *Personal jurisdiction* – Crucial in international cases is the issue of *personal jurisdiction* over foreign parties – whether a court has judicial power over a person or company domiciled in another country. A court's personal jurisdiction is generally said to extend to all physical persons present, residing or domiciled in the forum state, as well as to any individuals who have *consented* to such jurisdiction. A foreign party manifests *express* consent to jurisdiction by signing an appropriate forum selection clause. In the absence of a forum selection or choice of law clause, some courts resort to a theory of *implied consent* to assert personal jurisdiction over foreign parties. For example, US courts will consider whether the foreign party has sufficient "minimum contacts" with the US, such as a branch office or regular commercial dealings in the US.

Ultimately, one option which is almost always available is simply to bring the lawsuit in the jurisdiction where the defendant is legally domiciled (a return to the Roman law principle). Unfortunately, this can involve great expense and inconvenience for the plaintiff.

3.3.3 Choice of law and applicable law

The parties may choose the law which they wish to govern their contract so long as the law chosen is that of a place that has some substantial relationship to the parties and the business transactions, and is not contrary to a strong public policy of the place where suit is brought.

If the contract does not specify the applicable law, or if the choice of law is unreasonable or contrary to public policy, then the court which tries the case will have to choose the applicable law. In doing so, courts refer to a body of legal theory known as "conflict of laws," which can involve exceedingly complex analysis, far beyond the scope of this book. However, the basic elements of conflict of laws analysis are grounded in common sense – the court will primarily look to the place where the contract was negotiated and/or signed, the place where it is to be performed, and the domiciles of the parties involved. Some countries leave great latitude to the courts to decide the most appropriate law (commonly, the law which bears "the most significant relationship" to the contract). The Vienna Convention for the International Sale of Goods, for example, provides for a "substantial relation" guideline.

Various international treaties provide a certain measure of harmonisation of conflict of laws principles. Amongst the most important are the Rome Convention of 1980 on the law applicable to contractual obligations, which applies in most European Union courts, and the Hague Convention of 1986 on the law applicable to international contracts for the sale of goods.

3.3.4 Enforcement of judgements

Winning a law suit is not enough. The legal judgement must then be *enforced*. If the complaining party obtains a judgement directing the other party to pay money damages, the prevailing party must also apply for a court order compelling the loser to pay over the funds. The likelihood of ultimately being able to enforce a judgement is something that must be thoroughly considered before the law suit is begun. It may be completely useless to receive a money judgement against a party who is likely to simply declare bankruptcy or disappear. Thus, a party wishing to begin a law suit will normally assure himself that the other party has sufficient assets to satisfy a money judgement. It may be necessary to apply for an *injunction* – a court order – freezing those assets until the case is decided.

Difficulties often arise when a judgement is obtained over a foreign party who has no assets in the jurisdiction where the judgement is rendered. In this case, the winner will look for countries in which the loser has assets to satisfy the judgement. Such assets can often be found in the jurisdiction where the losing party is domiciled. A court procedure commonly known as an *exequatur* or "execution of judgement" must then be held in that country. An exequatur involves a hearing by a court which has been asked to recognise a foreign court judgement. Will the exequatur result in enforcement of the foreign judgement? The situation varies widely from country to country. In Europe, the Brussels and Lugano

Conventions have made enforcement of foreign judgements from other signatory countries a fairly routine matter. In other countries, the courts will often ask whether there is a relationship of *reciprocity* between the courts of the two countries. In essence, this means, "we will enforce your judgements if we find you have enforced ours".

3.4 International commercial arbitration

3.4.1 Benefits of international commercial arbitration

International commercial arbitration is often the most appropriate dispute-resolution mechanism for major international transactions. The advantages of arbitration are numerous:

a. **Neutrality** – The choice of arbitration allows the parties to deal with the otherwise troublesome negotiating point of deciding where a law suit should be brought in the event of a dispute. Many traders may hesitate to take the risk that they would have to sue in a foreign court, where they may not only be unfamiliar with language, procedure, law and customs, but where they may even have doubts about the potential bias of the judges or judicial system. With arbitration, the parties may agree that the case will be heard in a neutral country (although arbitration can take place anywhere, including the country of one of the contract parties).

b. **Confidentiality** – Arbitration is private, confidential, and does not generate precedents or binding jurisprudence. Large multinationals may not wish to take the risk that unfounded charges against them gain publicity by being debated in open court. The lack of precedential value for an arbitral award reduces the downside risk for a party which enters into many similar or related contracts. With litigation, losing a case may mean establishing a precedent which might then lead to automatically losing an entire series of similar or related cases.

c. **Expense and timing** – Arbitration is generally faster and cheaper than litigation. Experienced lawyers can sometimes take advantage of complicated court procedures to stall and delay the resolution of a case, while simpler arbitral procedures are less amenable to dilatory tactics. In many countries the court dockets are so backlogged that even getting to the initial phases of hearing a case can take years. Moreover, arbitral awards are normally final, whereas court judgements may be appealed to several higher courts.

d. **Language** – Arbitrations can be held in a convenient language. Language can otherwise be a substantial hidden expense of foreign court proceedings.

e. **Arbitrator's expertise** – The parties in a dispute may be able to designate an arbitrator who is an expert in the relevant technical field, or who is at least familiar with international business cases. Experienced trial attorneys often complain that judges, on the other hand, do not really understand the technical cases they are called to rule upon. The expertise of the arbitrator may also contribute to obtaining a more rapid final decision, because the arbitrator will not have to receive as much "education" as would a judge.

f. Enforcement – The enforcement of international arbitral awards is supported by an international treaty[2], rendering arbitration to some extent more reliable in this respect than litigation.

3.4.2 Potential disadvantages

Despite the foregoing, certain reservations are also commonly voiced about arbitration.

a. Cost and delay – Although it is said that arbitration is relatively cheaper and faster than litigation, there are many examples of arbitrations which were very expensive or dragged on for many years (which is not to say that those cases, had they been litigated, would not have been even more expensive and time-consuming). With litigation, by comparison, there is no need to pay for the judges' salaries nor the rental of the courtroom. Nonetheless, arbitration is widely believed to be less expensive than litigation because the procedure is swifter and not open to appeal. Moreover, arbitration permits greater flexibility and party control over the procedures. In a sense, with arbitration "you get what you pay for"[3]. However, parties are well-advised to understand that the assertion that arbitration is cheaper and faster that does not necessarily mean it is cheap or fast. Parties that wish to assure themselves that the time and cost of dispute-resolution be kept to a minimum may wish to specify in advance certain ways of expediting the process (see below, *"Fast Track Arbitration"*).

b. Procedural safeguards – The many procedural devices allowed in litigation, while often having the effect of slowing down the progress of a case, are not without potential benefits for both sides. In complicated cases, it may be helpful to be able to have complete access to documents in the possession of the other side. Some legal systems (particularly the "common law" ones derived from English and American principles) have much more highly-developed rules for this *"discovery"* than are available with arbitration. Some lawyers experienced in civil litigation have found themselves frustrated by what they perceived as the relative informality of arbitration, which in their eyes constituted a lack of "rigor" or "order". However, the inherent flexibility of arbitration means that whenever the parties' agree that it is in their interests, arbitrations can be pre-structured so as to have a high degree of procedural safeguards. For example, complex arbitrations can be conducted with transcripts or written records.

c. Finality – Arbitral awards are more final than preliminary judicial awards in that arbitral awards cannot be appealed to higher tribunals. Losing parties may, however, seek to overturn or delay the enforcement of an arbitral award by going to court to challenge the validity of the arbitration. In general, recourse against an arbitral award is much more limited than against an initial court judgement.

3.5 ICC Arbitration

3.5.1 Introductory

Arbitration under the auspices of the ICC International Court of Arbitration ("ICC arbitration") is probably the most widely-used form of international arbitration. More than 8500 cases have been submitted for ICC arbitration since it was first made available in 1923. Currently, approximately 400 cases are received per year. More than 800 cases are currently pending, with a total amount-in-dispute value of approximately $20 billion. This caseload is growing at a rapid annual rate.

In 1996 and 1997 the ICC undertook a significant revision of its rules of arbitration, with the new rules to go into effect on 1 January 1998. Amongst the key changes adopted include specific articles dealing with multi-party arbitration, correction and interpretation of arbitrators' awards, and truncated tribunals. In general, the revision aims to increase the precision and speed of operations of ICC arbitrations. The discussion below is based primarily on the current version of the rules (pre-1998), since the general character and overall structure of ICC arbitration will remain the same.

ICC arbitration commends itself by certain key features:

a. **Universality** – Unlike certain other arbitral fora, the ICC is not limited in terms of technical or geographical scope. ICC arbitrations have covered the full range of business sectors, involving parties from all corners of the globe, including both private and governmental entities. Although the International Court of Arbitration (the "Court") is based in Paris, and has meeting rooms and other infrastructure support there, the proceedings may take place anywhere in the world. In fact, the majority of proceedings take place outside of Paris. Arbitrators and counsel may come from almost anywhere; more than 75 nationalities were represented among ICC arbitrators over a 9-year period in the 1980s. Currently, ICC arbitral proceedings are pending in approximately 30 countries.

b. **Supervision** – Especially as compared with ad hoc arbitration, ICC arbitration distinguishes itself by virtue of its support from a professional staff. ICC arbitration is the most highly-supervised form of institutional arbitration. The Court employs approximately 30 staff members, including a Secretary General and six legal counsel. The ICC staff relieves the arbitrators of the need to oversee such case management issues as supervising payment of fees and expenses, and the Secretariat also handles much of the work involved in distributing necessary documentation. The Court scrutinises and approves the arbitrator's award – a unique and important feature (new arbitration rules which are intended to go into effect in 1998 will increase the ambit of the Court's power to interpret arbitral awards and/or correct them for reasons of legal error). Moreover, it is the Court, rather than the arbitrators, that notifies the parties of the ultimate award. The Court relies on a state-of-the-art computer system to file and track all arbitration documents.

c. **Stature** – After seven decades as the world's pre-eminent arbitral institution, the ICC has acquired an imposing aura of neutrality and respectability, which may be of practical relevance in certain cases. For example, during negotiations parties do not need to convince their counterparties of the neutrality of ICC arbitration.

3.5.2 The ICC arbitration clause

Although it is possible for parties to mutually decide on submitting a case for ICC arbitration after the dispute has arisen, it is preferable that the choice of ICC arbitration be made earlier, via inclusion of the appropriate *arbitration clause* in the contract. The ICC recommends the use of the following standard clause:

> "All disputes arising in connection with the present contract shall be finally settled under the Rules of Conciliation and Arbitration of the International Chamber of Commerce by one or more arbitrators appointed in accordance with the said Rules."

This clause can be complemented by the addition of stipulations as to the place of arbitration, the number of arbitrators (one or three), the applicable law, and the language to be used. In particular, parties who wish to make sure that the process is as expedited and inexpensive as possible should seek to incorporate these precise stipulations in the contract. Thus, if parties can agree on an applicable law, it will save much time wrangling about applicable law in the event of a dispute. One common solution is to stipulate the applicable law of a neutral country. The stipulation of a sole arbitrator is one way to make sure that the cost of arbitration is kept to a minimum.

If the contract involves multiple (i.e., more than two) parties, special provisions should be considered.

However, parties should take care that any additions to the basic standard clause do not create ambiguity. For example, parties have been known to add the words "in Paris" after "International Chamber of Commerce". Unfortunately, this may cause confusion as to whether they mean that the place of arbitration should be Paris.

3.5.3 The ICC Court and Secretariat

The Court consists of a Chairman, several Vice-Chairmen, and approximately 50 members. The Secretariat is composed of a Secretary General, a General Counsel, and six Counsel, plus other special Counsel and support staff.

The Court does not itself decide disputes; rather it oversees the conduct of proceedings and ensures that they conform to the ICC Rules. The Court's main tasks are:

1) To decide whether a prima facie agreement to arbitrate under ICC Rules exists.
2) To appoint the arbitrators. For sole arbitrators and chairmen, the Court first determines that a particular nationality is desirable (often that of the place of arbitration), then requests the relevant ICC National Committee to recommend an arbitrator; the recommendations are usually, although not obligatorily, followed. The Court also reviews and decides on parties' challenges to arbitrators on grounds of alleged bias or incompetence.
3) To determine the place of arbitration, unless the parties have made a specific provision.
4) To approve the arbitrators' Terms of Reference (see below).
5) To determine the arbitrators' fees and expenses, and establishment of deposits.

6) To decide on any necessary extension of time limits.

7) To approve the draft Awards.

3.5.4 The Arbitrator(s)

One of the potential benefits of ICC arbitration lies in the parties' freedom to choose the arbitrators. If the Court is called upon to appoint a sole arbitrator or chairman, it will choose a national from a neutral country. The Court requires arbitrators to be completely independent from both parties and the arbitrators must make an initial statement to this effect.

As for the number of arbitrators, the basic option is for either one or three arbitrators. If the parties do not specify, the Court will appoint a sole arbitrator except in cases of complexity or amount justifying the appointment of three arbitrators. The choice of three arbitrators is very common, perhaps because it allows each party to appoint one arbitrator. When drafting an arbitration clause specifying the number of arbitrators, the parties should also keep in mind that stipulating three arbitrators will clearly increase the overall cost of handling a dispute, and will in addition often cause delay. Parties who believe that an arbitrator is not completely neutral and independent may challenge the arbitrator by submitting the matter to the Court. If the Court finds that the arbitrator in fact is not neutral or is not otherwise properly fulfilling his duties, the arbitrator will be replaced.

3.5.5 ICC arbitration procedure

Pursuant to the ICC Rules of Arbitration (the "Rules"), procedure is as follows:

a. **Request for arbitration** – At least one party (the "claimant") must send a written Request to the Secretariat of the Court (the "Secretariat"), accompanied by a non-refundable advance of $2000 USD on administrative costs. The Rules require that the Request identify all the relevant parties and describe the case. The Secretariat will then notify the "defendant" of the Request, forwarding all relevant documents. The defendant must answer the request within 30 days, setting forth its defence, any counterclaims, and any comments on the constitution of the arbitral tribunal. The claimant is allowed 30 days to reply to a counterclaim. Assuming that it has been established that there is a valid ICC arbitration clause, the Secretariat submits the case to the Court. The Court reviews the relevant documents and, unless the parties have made specific provisions, sets the place and language of the arbitration and chooses the arbitrator(s).

b. **Terms of Reference** – A key feature of ICC arbitration is found in the Terms of Reference drafted by the arbitrator (the singular will be used henceforth, although arbitral tribunals may involve three arbitrators), which describe the case, define the issues, and indicate the place and applicable rules for the arbitration. The Terms of Reference are submitted to the parties for signature and comment (the arbitrator may or may not amend the document according to the parties' input), then submitted to the Court. If one of the parties has not signed the Terms of Reference, the Court will decide whether or not to approve them. If both parties sign, the Court will only scrutinise and take note of the Terms. The arbitration goes forward regardless of the refusal of a party to sign the Terms of Reference.

Whether or not the Terms of Reference are a necessary or advisable part of arbitral procedure has been a long-standing debate within the international community of arbitration practitioners. It has been claimed that the usefulness of Terms of Reference is not sufficient to justify the expenditure of time on their preparation. In recent years, however, there has developed an emerging international consensus that some form of preliminary procedure – such as that of the ICC Terms of Reference – is useful. The ICC position is that Terms of Reference are an essential part of the ICC procedure and that they contribute significantly to focusing the issues, thereby increasing the effectiveness of later hearings. Moreover, anecdotal evidence from so-called "fast-track" arbitrations would appear to indicate that Terms of Reference can be prepared very quickly indeed if it is truly the desire of the parties to do so.

c. **Time Limits** – The Terms of Reference must be submitted to the Court within two months after the arbitrator receives the case file, and the arbitrator must make his award within six months after the signature of the Terms of Reference or the payment of the advance to cover administrative expenses (whichever comes later). However, the Court may authorise extensions of the time limits, and in practice such extensions are fairly common.

d. **Proceedings** – Although the parties are free to agree on rules of procedure, if they fail to do so these will be set by the arbitrator, who will further decide on the need for hearings (although the parties have a right to a hearing, if either so requests), examination of witnesses, or the appointment of experts. The parties may apply to any competent tribunal for a court order or injunction to freeze assets or force the other party to refrain from certain actions. The parties may also request such measures from the arbitrator, who may order different measures from those ordered by another judicial instance (this will depend on the law governing the proceeding; thus, such measures are not possible in Germany or Italy).

e. **Applicable law** – If the parties do not specify the applicable law, as by a choice of law clause, the arbitrator will decide.

f. **Award** – Final judgements by the arbitrator(s) are called awards. They must be in writing and are rendered either by unanimous decision, by majority, or failing these, by the Chairman. Dissents may be permitted in certain cases. If the parties are able to work out a settlement between themselves, they may wish to have such a settlement formalised as an award by the arbitrator, thereby facilitating enforcement. The award also decides the apportionment of costs for the arbitration, and whether one side must pay the other's legal fees.

The award is first submitted in draft form to the Court, which may modify the form of the award or make substantive suggestions to the arbitrator – without affecting the arbitrator's liberty of decision – before granting its approval. The parties are then notified of the award, but only after they have fully paid the costs of the arbitration.

If one of the parties refuses to comply with the award, the other party may seek enforcement by a competent court. Such recourse is considerably facilitated by the existence of the 1958 New York Convention on the Recognition and Enforcement of Foreign Arbitral Awards, which has been signed by more than 100 countries.

g. Costs – Costs include arbitrators' fees and expenses, administrative charges, and lawyers' fees and expenses.

The ICC's administrative expenses are calculated according to a fixed Schedule of Costs (the "Schedule") on the basis of the amount in dispute. The court estimates total expenses and fixes the amount for the required advance. Each party is required to pay 25% of the advance before the file is transmitted to the arbitrator(s); the balance of the advance must be paid for the Terms of Reference to come into force. If one party fails to pay its share, the other party must pay it or supply a bank guarantee. Arbitrators' fees are also fixed by the Court in accordance with the scale appended to the Schedule, although the court may in exceptional cases vary the fees or expenses.

h. Costs of ICC/other arbitrations – The criticism is sometimes heard that ICC arbitration – and arbitration under the rules of other private arbitral bodies – is "expensive" or "too expensive". It is also sometimes claimed that ICC arbitration is only suitable for "really big" cases, with minimum amounts in dispute of several hundred thousand dollars. Careful analysis shows that these observations, while not entirely devoid of substance, must be received with some scepticism.

First of all, in order to judge whether ICC arbitration is "expensive", some kind of pertinent comparison must be made. Very few figures are available on the costs of similarly complex international arbitrations by other arbitration institutions. The cost of "comparable" litigation is virtually impossible to estimate, because some litigated cases may be appealed repeatedly, for years, whereas other court judgements are immediately complied with. Although the diversity of cases is such that statistics on an average duration for arbitration would not be very helpful, it would appear that a typical ICC arbitration will often be completed within 1 to 3 years. This would suggest that ICC arbitration (like other forms or private commercial arbitration) is extremely competitive in terms of time and expense as compared to litigation before public tribunals, where cases commonly drag on many times longer, with a multiplication of legal fees and total expenses.

It is true, nonetheless, that the bulk of ICC arbitration concerns fairly large cases. In recent years, up to 60% of cases concerned amounts in excess of $1 million dollars. However, there is no minimum amount for ICC arbitration, and in fact the ICC regularly receives cases for very small amounts. Of course, when the amount in dispute is beneath a certain level, the cost of arbitral proceedings may end up being greater than the amount the claimant could hope to win in the award. However, this is equally the case with litigation and all other forms of institutional dispute resolution. It does happen that parties wish to arbitrate or litigate cases even for small amounts-in-dispute; these cases may involve a matter of principle, or may be linked to a larger commercial issue.

i. ICC "Fast-Track" Arbitration – The ICC is highly sensitive to the desire of multinational firms and legal counsel to have recourse to accelerated or expedited forms of arbitration. Of course, ICC arbitration is itself intended to be an accelerated or expedited procedure. A series of time limits are built into the arbitral process under the ICC rules, so that an arbitration that moves forward without time extensions should be completed within one year. Time extensions, however, are allowed and are quite common, especially in complex cases. Other arbitral institutions (such as the American Arbitration Association) have seen fit to draft specific rules for expedited arbitration.

Loosely, a fast-track arbitration is one where both parties have agreed to a specific form of expedited arbitral proceeding. What distinguishes a fast-track arbitration from one which is merely fast is that in the fast-track case the two parties "select a subset of disputes from the universe of potential disputes and agree that, if a dispute in this category arises, it will be resolved within a non-extendible time limit"[4]. The two components of fast-track arbitration are therefore: 1) *segmentation* – only a *subset* of possible disputes will be submitted, and 2) *time limits*.

These two components must be handled with caution. Both segmentation and time-limits can create considerable legal and procedural difficulties unless the contract is carefully and precisely drafted by experienced legal counsel. Thus, fast-track arbitration is not for everybody. If parties truly have a strong interest in providing for expedited procedures, they should invest time and forethought into crafting suitable arbitration provisions. Legal counsel are well-advised to consult the literature on fast-track arbitration, and to set aside sufficient time for negotiating and drafting the appropriate clauses.

Although it is not possible in this text to provide a detailed guide to the drafting of fast-track arbitration clauses, a few general rules may be of use. As indicated in a prior section, any arbitration, fast-track or other, will move more quickly if the parties have agreed in the arbitration clause on the basic questions of *place* and *language* of arbitration, *number of arbitrators*, and *applicable law*. With respect to the question of time-limits, parties should be aware of the dangers of setting a general or global time-limit for the entire arbitration. Should the time-limit subsequently prove impractical or impossible for the arbitrators to respect, the time-limit may put the entire arbitration into jeopardy. Therefore, it may be preferable to simply draft an arbitration clause which invests the arbitrator with the authority to "set an accelerated procedure within the arbitrator's sole discretion". This alternative is more likely to adapt itself to the procedural and factual particularities of the case.

For parties unwilling or disinclined to draft the precise conditions necessary for fast-track arbitration, there may be some value in including a general statement that the two parties "strongly desire" that arbitral proceedings be conducted in the most expedited manner possible. This may allow the arbitrator certain leeway to take measures to push the arbitration along, while protecting the final award from an attack by the losing party on due process grounds.

3.6 Other arbitration institutions and rules

There are various alternatives to ICC arbitration. Other well-known arbitration institutions include the London Court of International Arbitration (LCIA), the American Arbitration Association (AAA), the Stockholm Court of Arbitration, the China International Economic and Trade Arbitration Commission (CIETAC), and many others around the world. The AAA, for example, handles a large number of international cases, but this number is still relatively small in proportion to their domestic cases. The AAA was not specifically set up to handle international cases, but has nonetheless developed a set of supplemental rules for international arbitrations.

The United Nations Commission on International Trade Law (UNCITRAL) has promulgated a very important set of rules for international commercial arbitration which allow the arbitration to be handled by any arbitration institution, or independently of an arbitration institution ("ad hoc" arbitration). Thus, the AAA and the ICC will supervise arbitrations conducted under UNCITRAL rules. Since the UNCITRAL rules were developed without reference to a specific arbitration institution, they are somewhat general as regards costs and fees, merely establishing a standard of "reasonableness". A notable success of the UNCITRAL rules involved their use as the basis of proceedings at the US – Iranian Claims Tribunal at the Hague.

"Ad hoc" arbitration refers to an arbitration that is structured by the parties themselves. The parties may base themselves in part on rules and procedures such as those of the ICC or UNCITRAL, or they may create their own "custom-made" procedure. Although ad hoc arbitrations can be useful in some contexts, parties should be aware that they require the utmost level of expertise on behalf of the legal counsel who negotiate the arbitration structure and draft the arbitration clause. The absence of institutional supervision means that the only safeguard against intentional dilatory tactics or other abuse of process must be found in the arbitration clause and its provisions.

Notes

[1] "the plaintiff follows the forum of the defendant."

[2] The New York Convention on the Recognition and Enforcement of Foreign Arbitral Awards – more than 100 countries are parties; for a full list of signatory countries contact the UNCITRAL Secretariat.

[3] Notes to the author from Eric Schwarz, former Secretary General of the ICC International Court of Arbitration.

[4] "When Doctrines Meet – Fast-Track Arbitration and the ICC Experience", Davis et. al., p. 70.

Chapter Four
International Contracts of Sale and General Conditions

The basics: The international sale contract is the central contract in export transactions. In law, a contract is created by the conjunction of offer and acceptance. In international trade, this offer and acceptance may be manifested in a variety of fashions, such as by the exchange of exporter's pro forma invoice (offer) and importer's purchase order (acceptance). A more sophisticated alternative is a sale contract specifically designed to suit the circumstances of the transaction, signed by both parties. A good sale contract or set of general conditions of sale will cover all the principal elements of the transaction, so that surprises and uncertainties are avoided. The parties' respective duties as concern the payment mechanism, transport contract and insurance responsibilities, inter alia, will all be clearly detailed in the contract.

4.1 The law governing the contract of sale

The rights of buyers and sellers in international transactions are governed either by *national law* (usually, the law of either the seller or the buyer's domicile) or by an international treaty, the *Vienna Convention on the International Sale of Goods* (described below). Since the Vienna Convention and most national sales laws are based on the distilled experience of centuries of commerce, it should not be surprising that they exhibit a great degree of similarity. This substantial international uniformity in commercial practice is at the heart of the concept of *lex mercatoria*, the international law of merchants. The lex mercatoria, according to its proponents, is a massive body of international custom and experience which can assist traders and judicial bodies in resolving commercial disputes.

Despite the emergence of a certain level of international uniformity as regards national commercial laws, there remain important differences. Such differences can be determinative of the outcome in a particular case, so that redress for a particular party may depend on which national law applies. For this reason, it is still quite common for the party in the stronger negotiating position to seek to impose a choice of law clause stipulating that its national law governs the contract.

4.1.1 The Vienna Convention on Contracts for the International Sale of Goods (CISG)

Commonly referred to as «the Vienna Convention», or by its initials (CISG), this treaty is well on its way to providing a universal legal infrastructure for international commerce. As of 1996, 46 countries had ratified CISG, including most of the major trading nations. The pace of ratification has been such that it is possible to hope for near-global coverage in the coming decades. Consequently, all international trade professionals should acquire a basic familiarity with the provisions of this key document.

a. Scope – CISG is in effect a sales code for international commercial transactions. Four important constraints limit its application:

1) *It only applies to international sales* – CISG applies if both parties to the contract are in different Contracting States (countries which have ratified CISG), or if only one of the parties is in a Contracting State but conflict of laws rules point to the application of the law of that state, or if both parties expressly agree to submit their contract to the application of CISG (conceivably, even if neither is in a Contracting State).

2) *CISG expressly <u>excludes</u> coverage of:* consumer sales; sales of ships, aircraft and electricity; securities transactions; sales where services play a preponderant role (although in this latter case the two parties may specifically state that they wish to override the exclusion and subject their contract to CISG).

3) *CISG does not cover certain important aspects* of international sales, most notably:
- *trade terms* (terms for the delivery of the goods and the fixing of the price, such as FOB and CIF, where CISG defers, inter alia, to *Incoterms* – see below); and
- *the passing of property* in the goods (the point at which the title to the goods is transferred from the exporter to the buyer – see below).

4) *CISG provides that parties may "contract out" of CISG* or any of its provisions; this is in recognition of the principle of freedom of contract. Parties may also use CISG as a primary law governing the contract, but agree to resort to a specific national law [1] as a "gap-filling" device.

b. Key provisions – CISG is composed of 101 articles which take up approximately 20 printed pages. Exporters and importers should especially be aware of the following points (keeping in mind that it is possible to expressly vary or exclude CISG provisions if both parties agree):

1) *Oral contracts* – These are permitted and enforceable under CISG; signed writings are *not* required.

2) *Prior course of dealings and trade usages* – CISG provides that the «parties are bound by any usage to which they have agreed and by any practices they have established between themselves».

3) *Contract formation* – An offer is any proposal that is «sufficiently definite,» meaning that it at least "indicates the goods and expressly or implicitly fixes or makes provision for determining the quantity and the price". Acceptance of an offer is effective when it reaches the offeror; however, the offeror may not revoke an offer once the offeree has dispatched his acceptance.

4) *The "Battle of the Forms"* – When the parties exchange printed forms which differ on certain terms, the question arises, which form prevails, the seller's or the buyer's? The CISG rule is that a buyer's acceptance which differs *materially*

(e.g., on a key point such as price, quantity, quality or delivery date) from the seller's offer amounts to a rejection and counter-offer, which the seller must expressly accept. If the buyer's acceptance only differs on points which are not *material*, then the acceptance is deemed to form a valid contract unless the seller objects. Ultimately, the easiest option is to try to always be the one who "fires the last shot". Thus, exporters may wish to provide a printed acknowledgement form – including the general conditions of sale – in response to buyers' purchase orders. Obviously, if either party believes that a provision contained in the other's general conditions is material and unacceptable, they should openly negotiate for a modification of that provision (see further discussion below on general conditions of sale).

5) *Delivery and risk of loss/Incoterms/UCP 500* – Delivery and risk of loss are covered much *less fully* than by Incoterms 1990; traders, therefore, should explicitly incorporate Incoterms into the sale contract (see below). Moreover, in contracts involving letters of credit, banks will generally follow rules in the International Chamber of Commerce's UCP 500, which require that "all parties deal in documents, not goods". To avoid discrepancy between CISG and the UCP 500, a prudent approach would be to specifically refer to UCP 500 in that part of the sale contract setting out the seller's documentary duties.

6) *Passage of property/title* – Not covered by CISG (nor Incoterms), therefore a matter of applicable domestic law; traders should specify the point at which they wish title to pass, after having checked the compliance of said provision with domestic law.

7) *Warranties* – CISG provides that the seller must deliver goods which are "of the quantity, quality and description required by the contract... The goods do not conform with the contract unless they...are fit for the purposes for which goods of the same description would ordinarily be used [or] are fit for any particular purpose expressly or impliedly made known to the seller at the time... of the contract".

8) *Inspection of the goods* – The buyer must inspect the goods and "loses the right to rely on a lack of conformity of the goods if he does not give notice... within a reasonable time after he has discovered [the non-conformity] or ought to have discovered it". The exporter may wish to expressly specify a limited period for notification of defects. Moreover, the exporter may wish to expressly override the CISG article 27, under which the exporter bears the risk of delay or non-receipt of notices from the buyer.

9) *Remedies* – CISG allows for the full scope of remedies, including specific performance, delivery of substitute goods, price reduction, and compensatory damages. Exporters may wish to expressly limit recourse to these remedies, as, for example, by limiting liability and by excluding consequential damages, price reduction or specific performance options.

As is inevitably the case with attempts at international harmonisation, CISG may not be to the benefit of all traders in all sales transactions. CISG is sometimes said to be more favourable to buyers and to parties in developing countries than to sellers or parties in industrialised countries. Nonetheless, CISG is undeniably a landmark document which will play a central role in international commerce in the decades to come. It is sufficiently comprehensive and balanced that more and more parties are likely to turn to it as an alternative to protracted negotiating contests in which each side seeks to impose its own domestic law.

4.2 The contract of sale

4.2.1 Basic elements

Under most legal systems, an international contract of sale comes into existence when a sufficiently precise offer by one party is accepted unconditionally by the other party. A sufficiently precise offer generally includes:
- a clear description of the goods
- price and payment terms
- delivery terms, including packing, invoicing, transportation and insurance instructions.

Whether or not an offer in a particular case is adequately precise will depend on the applicable law and circumstances of the case. Even if one or more of the above "essential" terms is absent from an agreement, a court may nonetheless find a binding contract. A variety of devices can be used to "fill in the gaps".

Either the exporter or importer can be the one who makes the first legally-binding offer. To take one example: an exporter replies to an inquiry from a prospective importer with a quotation which is clearly only intended to be an invitation to contract (and therefore not a binding offer). In such a case, the importer's purchase order is considered the offer. If the exporter wishes to conclude a contract, he will accept the offer, which is usually done via a confirmation.

However, to take a slightly different example, suppose that the exporter's sales proposal is extremely concrete, contains all the above essential elements, is addressed to a specific importer and the exporter clearly intends to be bound thereby. Here, the exporter's proposal amounts to a legally binding offer and the importer's purchase order constitutes an acceptance, concluding a binding contract.

4.2.2 Checklist – Key clauses in international sales contracts

The following clauses are often included in international contracts of sale and general conditions of sale:

- preamble
- identification of parties
- description of goods
- price and payment conditions
- delivery periods and conditions
- inspection of the goods – obligations and limitations
- quantity or quality variations in the products delivered
- reservation of title and passing of property rights
- transfer of risk – how accomplished
- seller's warranties and buyer's complaints

- assignment of rights
- force majeure clause
- requirement that amendments or modifications be in writing
- choice of controlling language of the contract
- choice of law
- choice of dispute resolution mechanism

4.2.3 Elements of a sale contract; the ICC Model Contract

The discussion below of sale contract clauses will frequently refer to the ICC Model International Contract of Sale (hereafter, the "ICC model"). Note, however, that the ICC model contract is two-part in nature. The first part, the *Special Conditions*, contains the basic information commonly found in export quotes or pro forma invoices. The second part, the *General Conditions*, establishes a general legal framework. Many international contracts, however, do not follow this two-part structure. Therefore, the discussion below assumes a contract based on a single set of clauses. We will examine the specific ICC provisions in greater detail in section 4.3.3 on general conditions of sale or purchase.

a. **Parties to the contract; preamble –** These introductory types of clauses generally identify the parties and the effective date of the contract. It is important that the parties, and their correct legal denomination, be carefully and exactly specified. In some countries corporations, especially family-owned ones, can be knit into a network of cross-owned companies. Some of these companies may be mere "shells" without assets, which means that a lawsuit against them could prove fruitless. Therefore, the party identified in the contract should be exactly the same company for which credit and bank references have been fully checked, and not one of its sister companies with a similar name. Likewise, an individual signing a contract on behalf of a company should do so in such a fashion that it is clear which party is to be bound by the contract, the company or its representative.

b. **Subject matter; product description and/or "scope of work" –** In a sale contract, the minimum "scope of work" is the seller's supply of the specified products. Where the contract calls for a *preponderant* part of the seller's obligations to involve services or labour, CISG (the Vienna Convention) is no longer applicable, unless the parties expressly decide to incorporate CISG notwithstanding the non-merchandise characteristics of the contract. As in the ICC model contract, introductory clauses may set forth basic definitions and/or explanations of the structure of the contract.

c. **Description** – The question of preciseness of description of the contract goods is worthy of attention. Generally, exporters should be cautious and brief in describing products. In some legal systems, if the goods delivered vary from the description given in the contract it may be possible for an importer faced by a falling market to terminate the contract, claiming that the seller has not fulfilled the contractual duty to deliver goods of the contract description. A buyer acting in bad faith might seek to seize upon irrelevant details which the seller has unwisely and unnecessarily placed in the contract. Thus, it can be dangerous to deliver goods which are "too good" – that is, goods of a superior but slightly different nature to that specified in the contract. Example: a buyer contracts to buy a shipment of used personal computers containing Intel "386" chips. The seller ultimately delivers – for the same price – computers containing "486" chips (which are technically superior). The buyer, for commercial reasons, is no longer able to pay for the shipment. Some systems of law would allow the buyer to terminate such a contract, on the grounds that the seller has delivered goods which are different to those required by the contract.

Risks resulting from excessively detailed product description can also arise in connection with a letter of credit. If a contract of sale is based on a pro forma invoice which contains an excessively detailed description of the products, the chances are increased that some aspect of that description will conflict with other documents required under the credit, thereby leading to a discrepancy and rejection by the bank of the documents. Certainly, if the seller delivers merchandise which is "too good" as in the previous paragraph, and the commercial invoice then differs from the product description in the letter of credit, the bank will initially reject the documents and it will be up to the importer to decide whether or not to waive the discrepancy.

The importer, on the other hand, is faced with contrary imperatives. She will want to negotiate a description which identifies the goods with sufficient precision such that the exporter cannot deliver goods which are "almost" good enough. Vague and general locutions are not helpful in the event of a later dispute and should be replaced by objective or documentary criteria (e.g., «top quality fish meal» will not be as useful in a court dispute under a documentary credit as "inspection certificate issued by XX company to indicate fish-meal with a minimum 70.75% protein content"). Some contracts include a separate Definitions section, for technical terms or terms with legal connotations, such as "delivery", "shipment", "acceptance", or "confirmation".

Exporters may wish to stipulate in their sale contracts or general conditions of sale that variations in quality or quantity which are of minimal importance should not be grounds for termination of the contract. For minor defects in the products, which do not prevent the buyer from using them more or less as intended, the buyer and seller may agree that it is fair that the buyer pay a reduced price or get a refund, because the goods delivered were of lesser quality than those specified in the contract at the contract price.

For defects which make it impossible for the buyer to use the goods at all, the buyer will commonly wish to negotiate for a right to a full refund, although she may find herself obliged to accept a corresponding duty to take care that any goods under her control are not improperly stored or disposed of, assuming that they have any residual value. The question of whether or not the buyer should also be entitled to consequential damages (damages which result from the contract breach, such as lost profits or production) is one that will vary according to the commercial context and legal system.

Export and the law: In a case in which the contract had called for "timber staves one-half inch thick", goods were ultimately delivered which were either more than five-eighths of an inch thick or between one-half and five-eighths of an inch thick. Despite testimony that the goods' quality had no negative practical consequence, the court observed:

> *"If the written contract specifies conditions of weight, measurement and the like, those conditions must be complied with. A ton does not mean about a ton, or a yard about a yard... If the seller wants a margin he must and in my opinion does stipulate for it. Of course by recognised trade usage particular figures may be given a different meaning, as in a baker's dozen...*
>
> *If a condition is not performed the buyer has a right to reject... No doubt, in business, men often find it unnecessary or inexpedient to insist on their strict legal rights. In a normal market if they get something substantially like the specified goods they may take them with or without grumbling and a claim for an allowance. But in a falling market I find that buyers are often as eager to insist on their legal rights as courts of law are ready to maintain them."*
>
> – Arcos Ltd. v. E.A. Ronaasen & Son (1933) AC 470 HL[2]

d. Pricing – Whenever the contract is one for long duration, or when inflation or currency fluctuations otherwise make it wise, exporters should consider including *price escalation* or *adaptation* clauses. One possibility is to make the price firm for a given period of time, and beyond that time to peg the price to publicly available labour and/or commodities indexes. There are thus situations in which it is acceptable to the parties to leave some uncertainty in the price – as of the date of conclusion of the contract; but the mechanism for fixing the price later should be clear.

For examples of price escalation clauses and formulae there are numerous industry and trade-association instruments. Thus, the Federation of British Electrotechnical and Allied Manufacturer's Associations (BEAMA) has issued a series of Contract Price Adjustment (CPA) clauses, which set precise arithmetical formulae for calculating price variations resulting from fluctuations in the cost of materials and labour. The United Nations Economic Commission for Europe has issued a series of general conditions of sale for the erection of plant and machinery abroad (sometimes called «turnkey» contracts), which contain a straightforward price revision formula which allows the parties to negotiate the degree of price adjustment and to agree on the public indexes or other sources of economic statistics upon which the revisions will be based.[3]

e. Delivery, transport, insurance – In international contracts, these items are best covered by reference to *Incoterms 1990*, trade terms defined by the ICC (see section on Incoterms 1990 below), such as FCA (Free Carrier), FOB (Free on Board) or CIF (Cost, Insurance and Freight). Incoterms 1990 principally cover allocation of international transport costs, transfer of risk, responsibility for customs clearance and duties, and responsibility for obtaining insurance coverage. Incoterms 1990 are nonetheless fairly general terms, and parties may be well-advised, particularly when dealing with new counterparties, to make additional specifications with respect to the exact manner of delivery, the amount and duration of insurance, and necessary limitations on suitable transport. The ICC model stipulates the Ex Works (EXW) term as a fallback provision when the parties have not otherwise chosen a specific trade term.

The importer will be wise to describe precisely the point of delivery. A failure to do so will allow the exporter to exploit general terms – thus, "FOB Spain" will ultimately allow the exporter to deliver at any Spanish port.

The question of timeliness of delivery is often dealt with by specific provisions in the contract of sale. With some products, late delivery is not a cause of concern, and the payment of a small percentage penalty by the exporter in such cases seems reasonable. However, with other products (e.g., a birthday cake), late delivery is a serious breach, depriving the importer of the entire value of the product. In such cases, the importer will want to insist in the contract that time of delivery is "of the essence". The importer may further wish to make the exporter liable for consequential damages flowing from late delivery. Such provisions will be strongly resisted by exporters, but in certain jurisdictions some liability for consequential damages may be inescapable regardless of contractual provisions.

f. **Retention of title and passage of property** – The transfer of legal title to goods in international transactions is, perhaps somewhat surprisingly, covered neither by Incoterms nor the Vienna Convention; it is purely a matter of national law. Consequently, the parties are free to specify how title passes provided they do so within the limitations fixed by the applicable national law. In this area the ICC has published a highly useful *Guide to Retention of Title*, and will publish in 1997 an in-depth comparative guide to national legislations on the *Transfer of Ownership in the International Sale of Goods*.

The *retention of title* clause (also called reservation of title) is a common one in international trade. It provides that the seller retains the property in the goods until the full purchase price is paid. In a sales transaction without a retention of title (*ROT*) clause, title passes from the seller to the buyer independently of the payment of the purchase price. In some countries, title will pass at the moment of physical delivery of the goods, while in others title passes according to the agreement is reached between seller and buyer. If a buyer who has received goods is unwilling or unable to pay the price, the seller may find himself barred from claiming title to the goods. These considerations become crucial when buyers become insolvent and other creditors are competing for the buyer's remaining assets. With a valid ROT clause, the seller can reclaim the goods even if the buyer is bankrupt.

There are several variations of the ROT clause, but two major types can be distinguished:

1) *The simple ROT clause*, under which the seller retains title until the price is paid, and

2) *The extended clause*, under which the seller seeks to extend its title to include:

    ii) the proceeds from any sale of the goods

    ii) any goods commingled with, or manufactured from the contract goods

    iii) any other indebtedness owed to seller by the buyer

    iv) any combination of the foregoing

The availability of recourse to extended-type clauses will depend on the applicable national law. Contract drafters therefore should prepare the ROT clause in light of the national law as regards the transfer of title.

g. Penalty and Liquidated Damages Clauses – The contract may provide that a party which fails to comply with obligations, or is late in doing so, will pay a fixed sum. The purpose may be to compensate the damaged party (liquidated damages) or to stimulate compliance via the threat of punishment (penalties). In some jurisdictions, penalties are not allowed and consequently liquidated damages which are held to be punitively harsh will be invalid. It is therefore prudent to provide a pre-estimate of likely damages, even if these are difficult to calculate, so that courts will be more likely to respect the fixed sum as a form of liquidated damages. A liquidated damages clause makes it unnecessary for a court to calculate damages. This can work to the advantage of both parties: for the buyer, because it provides an easy way to calculate damages; for the seller, because it limits the potential extent of those damages.

h. Force Majeure and Hardship/Excusable Delays – Under most systems of law, a party can be excused from a failure to perform a contract obligation which is caused by the intervention of a totally unforeseeable event, such as the outbreak of war, or an "act of God" such as an earthquake or hurricane. Under the American commercial code (UCC) the standard for this relief is one of "*commercial impracticability*". In contrast, many civil law jurisdictions apply the term *force majeure* to this problem. Under CISG, the standard is based on the concept of "*impediments*" to performance. Because of the differences between these standards, parties might be well advised to draft their own *force majeure, hardship,* or *excusable delays* clause. The ICC publication, "Force Majeure and Hardship" provides a sample force majeure clause which can be incorporated by reference, as well as a hardship clause which must be expressly integrated in the contract. In addition, the ICC Model provides a similar, somewhat more concise formulation of a force majeure clause.

When the seller wishes to devise his own excusable delays clause, he will seek to anticipate in its provision such potential difficulties as those related to obtaining government authorisations, changes in customs duties or regulations, drastic fluctuations in labour, materials, energy, or transportation prices, etc.

4.3 General conditions of sale (or purchase)

4.3.1 The purpose of general conditions of sale (or purchase)

Many international contracts are made up of two parts: 1) a precise commercial offer in the form of a pro forma invoice or memorandum, which is subject to 2) certain standard legal terms known as "*general conditions,*" "general conditions of sale/purchase," or "general terms and conditions". The general conditions often appear as a pre-printed set of clauses on the back of, or attached to, specific tenders, proposals, price lists, catalogues, acceptances, confirmations or purchase orders.

The purpose of general conditions is to complement bare exchanges of business forms or correspondence which do not cover all important legal aspects of the transaction. General conditions are *not* used whenever a unique, detailed contract is to be specifically drafted. General conditions save time by establishing a standard legal framework which will then apply to a multitude of repeated, individual transactions. This enables exporters to carry on and conclude negotiations on the key practical issues of price, delivery terms and quality, leaving the legal "fine points" to be covered by the general conditions. Those contractual provisions which are *not* appropriate for inclusion in general conditions are those that will vary from contract to contract, such as price, product specification and delivery details.

4.3.2 The "battle of the forms": obtaining agreement to general conditions

With general conditions, as with other provisions of the contract of sale, one must obtain the agreement of one's counterparty. Thus, if a seller were to send the general conditions along with the commercial invoice after the goods had been dispatched, the conditions would have no legal effect. However, if one party transmits general conditions along with the offer or acceptance, the *silence* or *performance* of the contract by the other party may be construed as *acceptance* of the general conditions. It is nonetheless preferable that the counterparty agree to the general conditions *in writing*. One way to obtain written agreement is to include a *confirmation slip* along with the order or acceptance form (to which the general conditions are attached). The counterparty is requested to return the confirmation slip, duly signed. As a result, some exporters have a rule that sales personnel are not authorised to sign customer purchase orders without management review (because to do so could indicate assent to the buyer's general conditions of purchase).

Many international traders do not systematically address the battle of forms issue. Instead, a series of printed forms are exchanged between seller and buyer (proposal, purchase order, acknowledgement, confirmation, etc.), and performance follows without further reflection. Only when a dispute arises and the lawyers are called in do parties begin to consider the significance of discrepancies between their general conditions.

> **Example:** An exporter's general conditions (printed on the back of the sales offer) contain a broad clause admitting various possible excuses for minor delays, whereas the importer's general conditions (printed on the back of the purchase order) contain a much more restrictive *Force Majeure* clause under which most foreseeable delays are inexcusable. The exporter's shipment arrives late, for reasons excused by the exporter's clause – but not the importer's. In such a case, the exporter who has not bothered to demand written confirmation of acceptance of his general conditions could find himself faced with a suit for damages (which can be surprisingly large in jurisdictions allowing for consequential damages)[1].

The only absolutely "safe" procedure is to refuse to conclude the contract until the other side signs your general conditions. However, since this may be viewed as impractical or unwieldy, some traders resort to the "last shot" theory. Under this approach, whichever party transmits the last printed form ("fires the last shot") has a better chance of imposing its general conditions. This is by no means as legally secure as a negotiated, signed agreement, since the availability of the last-shot theory will depend on applicable law.

1. See International Contract Manual, Kritzer ed., Kluwer, Farrington Looseleaf.

4.3.3 ICC Model General Conditions of Sale, a balanced set of clauses

As described in the preceding sections, the ICC has developed a set of Model General Conditions of Sale in conjunction with the ICC Model International Sales Contract (the "ICC Model"). The ICC Model consists of two parts:

Special Conditions – This part corresponds to the role of a form sale contract or pro forma invoice; and

General Conditions – This part provides a detailed legal background to complement the basic provisions on price, product description, payment and delivery terms contained in the Special Conditions.

It is intended that parties be free to use the ICC General Conditions independently, even if they do not use the Special Conditions.

The ICC Model as a whole is intended to dovetail with the provisions of the Vienna Convention, thereby creating a "CISG-compatible" instrument. Although the ICC Model differs substantially from other, more specifically-targeted general conditions, it can serve as a useful example of one way of dealing with the issues usually covered by general sales conditions.

a. **Scope** – Because general conditions will vary according to the nature of the products, the ICC decided to focus on a single key sector of international trade: mass-produced manufactured goods intended for ultimate re-sale to consumers. This would cover everything from toasters to toothbrushes, but would not apply to goods for industrial use such as large machine-tools, nor to custom-made goods, raw materials or commodities.

b. **Incorporation by reference** – It is intended that parties be able to incorporate the ICC Model by a simple reference, such as: "This contract is subject to the general conditions of the ICC Model International Contract of Sale". Theoretically, an exporter could make a sales offer, "100£/container blue widgets FOB London Incoterms 1990 under the general conditions of the ICC Model International Contract of Sale", and expect thereby to conclude, with buyer's accepance, a detailed and complete international contract of sale. However, whether or not courts would enforce the reference to the ICC General Conditions could depend on whether it could be established that the buyer was familiar with those terms. So it is probably better to include the full text of the general conditions, at least in early communications to the counterparty. Moreover, in light of the discussion above on the battle of forms, it is preferable to obtain the counterparty's signed agreement to the general conditions.

c. **Product characteristics** – How strictly will the exporter be bound to deliver the exact qualities and specifications he mentions in his sales literature and in his catalogues? The ICC Model provides that product characteristics (e.g., dimensions, capacities, prices, colours, etc.) contained in catalogues and brochures, or evidenced in samples, will only be binding upon the seller if they are expressly referred to in the sales contract.

d. **Pre-shipment inspection (PSI) and examination of the goods** – The ICC Model provides the following rule: if the parties have agreed to PSI, the seller must notify the buyer within a reasonable time before shipment that the goods are ready for inspection.

e. **Price and payment conditions** – Under the ICC Model, the current list price of the seller applies unless otherwise agreed. The price is net of VAT and is not subject to price adjustment.

The ICC Model permits use of all payment modes, including open account, documentary collection, documentary credit, and payment in advance. If the parties fail to specify any form of payment, a default provision is based on an open account payment by electronic funds transfer.

f. **Retention of title** – If the parties have agreed on retention of title, the goods shall remain the property of the seller until the complete payment of the price or as otherwise agreed (see discussion of retention of title in preceding section).

g. **Delivery** – Unless otherwise agreed, delivery is at seller's place of business (EXW Incoterms 1990). The ICC Model also makes highly specific provisions with respect to calculation of liquidated damages in the event of buyer's claim for lateness or non-delivery, the idea being to limit the amount of damages available to the buyer in the event of a delayed shipment. In essence, the seller must pay liquidated damages of 0.5% of the price per week of lateness up to a maximum of 5% of the price.

h. **Transfer of risk** – According to the rule of Incoterms.

i. **Non-conformity of the goods** – Products with tolerances which are reasonable or within the range of usages or common practices shall not be deemed non-conforming. The buyer must notify the seller in writing of any non-conformity within a specified period of time.

j. **Force majeure** – Failure of performance by either party is excused in the event of "force majeure", which in essence amounts to reasonably unforeseeable and unavoidable circumstances which make it substantially impossible for a party to fulfil its obligations.

k. **Applicable law and arbitration** – Any questions not covered by the ICC Model are to resolved by reference to CISG, and if these are not covered by CISG, to general principles of international trade (see above, lex mercatoria) or to principles common to the national laws of the parties. Dispute resolution is by arbitration under the ICC Rules of Conciliation and Arbitration.

4.3.4 Industry-specific general conditions – UN ECE and others

Many trade associations and international organisations have developed general conditions which are specifically suited for a particular industrial sector. The United Nations Economic Commission for Europe (UN ECE), in particular, has developed a series of these instruments. A typical example is UN ECE 188, entitled "General Conditions for the Supply of Plant and Machinery for Export". UN ECE 188 resembles the ICC Model in many key respects, but is understandably much more detailed when it comes to such items as delivery (which can be particularly complicated when the product is an entire manufacturing plant), technical drawings, and guarantees. Traders should check with their relevant industry association for the existence of specifically-adapted general conditions.

4.4 Trade terms for international contracts – Incoterms 1990

The basics: Incoterms are internationally standardised "trade terms" (such as FCA, FOB, and CIF), which enable exporters to quote prices that clearly allocate the costs and risks of international transport between seller and buyer. Insurance responsibilities (under CIF and CIP) and customs formalities are also covered by Incoterms.

Incoterms should be explicitly incorporated into contracts of sale by reference, e.g., "FOB Rotterdam Incoterms 1990". Incoterms govern certain responsibilities between *seller* and *buyer* under the *contract of sale*; they should not be confused with the allocation of responsibilities between *shipper, carrier* and consignee under the *contract of carriage.*

When goods are containerised, transport is multi-modal, or delivery is to an inland terminal, traders should *not use* the traditional set of maritime terms, FOB – CFR – CIF, but should instead use the more appropriate terms, FCA – CPT – CIP.

Reflecting the general trend in international trade and transport to "house-to-house" service, the "delivered" or "D-terms" Incoterms (especially DDU and DDP) are becoming more prevalent.

4.4.1 Introductory

a. **How were Incoterms developed? How are they used?** The ICC derived Incoterms (*International Commercial Terms*) from studies of prevailing international trade practices, publishing the first version of Incoterms in 1936. Subsequent revisions were published in 1953, 1967, 1976 and 1980. The current valid version is Incoterms 1990, and the next revision will probably not appear before the year 2000. Incoterms can be incorporated into contracts by simple reference, e.g. "FOB Liverpool Incoterms 1990".

The Incoterms tell the buyer what is «included» in the sales price, by allocating transport costs and risks, as well as the responsibility for insurance and customs formalities, between the seller and buyer.

There are 13 Incoterms. They can be thought of as representing a stepladder of increasing responsibility from seller's premises to buyer's premises. Thus, the Incoterm which represents the minimum responsibility for the seller is EXW (Ex Works), which is generally used in cases involving delivery at the seller's factory or warehouse. At the other extreme, the Incoterm DDP (Delivered Duty Paid) represents maximum responsibility on the part of the seller, with delivery generally at the buyer's premises.

A buyer on EXW terms knows that nothing "extra" (in terms of transport, customs clearance or insurance) is included in the sales price – the buyer must handle the entire transport operation herself. A buyer on DDP terms ("Delivered Duty Paid"), knows the quoted price includes all transport costs, risks and formalities up to the final destination. In between these two extremes, there are

11 other Incoterms, representing a range of options for the division of costs/risks between the parties.

b. How does one incorporate Incoterms into a contract?

> **Key reminder:** traders should explicity refer to "INCOTERMS 1990". Traders should link their contracts to Incoterms by explicitly referring to Incoterms. The common practice of quoting a price as follows, "$100/ton FOB New York" (without an explicit reference to "Incoterms 1990") can be DANGEROUS. In the absence of a specific reference to Incoterms the trader may lose the right to apply Incoterms to the contract. The contract may consequently be subjected to a national legal definition, with surprising results [e.g., the American definition of FOB can be quite different from the "Incoterms" definition]. The correct formulation of the above contract would be "$100/ton FOB New York Incoterms 1990".

c. Are Incoterms the law? The legal nature of Incoterms is frequently misunderstood. Incoterms are creatures of contract, not legislation. Incoterms apply to a contract whenever the parties can demonstrate that they both intended Incoterms to apply. If the parties fail to incorporate Incoterms into the sale contract, they may not be able to invoke Incoterms once a dispute has arisen; instead, national legal interpretations may apply.

There are, however, exceptions. If trade customs, general sales conditions, commercial usages or previous contractual dealings indicate that the parties intended to use Incoterms, then Incoterms may apply even in the absence of a specific mention in the sale contract. Under some legal systems great weight is given to customs of trade and there may be a presumption that Incoterms constitute a custom of trade. In such countries, courts or arbitrators might take judicial notice of an Incoterms rule to resolve a case although Incoterms had not been incorporated into the contract.

d. Why should importers and exporters understand the Incoterms in detail? Many international traders, unfortunately, have only a general idea of the differences between such Incoterms such as EXW, FOB, CIF or DDP. As a result, they are unprepared for certain common contingencies with respect to transfer of risk, loading/unloading, customs clearance and insurance. For example, one of the more common uncertainties arising in international sales is, who is responsible for loading (or unloading) the goods? An understanding of Incoterms will generally allow the matter to be solved.

e. What important matters are not covered by Incoterms? The Incoterms do not cover all possible legal or transport issues arising out of an international sale. Incoterms are a sort of contractual shorthand which allows the parties to easily specify their understanding as to: 1) the transport costs which the seller will cover; 2) the point at which risk of loss will be transferred from seller to buyer; 3) who must handle customs formalities and pay duties; and, 4) in the case of CIF and CIP, the seller's responsibility to provide insurance cover.

Other details must be dealt with specifically in the contract. Thus, there is nothing in the Incoterms on how the seller should transport the goods to the agreed delivery point. If the sale is "FOB Buenos Aires Incoterms 1990" the buyer has no control – under Incoterms – over how the seller gets the goods to Buenos Aires. But it may be very important to the buyer that the goods be transported in a certain way, for example, in refrigerated containers. If this is the case, the buyer should specify in the contract how the goods must be transported to the delivery point.

> **Key reminder:** The Incoterms cannot be expected to make up for a contract which is not sufficiently precise. In many cases it is advisable to include in the sale contract precise details on exact place and method of delivery, loading and unloading charges, extent of insurance, and mode of transport.

Moreover, Incoterms only cover those cases where one party has an *obligation* to the other party to do something. Incoterms do not indicate when a trader should do something because it is *prudent* or advisable. Thus, a buyer of merchandise in an FOB contract has no obligation to take out insurance, and Incoterms are silent on this matter. But since the risk of loss is on the buyer once the goods have been loaded, she would be very foolish not to take out insurance.

f. Transfer of property or title – One of the key areas *not* governed by Incoterms is that of the transfer of property or title to goods. In fact, there is no international legal harmonisation as regards the transfer or title or property in international transactions. Thus, the matter is not resolved by the Vienna Convention on the International Sale of Goods.

Since the law on transfer of property rights differs from country to country, the parties to a contract of sale may wish to specifically provide for this matter in the contract, but only after determining what is permissible under the applicable law. Under many jurisdictions it is possible for the seller to retain title and ownership of the property until the purchase price is paid in full, even if this takes years. This "*retention of title*" by the seller is usually set out in a clause in the contract of sale (see discussion above in section on Contract of Sale).

4.4.2 The contract of sale and the contract of carriage: Incoterms, Liner terms and Charter party terms

Perhaps the most common misunderstanding related to Incoterms involves confusing the *contract of sale* with the *contract of carriage*. Note the distinction:

• *Contract of sale* – Incoterms are embedded in this contract, an agreement between the *seller* and *buyer*.

• *Contract of carriage* – This contract is between the *shipper* and the *carrier* (or his agent). Depending on the contract of sale and the chosen Incoterm, the shipper may be either the seller or the buyer.

Incoterms are not part of the contract of carriage. However, the choice of Incoterm may oblige the shipper to obtain a contract of carriage with particular conditions. One cause of confusion in this area is that terms in the contract of carriage resemble Incoterms (for example, in their usage of the word "free" as in "free in and out") – but traders should remember that these are separate contracts with separate sets of responsibilities.

Many traders appear to expect that the transport contract will automatically accord with the Incoterm in the sales contract. Although it is indeed important that the transport responsibilities required by the Incoterm in the contract of sale accord with the terms of the contract of carriage, there is nothing automatic about it. It is up to the shipper to give precise instructions to the carrier or freight forwarder so that the proper transport arrangements are made and so that the invoices are prepared accordingly. In some cases, inexperienced traders do not even inform the carrier as to the Incoterm in the contract of sale, then profess surprise later when the billing for transport services does not accord with the Incoterm.

a. **Liner terms** – With "liner" transport the shipper entrusts his goods to a "shipping line" which often is a member of one of the large "conferences" (groups of shipping companies that have associated to assure levels of service at specified price ranges on particular ocean routes). Not all shipping companies belong to the conferences – the ones that do not are called "outsiders" or "tramps". Certain costs may be included in the freight (such as loading or unloading charges) charged by regular shipping lines – hence, "liner terms". With liner terms, for example, discharging expenses are frequently included in the freight. Shippers should take care to ensure that the charges included in the liner terms accord with the shipper's transport responsibilities under the given Incoterm (see also Chapter 9 on sea freight).

b. **Charter parties** – Another basic form of maritime transport is via charter party, under which the shipper hires a ship or part of a ship. In this context, "free in" and "free out" mean that the loading or unloading obligations are not included in the charter party hire.

Thus, when a seller under CIF has chartered the vessel on "free out terms", he will have assumed the costs of loading and discharge vis-a-vis the shipowner. It will be in the seller's interest to require the buyer to discharge the goods within a certain number of days (referred to as the «laytime»). Conversely, a shipowner may provide for a bonus (known as « dispatch money) to the seller (when seller is charterer) for timely discharging, which the seller may pass on as an incentive to the buyer. The relationship of these charter party arrangements to the agreement between seller and buyer should be clarified in the contract of sale.

Finally, under CFR and CIF Incoterms, where a bill of lading "contains a reference to a charter party", the charter party must also be tendered by seller to buyer. In this requirement Incoterms departs from the rule under certain national legal systems, such as that of the United Kingdom.

4.4.3 Summary of the Incoterms 1990

The Four Basic Incoterms Groups: E-, F-, C- and D- Terms

"E"- terms: The goods are placed at the disposal of the buyer at the seller's premises/factory.

"F"- terms: The buyer is responsible for the cost and risk of the main international carriage.

"C"- terms: The seller pays for the main international carriage, but does not bear the risks during that carriage.

"D"- terms: The seller bears all costs and risks up to the delivery point at the agreed destination, which may be in buyer's country or even at the buyer's premises.

Brief definitions - the 13 current Incoterms

Please note: The summary below is provided only as a general introduction; it should in no way be relied upon by traders as an alternative to the full text of Incoterms 1990, which is far more detailed and precise (available from ICC Publishing or from your local ICC National Committee or Chamber of Commerce).

- **"E"- Terms**
  EXW – Ex Works: the seller makes the goods available at his premises.

- **"F"- Terms**
  FCA – Free Carrier: the seller hands over the goods, cleared for export, into the custody of the first carrier (named by the buyer) at the named place. This term is suitable for all modes of transport, including carriage by air, rail, road, and containerised/multi-modal transport.

  FAS – Free Alongside Ship: the seller must place the goods alongside the ship at the named port. The buyer must clear the goods for export. Suitable for maritime transport only.

  FOB – The classic maritime trade term, Free On Board: seller must load the goods on board the ship nominated by the buyer, cost and risk being divided at ship's rail. The seller must clear the goods for export. Maritime transport only.

- **"C"- Terms**
  CFR – Cost and Freight: seller must pay the costs and freight to bring the goods to the port of destination. However, risk is transferred to the buyer once the goods have crossed the ship's rail. Maritime transport only.

  CIF – Cost, Insurance and Freight: exactly the same as CFR except that the seller must in addition procure and pay for insurance for the buyer. Maritime transport only.

  CPT – Carriage Paid To: the general/containerised/multimodal equivalent of CFR. The seller pays for carriage to the named point of destination, but risk passes when the goods are handed over to the first carrier.

  CIP – Carriage and Insurance Paid To: the containerised transport/multimodal equivalent of CIF. Seller pays for carriage and insurance to the named destination point, but risk passes when the goods are handed over to the first carrier.

- **"D"-Terms**
  DAF – Delivered At Frontier: the seller makes the goods available, cleared for export, at the named place on the frontier. Suitable for rail/road transport.

The distinction between two key groups of Incoterms

FCA · CPT · CIP

(general, multimodal /containerized transport)

FOB · CFR · CIF

(maritime transport only)

The key difference is in the point of **TRANSFER OF RISK** :

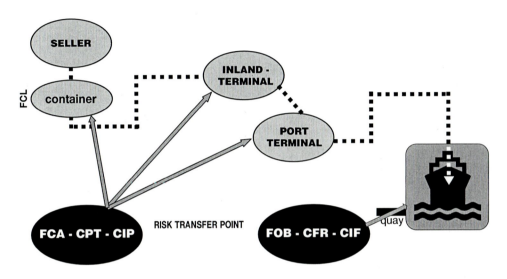

Since containerized and multimodal shipments are often delivered to the carrier far <u>inland</u> from the ship's rail, it makes sense to move the point of risk transfer accordingly. Pursuant to the sale contract, delivery may take place at any one of a number of stipulated points.

Risks are transferred at ship's rail

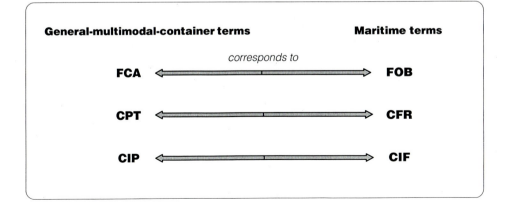

DES – Delivered Ex Ship: the seller makes the goods available to the buyer on board the ship at the port of destination, uncleared for import.

DEQ – Delivered Ex Quay: one step further than DES — the goods must be unloaded onto the quay at the port of destination, and import clearance must be obtained by the seller.

DDU – Delivered Duty Unpaid (new in Incoterms 1990): the seller must deliver the goods all the way to a named place in the country of destination. However, the buyer must clear the goods for import and pay the necessary duties.

DDP – Delivered Duty Paid: maximum obligation for seller — seller pays for all costs, charges, and official formalities up to destination.

Note: Certain previously used terms were dropped in the 1990 revision of Incoterms:

FOB Airport – replaced by FCA (Free Carrier), which is appropriate for all modes of transport

FOR/FOT – "Free on Rail/Free on Truck" – replaced by FCA

4.4.4 Incoterms categories

In order to understand how to properly use Incoterms, it is helpful to be familiar with certain fundamental distinctions in Incoterms.

a. Maritime Terms vs. General/Multimodal Terms

"General/Container/Multimodal" Incoterms: FCA – CPT – CIP
These Incoterms are the modern counterparts of older, maritime terms (FOB – CFR – CIF) and were specifically developed for containerised and multi-modal transport – but they are suitable for all modes of transport. FCA, CPT or CIP should be used when transport is containerised or multi-modal. Multi-modal transport refers to that which involves a sequence of different modes of transport – e.g., goods are first hauled by road carrier, then shipped on a container vessel, then transferred to rail transport. However, it should be noted that these modern terms were designed for a maximum of flexibility, so that they can be used for virtually all modes of transport, including traditional bulk maritime transport.

The terms DDU and DDP are suitable for all forms of transport, but their use often implies multi-modal transport.

The DAF term is a unique case, used primarily for road/rail transport.

"Maritime only" Incoterms: FAS – FOB – CFR – CIF – DES – DEQ
These six Incoterms have derived from long-standing tradition in sea transport. Today, they should be used only for sales in which the principal international transport will be by seagoing vessel. Nonetheless, the three most common terms, FOB, CFR and CIF, are widely over-used and mis-used by exporters, who quote them even in regard to transactions in which the goods are containerised or will be delivered at an inland point rather than on board a vessel.

The key distinction between the maritime terms and the multimodal terms is the different point of transfer of risk and division of cost. With the traditional maritime terms, FOB, CFR and CIF, the division of risks and costs between seller and buyer is at the ship's rail. If a crate, being hoisted over the ship's rail by means of a crane, were to slip and fall onto the wharf, destroying the merchandise, the loss would be the seller's, and *the seller would not have fulfilled the sales contract.*

In modern transport practice, non-bulk goods are frequently shipped in containers that are mechanically stacked in immense container yards. Furthermore, "roll-on roll-off" (RO-RO ships) allow lorries to drive container loads directly onto the ship. With the increasing prevalence of these practices, it was no longer appropriate to divide responsibilities at the ship's rail, for reasons linked to both risk and cost.

With containerised transport, the seller commonly delivers the full container (FCL) or the goods to be grouped into a container (LCL) at a point *inland* from the ship's rail. Often the goods are delivered to a container terminal, which may be located at the port or even far inland. Since goods are leaving the sellers' control earlier, it no longer makes sense to divide risk at the ship's rail. Goods may be lost or damaged in between the time they are delivered to the container terminal and the time they are loaded on board (it does happen that port terminals suffer from fire damage). In such a case, the unwary seller who has not required a sufficiently inclusive insurance policy may find that he is not insured for the loss of the goods.

However, even if the goods have been fully insured under an "open" cover or "floating" policy, the seller who is unable to load goods in good condition on board commits a breach of the sale contract. Under FOB, CFR, or CIF, seller is required to deliver the goods *on board.*

Moreover, the seller of a containerised shipment under FOB or CIF may not be able to comply with the requirement to furnish the "usual" transport contract required under clause A3 of Incoterms, because the buyer will not receive complete legal rights against the carrier. That is, there may be a *gap* in the coverage provided by the bill of lading, between the delivery to the inland container terminal (which may be operated by someone other than the carrier) and the loading on board the vessel provided by the carrier.

In response to the difficulties of adapting traditional Incoterms to modern transport practices, the ICC developed the "modern" trade terms appropriate for containers, RO-RO ships, and multi-modal transport. Under these terms, delivery is considered to occur when the goods are received into the transportation system. Thus, the FCA, CPT , and CIP terms move the crucial transfer point inland, to the point where the seller hands the goods over to the carrier, as at a container or port terminal.

The ship's rail had proven troublesome not only with respect to the transfer of risks, but also to the division of costs. Technically, costs under FOB, CFR and CIF are to be divided precisely at the ship's rail. But it is virtually never the case that port authorities or stevedores divide the charges for loading operations at the ship's rail. Thus, either the seller or buyer will pay entirely for these operations, although technically not required to. The only alternative is a cumbersome division between the parties. In contrast, FCA, CPT and CIP shift the transfer point inland, allowing for a simpler allocation of costs.

Problems with division of cost under FCA– CPT– CIP: Terminal Handling Charges (T.H.C.) – Although the division of costs under FCA, CPT and CIP may be simpler than under FOB, CFR and CIF, problems may arise. A buyer who has regularly bought from a seller under FOB may find herself disconcerted at the cost distribution if the seller switches to FCA. Recall that FCA not only moves the risk point inland, it does the same for the division of costs. Thus, under FCA the buyer may find herself invoiced for "terminal handling charges" which she was not accustomed to pay under FOB. Should this prove to be a source of dispute, one compromise is to provide that the seller will be responsible for all costs "up to ship's side", e.g., "100$/ton FOB Veracruz Incoterms 1990 costs up to ship's side for seller's account". This compromise allows the seller to retain the risk-transfer benefit of FCA (the risk is still transferred earlier), while allowing the buyer a concession in that buyer does not have to pay for terminal handling or loading charges.

b. Shipment vs. Arrival Contracts

Incoterms can be divided into those that dictate *shipment* or *arrival* contracts.

1) *Shipment Contracts* – E-, F-, and C- terms – The seller fulfils his delivery obligation at the point of shipment, hence, "shipment contracts". Shipment contracts were the norm of international trade in previous centuries, when the risks of ocean travel were much higher. Sellers did not wish to gamble that the goods would reach the overseas destination or that foreign buyers would pay after receipt. Instead, sellers preferred to be paid (and to transfer all risks) once they had delivered the goods on board a ship at the port of loading.

The letter of credit system developed in tandem with the practice of shipment contracts, allowing the seller to receive prompt payment against documents proving that the goods had indeed been shipped. However, it is a very common misconception amongst traders that there is a difference between F-terms and C-terms contracts with respect to transfer of risk. Both FOB and CIF terms dictate shipment contracts.

2) *Arrival Contracts* – Only the D-terms make for arrival contracts. Under D-terms, the seller is responsible for the goods until they arrive in the country of destination (hence "arrival contracts"). The seller not only pays the cost of transport to the ultimate destination, he is also at risk for any damage that may occur to the goods up to that point.

Compare CIF (a shipment contract) and DDU (an arrival contract) in the case of a maritime shipment to a foreign port. Under CIF, there are two critical points: i) the point of division of risks (at the ship's rail in the port of loading) and ii) the point to which freight is paid, the destination port. With DDU, on the other hand, the seller bears all risk until the goods arrive at destination, and he also pays for the carriage all the way to the destination. This distinction becomes crucial if the goods are lost or damaged in transit. Under CIF, the seller is safe, because he fulfilled his delivery obligation when the goods were loaded on board the ship. The buyer must pay the contract price even if the goods arrive damaged or are lost. The buyer can rely only on the insurance to recompense herself (and bear any losses not covered by insurance, should the insurance prove insufficient).

Note the Difference between C- and D- terms !

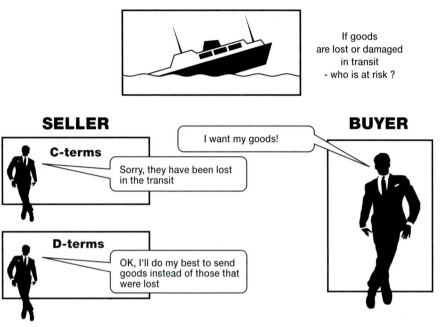

The basic distinction between C- and D- terms becomes crucial when goods are lost or damaged in transit. With C-terms, the seller has already fulfilled his delivery obligations, while with D-terms the seller may be liable for breach of contract.

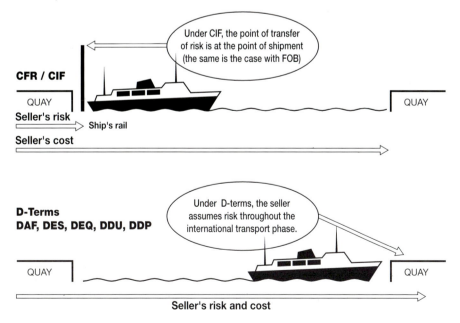

Under DDU, on the other hand, if the goods are damaged in transit, the seller has not fulfilled his delivery obligation under the contract. He may, therefore, be liable for breach of contract, meaning he would be required to pay damages, provide substitute goods, or make some other kind of restitution.

Since D-terms thus involve greater risk for the seller than C-terms, this will generally be reflected in higher prices.

4.4.5 Division of costs, risks and responsibilities

Incoterms allocate costs, risks and responsibilities between seller and buyer according to the provisions of 10 numbered articles, divided into two parallel series – "A" for seller's responsibilities, and "B" for buyer's responsibilities:

A – Seller's responsibilities	B – Buyer's responsibilities
A1 Provision of goods in conformity with the contract	Payment of the price **B1**
A2 Licences, authorisations and formalities	Licences, authorisations and formalities **B2**
A3 Contract of carriage and insurance	Contract of carriage **B3**
A4 Delivery	Taking delivery **B4**
A5 Transfer of risks	Transfer of risks **B5**
A6 Division of costs	Division of costs **B6**
A7 Notice to the buyer	Notice to the seller **B7**
A8 Proof of delivery, transport document or equivalent electronic message	Proof of delivery, transport document **B8** or equivalent electronic message
A9 Checking – packaging – marking	Inspection of goods **B9**
A10 Other obligations	Other obligations **B10**

A1/B1 *Delivery of goods and payment of price* – The seller must deliver the goods specified in the contract, along with a commercial invoice. The buyer must pay the purchase price.

A2/B2 *Customs clearance and formalities* – Incoterms allocate the responsibilities for export and import customs clearance and formalities between seller and buyer. Traders should take particular care whenever the chosen Incoterm makes them responsible for customs formalities in the other party's country. For the buyer, this means taking care with EXW and FAS, and for the seller, DEQ and DDP. One possible precaution is to include in the sales contract the following two provisions: 1) the right to terminate the contract in the event that customs clearance is impossible due to quotas or prohibitions, and 2) an extension of the time for delivery should customs clearance be delayed.

A3/B3 *Contracts of carriage and insurance*

• *Contract of carriage* – Incoterms allocate between seller and buyer the responsibility for procuring a contract of carriage for the main international transport of the goods (with the exception of EXW; of course, the EXW buyer will normally procure the contract of carriage, unless acting as a broker or re-seller in a "string" transaction). The following are the range of options under Incoterms:

EXW – neither party is under an obligation.

FCA, FAS and FOB – the buyer is under an obligation to "contract at his own expense for the carriage of the goods". However, it is fairly common for the seller, at buyer's request, to contract for carriage at the buyer's risk and expense – although the seller is under no obligation to do so.

CFR, CIF, CPT, CIP – the seller is under an obligation to "contract on usual terms at his own expense for the carriage of the goods". The carriage must be for transport by a "usual route" and in a "customary manner" (or in the specific case of sea transport under CFR or CIF, "in a vessel...of the type normally used for the transport of goods of the contract description").

DAF, DES, DEQ, DDU, DDP – the seller is under an obligation to "contract at his own expense for the carriage of the goods by a usual route and in a customary manner" to the named place, port or quay at destination.

• *Contract of insurance* – Only under CIF and CIP is insurance *required*: the seller must obtain at his own expense cargo insurance entitling the buyer to claim directly from the insurer. The minimum insurance coverage required under CIF and CIP is 110% of the value of the goods (the extra 10% is meant to account for the potential profit to the buyer from the transaction). The Incoterms insurance requirements are based on the Institute Cargo Clauses drafted by the Institute of London Underwriters. There are three alternatives: clauses, A, B, or C, with clause A representing the so-called "all-risk" insurance (traders should not be deceived by this term into thinking that "all" risks are covered -- they are not; see below).

The Incoterms principle of minimum coverage is a potential trap for the inexperienced trader, because minimum coverage is only appropriate when the risk of loss is only from such casualties as collision or fire; such coverage does not include damage resulting from theft, pilferage or improper handling of the goods. Consequently, minimum cover is not suitable for manufactured goods, especially if they are of high value. The buyer may want to go even further than clause A, by requiring insurance against war, riots, and strikes (as in so-called "SRCC" clauses - coverage for "strikes, riots and civil commotions"), but these and similar items must be included specifically, and cannot be added simply by using a formula such as «maximum insurance». If the buyer agrees to a CIF or CIP term with «maximum insurance», he will in effect be leaving it to the seller to determine which of the possible and available covers this could be, with a resultant level of uncertainty.

Model Insurance Clause: In light of the foregoing, the ICC recommends that partners specifically agree in their contracts as to the precise extent of coverage, as in the following example clause:

Insurance cover on the basis of ...(clearly identified) conditions
from...(place of commencement of insurance)
to... (place of termination of insurance)

Extensions: plus... days of storage at buyer's option
plus... War, SRCC, etc.
plus... % profit anticipated
plus... (named currency – if not currency of contract)
plus... (other particularities)

A4/B4 *Delivery and Taking of Delivery*

Who is responsible for loading/unloading operations? One of the practical issues influenced by the different delivery provisions is that of determining who is responsible for loading and unloading/discharging operations. The loading/unloading obligation is also covered by clause A6/B6, which deals with the division of costs, because the party with a responsibility for loading or unloading will generally have to pay the costs as well. For reasons of unity of presentation, we will consider both aspects together.

Traders should understand that with certain Incoterms the loading or unloading obligations are generally clear, while with other Incoterms additional contractual provisions may be advisable.

• *Loading*

Delivery at seller's premises – Under EXW, the seller is *not required to load* the goods upon vehicles provided by the buyer; the buyer wishing to have the loading operations included in the seller's obligations should add a contractual stipulation to that effect (note that it is also possible to deliver at seller's premises with FCA, which is discussed below).

Delivery on board vessel – Under FOB, CFR, and CIF, the seller *must load* goods on board the named vessel. Technically, under Incoterms the cost of transport operations is divided at the ship's rail. However, in practice the attribution of the cost of loading and related operations (such as stowage and trimming) may vary according to local custom of port. Buyers who are unfamiliar with the custom of the port of loading should consider adding contractual stipulations as to the distribution of loading costs.

Delivery alongside ship – Under FAS, the seller is *not required to load* the goods on board the vessel (although he must do any unloading of the goods necessary to place them alongside ship).

Delivery into custody of the carrier – Under FCA, CPT, and CIP, the delivery is accomplished when the goods are placed "in the custody" of the carrier. The delivery provisions under FCA A4 form the longest article in all of Incoterms, specifying delivery under seven transport modalities (rail, road, air, sea, inland waterway, multimodal, unnamed). A common usage of FCA in international trade involves initial delivery to a transport or container terminal, with the main international transport thereafter to include sea transport. Here, Incoterms provide for a basic distinction between FCL (full container load) shipments and LCL (less than full container load) or non-containerised shipments:

FCL – delivery is completed when the loaded container has been "taken over" by the carrier; the seller is therefore generally responsible for loading ("stuffing") the container.

LCL – The seller must carry the goods to the transport terminal and delivery is completed when the goods have been "handed over" to the carrier.

• *Unloading/Discharging*

Delivery at buyer's premises – Under DDU and DDP, the seller must place the goods at the disposal of the buyer. *The seller is not specifically obliged to unload the goods.* Therefore, the buyer may wish to include a contractual stipulation placing the cost and risk of unloading upon the seller.

Unloading/discharging under C-terms – Under CFR, CIF, CPT and CIP the allocation of the costs for unloading at the point of destination can be complicated and even troublesome (note that, technically, this issue is not one of *delivery* under A4/B4 – *delivery* being accomplished when the goods are loaded on board or delivered to the carrier for shipment; rather this is a question of the division of costs under A6/B6). *Traders are, therefore, well advised to deal specifically in the sales contract with the question of discharging at destination.* In the absence of a precise contractual stipulation, Incoterms provide the following basic rule of interpretation for C-terms:

1) unloading costs *included* in freight – if the unloading/discharging costs are included in the freight (which must be paid by sellers under C-terms), then these costs are for seller's account.

2) unloading costs *not included* in freight – if unloading/discharging operations are not included in the freight, then they are for buyer's account.

A5/B5 *Transfer of risks* – The rule for the transfer of risks from seller to buyer directly follows upon the applicable rule under A4/B4 as to delivery. In general, the seller is liable for the risks of loss up to the delivery point, the buyer is responsible thereafter. The most significant consequence of the transfer point is that if goods fail to reach the point of transfer of risk, the seller has not fulfilled his delivery obligation and may in some legal systems be liable for breach of contract unless substitute goods can be procured within the contractual time for delivery.

• *Premature transfer of risk* – Under several of the Incoterms, the buyer is under a duty to take certain actions which will enable the seller to accomplish delivery. The buyer's failure to perform any of the duties necessary for the seller to accomplish delivery can result in a premature transfer of risk, provided that the contract goods have been "clearly set aside or otherwise identified as the contract goods".

A6/B6 *Division of costs* – Generally, seller pays costs up the point of delivery, buyer pays costs after that point. If a party is under a duty to perform a function, that party must normally pay the costs of accomplishing that function. However, in practice there are exceptions to the basic rule and particular commercial practices or trading customs may require a different principle. Thus, traders may wish to make specific contractual provisions so as to obtain absolute clarity between the parties with respect to the following cost items under specific Incoterms:

EXW – costs of loading

FCA – costs of loading/stuffing containers; terminal handling charges

FOB – terminal and port charges; loading charges; stowing and trimming

CIF/CIP – insurance costs; costs of additional insurance protection requested by buyer

all C-terms – unloading costs; quay dues and port dues at destination; warehousing and terminal charges at destination; demurrage

D-terms – import clearance; duties, taxes and official charges

• *Services and Assistance* – Often one party will be required to assist the other in performing a certain task, and may be entitled to reimbursement. Examples: 1) seller's assistance for the buyer's export clearance under EXW and FAS; 2) buyer's assistance for the seller's clearing of goods under DEQ and DDP.

A7/B7 *Notice Provisions*

• Buyer must give notice – Unless there is a specified time or place in the contract, the buyer must give the seller sufficient notice of the following:

– the time and place to take delivery under EXW or D-terms

– the nomination of the carrier and delivery time under F- terms

– the time for shipping the goods and /or the destination under C-terms.

• Seller must give notice – The seller must give the buyer notice of:

– when and where the goods will be placed at the buyer's disposal under EXW

– when and where the goods have been delivered to the carrier under F- and C-terms

– when and where the goods are expected to arrive under D-terms so that the buyer can take appropriate measures in time to receive them.

A8/B8 *Proof of delivery and transport document* – Under all Incoterms except EXW, the seller must submit proof of having fulfilled the delivery obligation. This proof is usually found in some sort of transport document, such as a bill of lading or waybill. Under CFR and CIF, as with FOB, the seller is under an obligation to deliver the goods on board the named vessel. Since the transport document should prove that delivery on board has been accomplished, the only acceptable transport document is an "on board" bill of lading.

However, with containerised or multimodal shipments, obtaining the on board bill of lading can be cumbersome. First, the container line will issue a "received for shipment" bill of lading; then, the seller will have to request that the "received for shipment" bill be converted to an "on board" bill by virtue of an "on board" notation once the goods have actually been loaded. The time which elapses while the seller waits for the onboard notation can be quite costly for the seller, because the seller may only have a very limited time to present the shipping documents in order to receive payment under a documentary credit.

There is only an absolute need for an onboard bill of lading, which may be a negotiable document, in those cases where the buyer intends to re-sell the goods afloat, by endorsing the bill of lading. If there is no such need, the seller would be well-advised to consider use of CPT or CIP instead of CFR or CIF, so that only a "received for shipment" bill of lading or waybill would be required under Incoterms Alternatively, it is possible to use CFR or CIF but with a specific stipulation to the effect that the particular transport documents envisaged will be acceptable.

A9/B9 *Checking-packaging-marking / Inspection of goods*

- Checking – the seller must "pay the costs of those checking operations (such as checking quality, measuring, weighing, counting)...necessary for...delivering the goods".

- Packaging – the seller must provide any packaging which is appropriate for the type of goods and the type of transport intended. Under EXW or F-terms, where the seller may not know what the type or conditions of international transport will be, the seller will only be required to provide appropriate packaging to the extent that the buyer has informed the seller of specific circumstances related to the transport.

   Pre-shipment inspection (PSI) – If the inspection is required by the authorities of the buyer's countries, then the buyer will normally bear the cost, unless otherwise specified in the contract.

   On the other hand, in cases where the inspection is performed to make sure that the goods are conforming or to make sure that there has been no maritime fraud, either the seller or buyer may pay, depending on trade customs or contractual stipulations. In any event, Incoterms section B9 specifies that the buyer will pay unless otherwise agreed.

A/B10 *Other obligations* – Both parties must render their counterparty – at the counterparty's cost – any assistance necessary for obtaining necessary documents or for performing their contractual obligations.

   Examples:
   - seller's assistance for the buyer's export clearance under EXW and FAS;
   - buyer's assistance for the seller's clearing of goods under DEQ and DDP.

Moreover, parties must provide all information necessary for their counterparty to obtain insurance for the shipment.

4.4.6 Miscellaneous points

a. **Optimal transport economy and the trend toward "D" Terms** – An essential principle of transport cost is that prices decline according to the amount or volume of transport services purchased. Thus, the total cost of transport between seller and buyer will in general be cheaper if it is arranged entirely either by seller or buyer. This would seem to militate in favour of either EXW or the D-terms.

   In fact, delivered terms have become more popular in international trade over the past decades. In addition to the advantage of optimising transport economy, D-terms allow for greater control by the seller of the quality of transport. In the case of high-value manufactured goods, it may be very important for the seller to be in a position to assure that the goods arrive in time and in good condition. Control of the entire transport chain is facilitated for seller under D-terms. Moreover, in highly competitive markets, buyers may insist on being quoted D-terms, which facilitates the comparison of offers from different countries.

b. **Ship arrives before bill of lading** – In cases involving documentary credit payments, the ship often arrives in the port of discharge before the buyer has received the bill of lading entitling her to take possession of the goods. Frequently, the ship's master accepts to hand the goods over to the buyer (despite the absence of a bill of lading) against the security provided by a bank guarantee, standby credit (sometimes called a "steamer" guarantee) or letter of indemnity (« LOI »). The ICC recommends avoiding this practice, as it reduces the security of the documentary credit transaction, which is based on the firm principle that under no circumstances should the goods be delivered except in return for an original bill of lading.

c. **Incoterms Variants and Additions: "stowed", "trimmed", "uncleared", "loaded", "landed", etc.** – Traders should note that Incoterms 1990 *do not* contain standard definitions of those additional terms which are sometimes appended to trade terms, as for example, "stowed" or "trimmed" in the common variation, "FOB stowed and trimmed".

> **WARNING:** Traders should be aware that the use of Incoterms variants can be dangerous, because the careless use of a variant can result in an ambiguous or even self-contradictory term. In particular, traders should be aware that by altering the cost element of a particular Incoterm, they may also be altering the transfer of risk.

To illustrate the difficulties which may arise from the use of an Incoterms variant, consider "FOB stowed". Incoterms do not define exactly what is meant by the word "stowed". Although it may seem clear that FOB stowed requires the seller to stow the goods aboard the ship (thereby shifting the point of division of *costs* from the ship's rail to the ship's hold), it is not clear whether the division of *risks* is similarly affected. Consequently, if the goods are damaged during stowage, traders will not be able to rely on Incoterms to determine whether the seller or buyer is responsible.

The only solution for the trader wishing to modify or vary the basic distribution of responsibilities or risks under Incoterms is to think carefully through the potential consequences, and in particular:
- are both cost and risk intended to be shifted?
- if the variant affects customs clearance or duties, is it intended to shift responsibility for a) customs duties, b) administrative clearance, c) risk of non-clearance or d) all of the preceding?

4.4.7 CHECKLIST – The Golden Rules of Incoterms

1. Explicitly incorporate Incoterms into your sales contracts, as by the specific mention "FCA...Incoterms 1990". Always include the words "Incoterms 1990" in your contracts.

2. Have access to a copy of the full set of definitions of Incoterms contained in the ICC publication "Incoterms 1990". This publication as well as "Guide to Incoterms 1990", "Incoterms in Practice", and ICC's new "Incoterms 1990 Software" tutorial may be purchased at ICC Publishing, Inc., 156 Fifth Avenue, New York, NY 10010, telephone: 212-206-1150.

3. Recognise the 13 valid Incoterms, and refer to them by their 3-letter abbreviations:

- **EXW** - Ex Works
- **FCA** - Free Carrier
- **FAS** - Free Alongside Ship
- **FOB** - Free On Board
- **CFR** - Cost and Freight
- **CIF** - Cost, Insurance and Freight
- **CPT** - Carriage Paid To (named place)
- **CIP** - Carriage and Insurance Paid To (named place)
- **DAF** - Delivered At Frontier
- **DES** - Delivered Ex Ship
- **DEQ** - Delivered Ex Quay
- **DDU** - Delivered Duty Unpaid
- **DDP** - Delivered Duty Paid

Note that the terms "FOB Airport" and "FOR/FOT" (free on rail/free on truck) have been replaced by the more general term, FCA. Avoid other, non-standard variations, such as "franco [named place]", "free [named place]", or C&F.

4. Distinguish between those Incoterms which should be used exclusively for traditional maritime transport (for example, bulk goods and commodities loaded over the ship's side), and the more general Incoterms which are appropriate for all modes of transport, particularly containerised and multimodal transport:

• *Maritime* – Use FAS, FOB, CFR, CIF, DES, and DEQ only for traditional maritime transport (goods lifted over ship's side).

• *Containerised/multimodal/general* – Use EXW, FCA, CIP, CPT, DAF, DDU and DDP for all modes of transport.

5. Understand that Incoterms are meant for use in the contract of <u>sale</u> between buyer and seller, which should not be confused with the related contract of <u>carriage</u> between the shipper and carrier/transporter. Traders should give precise directions to their transporters as to the Incoterm they have chosen in a particular contract of sale; this will ensure that the contract of carriage is in conformity with the contract of sale.

6. Understand that Incoterms cover the allocation between seller and buyer of risks and costs, as well as certain customs and insurance responsibilities. However, several other important conditions of a sales contract may need to be specified in addition to Incoterms. You may be well-advised to:

- Specify how delivery will take place, and specifically who must load and who must discharge.
- Specify how much insurance coverage you want, and the geographical and time extent of the insurance coverage (where and when coverage begins and ends).
- Specify any necessary limitations on what kind of transport is appropriate (i.e., refrigerated containers, not carried on deck, etc.).
- Make sure that your contract contains force majeure, exoneration, or time-extension clauses if you are responsible for customs clearance or foreign delivery at an inland point.

7. Understand that CIF, CFR, CIP and CPT are NOT "arrival contracts"; they are "shipment contracts". This means that the point of transfer of risk with these C-terms is the same as with F-terms: in the country of departure.

Chapter Five
Agency, Distributorship and Franchising Contracts

The basics: Agency, distributorship and franchising are three important and distinct modes for export and the international expansion of firms. Traders should be familiar with the benefits and disadvantages of each particular mode, and understand the differing legal frameworks underlying each of them. A foreign agent markets the exporter's products, leaving the contract of sale to be concluded directly between the exporter and the foreign customer. The agent's income is usually derived from a percentage commission on sales made in his territory. A distributor buys the exporter's products and then re-sells them in the distributorship territory. The distributor's earnings come from the difference between the purchase price from exporter and the re-sale price to the domestic customer. Exporters, agents and distributors may wish to refer to the model contracts developed by the International Chamber of Commerce (ICC).

5.1 Agency

5.1.1 Agency and distributorship in the range of possible distribution options

Agency and distributorship relationships represent a common phase in the internationalisation of the export firm. They require relatively more investment than mere direct exporting, because the exporter must go to the expense of evaluating and contracting with the representative, and must further concede an important share of the profits to the representative. However, the agency/distributorship option is cheaper and less risky than establishing a joint venture or a branch.

Agency and distributorship relations have traditionally been a good place for small importers to begin. By representing a high-quality foreign manufacturer, it may be possible to get a business off the ground with a small initial capital investment.

Let us consider the range of options for international distribution:

a. **Branch office** – An exporter could opt for a mode of commercial distribution with a high level of control, investment and risk, by opening a branch office. However, this might entail extensive formalities. The registration of the branch in some countries exposes the exporter's entire legal entity to taxation on world-wide profits (as in the *unitary taxation* systems of some US states).

b. **Subsidiary** – A subsidiary is an independent company set up under the laws of the foreign country. Subsidiaries are also a high-investment, high-risk form of internationalisation. Subsidiaries have several potential disadvantages: they may generate unwieldy overhead structures caused by the degree of centralised control

The difference between agency and distributorship relationships

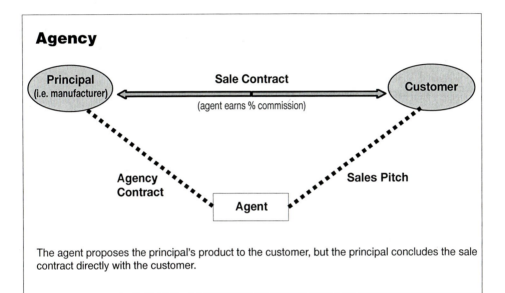

Agency

The agent proposes the principal's product to the customer, but the principal concludes the sale contract directly with the customer.

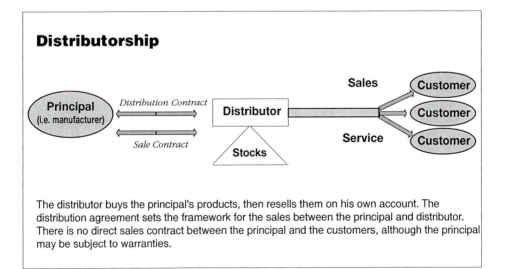

Distributorship

The distributor buys the principal's products, then resells them on his own account. The distribution agreement sets the framework for the sales between the principal and distributor. There is no direct sales contract between the principal and the customers, although the principal may be subject to warranties.

required from the home office; the exporter may have difficulty supervising and motivating local employees, who may have a work ethic distinct from that of the exporter's home country. Moreover, the employees of the subsidiary are frequently protected by strict labour laws, so that laying off employees may be difficult.

c. **Joint venture** – Another option is that of the joint venture, which encompasses structures ranging from a loose association to a separate company. The joint venture may be subject to national requirements of majority ownership by the local partner. Also, it may be difficult to legally withdraw from the venture. Moreover, because of the venture's limited legal liability, other parties may be unwilling to contract with it.

d. **Agent or distributor** – Thus, one arrives at the option of the agent or distributor – independent contractors who do not bind the principal. No partnership or joint venture is created. The exporter avoids the risks of unwanted contractual obligations, the need to register a branch office, and the possibility of local taxation. The exporter often hopes to rely on the expertise of the local agent to introduce a product rapidly throughout a market, but does not want to go to the expense or risk of investing more heavily, as via a subsidiary.

5.1.2 Choosing between agency and distributorship

Many international business executives do not observe any significant distinction between the terms "agency" and "distributorship". The two terms are often used interchangeably, as if they were synonymous and equivalent to yet another general term, "foreign representative". Both agents and distributors are, in a broad sense, "representatives". However, under many systems of law one finds important legal distinctions between agency and distributorship:

In commercial agency relationships, the principal will ultimately *contract directly* with the customers. The agent only, as it were, "introduces" them, by conducting marketing and prospecting activities in the territory. Conversely, in distributorship relationships, the distributor stands between the principal and the ultimate customers – the distributor buys the goods and then re-sells them on its own account to the final purchaser. The key difference is therefore that the agent does not buy the goods and take title to them in his own name.

In actual practice, the two roles may both be played by the same firm: a firm may act as an agent and a distributor at the same time, but for different products. It is even possible to be both agent and distributor for the same principal, acting as an agent for certain products and as a distributor for others. In the event of a dispute, the legal consequences of a particular transaction may turn on whether the representative was acting as an agent or a distributor.

Although there are no general principles applicable to all jurisdictions, the reader may find some guidance in the following simple rule of thumb for determining whether an agency or distributorship structure is more suitable for a given project.

- *Agency preferable*: **If the final purchasers are likely to want to *deal directly* with the principal (for example, as with products that are unique or must be customised, or machinery which is complicated, expensive, or maintenance-intensive), then agency is more appropriate.**

- *Distributorship preferable*: **If the representative needs to keep a very *large stock* of goods on hand for re-sale to a large number of customers, the appropriate contract is likely to be one for distributorship.**

The exporter's choice of distribution structure may change over time. A not uncommon development scenario is for an exporter to begin with direct export sales, then move to international sales via an agent, then later on to sales via a distributorship relationship, and then finally, if the market has become extremely well-developed, to a branch or subsidiary.

5.1.3 Drafting agency and distributorship contracts

Agency and distributorship contracts require careful drafting because they must govern long-lasting relationships and significant mutual investments. In comparison, a contract for the sale of a shipment of consumer goods may be precise and yet brief – the subject matter is more simple and straightforward. Agency and distributorship contracts must allow for a wide range of contingencies and a variable range of products over a period of time. Not only products but also parties may change over time – prospering or declining, or being purchased by third parties. How does the contractual agreement respond to such changed situations? The contract must be precise enough to provide clear solutions for predictable price and product-line variations, but flexible enough to adapt to contingencies.

Agency and distributorship commercial relationships usually require work, patience, and investment of time and money by both parties. Consequently, an eventual separation can be quite painful. Under some systems of law, the exporter is required to pay an *indemnity*, an equitable compensatory payment for the financial loss the agent is deemed to suffer as a result of the separation. If an exporter becomes unhappy with the agent and wishes to terminate the contract, he may be surprised to discover that an indemnity payment is necessary. The indemnity may be resented as unexpected or onerous.

Despite the above, it would appear that many representative relationships are negotiated in a casual manner. Some export manufacturers may be reluctant to negotiate in great detail their agency contracts, fearing to give the impression that they do not trust the other side. Agents, conversely, may be desperate for business and willing to sign any contract. Consequently, some agency and distributor relationships are indeed concluded by verbal agreements or "handshakes", or through the use of a very brief letter or memorandum. This is a risky approach. Contract negotiation should not be given short shrift: a thoroughly-negotiated and well-drafted contract is the best way of avoiding future disputes.

Good contracts are not enough, of course. Agents and distributors are like ambassadors. If they give customers a bad impression of the exporter's products and services, the exporter may be effectively barred from that market for years.

Moreover, an unsatisfied or dismissed agent may establish relations with a rival exporter. Therefore, representatives should be selected with extreme care, after a long analysis of the market and all potential partners and their respective competencies.

5.1.4 Legal principles of agency contracts

Agency contracts impose substantial legal commitments. The exporter should realise that agents may – in some jurisdictions and under certain conditions – acquire the authority to contract in the exporter's name. The exporter should, therefore, take care that the agent is a well-established professional with a good reputation. The exporter or manufacturer (called the "principal" in the agency context), may wish to provide for further contractual precautions, such as by requiring a trial period in which to evaluate the agent's competence. Another common precautionary measure is a minimum sales or turnover figure.

On the other side, the agent is likely to invest a great deal of time and energy in promoting the products of the principal, in creating a good reputation for them, and in advertising them throughout the national territory. If these efforts are properly executed, the principal's products will accumulate "goodwill" (a good professional reputation) worth a significant amount of money in future sales for the principal. Moreover, the principal may eventually acquire the names and addresses of the main customers the agent has prospected with his time and effort. At a later point in time, once the goods are well-established in the territory, the principal may seek to eliminate the agent and deal directly with the customers, saving himself the agent's commission fees.

From the foregoing, it may be seen that the termination provisions of the contract can provide certainty and protection for both sides. For the agent, a termination indemnity will ensure that if he is terminated he will at least receive a percentage of the financial value of the goodwill generated for the principal. Moreover, the contractual or legally-required length of notice – which the principal must give before termination – may allow the agent sufficient time to find other principals for whom to work. Conversely, the principal will generally wish for his own protection to have a short minimum notice period for termination, and if possible, to avoid paying any termination indemnity whatsoever. However, even in many cases where the principal has in a particular jurisdiction both the legal right and the negotiating leverage to impose an earlier termination or lower indemnity, he may still wish to provide for a "fair" period of notice and indemnity.

a. **Legal definitions of agency** – The use of the word "agency" in international trade does not always accord with the strict legal meaning of the term. For example, "buying agents" may or may not be agents in the legal sense.

b. **Disclosure of principal** – An agent may or may not disclose the fact that he is acting on behalf of a foreign exporter, his principal. This concept of "*disclosure*" reveals a key distinction between the "*civil law*" approach of continental Europe and the "*common law*" approach of the United States, United Kingdom, Australia and certain other countries. Under the common law approach, if the agent does not reveal to the customer that he is acting as an agent, then, in the event of a dispute, the customer may elect to sue either the agent or the principal (the agent may be easier to sue, because he is in the same jurisdiction as the customer). Likewise, the principal may elect to directly sue the customer. However, in many civil law countries, the principal may not be able to directly sue the customer if the agent has not disclosed the principal's existence to the customer – only the agent can sue the customer. If an exporter wishes to avoid this constraint, he should contractually require the agent to disclose during any sales or professional communications the fact that he is acting as an agent, or contractually require the agent to assign to the principal any relevant claims against customers.

c. **Actual and apparent authority** – The distinction between actual and apparent or ostensible authority is a legal concept of particular importance in common law jurisdictions. *Actual authority* refers to authority which the principal gives expressly to the agent; *apparent authority* (or *ostensible authority*) is the authority that an agent appears to have to others. Usually, an agent's apparent authority coincides with his actual authority (he does not exceed his contractual authorisation to bind the principal), and the distinction is not important. However, under certain circumstances, a third party may rely on an agent's apparent authority to bind the agent or principal to the contract. Thus, the principal should avoid giving the impression to third parties that the agent has full authority to bind the principal.

5.1.5 Basic duties of agent and principal

a. Duties of the agent

To use reasonable diligence -The agent must carry out his duties with customary and reasonable care, skill and diligence, and is responsible to the principal for any loss caused by a failure to observe such standards. For example, an agent cannot give a buyer any warranty unless the principal has given him the authority to do so.

To disclose all material facts – The agent must pass on all information likely to be of interest to the principal in deciding whether or not to accept the customer's order. Clearly, the agent may have a financial incentive to neglect this duty if he feels that certain information will result in the principal refusing to accept the order. However, such a violation of the duty to disclose makes the contract voidable at the principal's option. Thus, for example, the agent cannot act simultaneously as an agent for the buyer and seller, thereby receiving a double commission.

Not to make secret profits – The agent can not accept a bribe or make other secret profits. The standards of honesty that an agent must respect are very high.

Not to divulge confidential information – The agent must not reveal privileged information about the principal and the principal's business operations.

To account to the principal – The agent must keep proper business records so that the principal can verify the terms and obligations of the agreement. The agent must pay over all moneys received on behalf of the principal.

b. Duties of the principal

To pay commission – The commission system is meant to provide an incentive for the agent to maximise sales. The principal may provide in the contract that the commission will only be paid when the purchase price is received in cash by the principal. Another alternative is to arrange a contract on *del credere* terms, which means that the agent undertakes to indemnify the principal for losses resulting from sales made to customers who turn out to be insolvent or fail to pay for whatever reason. Obviously, the calculation of the agent's commission is at the very heart of the contract. It is vital that the parties express themselves with absolute precision on this point.

Agent's expenses and indemnity – The self-employed sales agent normally cannot claim his expenses from the principal unless they have agreed to this effect in the agency contract.

Orders emanating from the agent's territory but not procured by him – The basic principle is that the agent is remunerated for orders placed derived from his efforts. However, if the order is placed directly with the principal by a customer within the agent's territory, the agent may or may not be entitled to commission, depending on the law governing the contract and the specific contractual provisions.

Commission on repeat orders – The contract should provide whether the agent is entitled to commission on repeat orders during the period of the agency agreement, as well as after the termination of the contract.

Principal's ability to accept or reject orders – If the agent has not been given the authority to do more than introduce customers, then the principal may either accept or reject the customer's order. Commission will only be paid if the principal accepts the order.

5.1.6 Agency and law/regulation: the case of the European Agency Directive

The European Commission Directive on Commercial Agents – Under the European Commission Directive on Commercial Agents (the "Directive"), which is a key example of a regulation which provides protection for agents, an agency contract cannot be valid unless evidenced in writing. The Directive also has some important items concerning the agent's commission; notably, it shall not be paid any later than the last day on the month following the quarter in which the commission became due; derogations are not permitted.

The Directive also sets forth certain highly specific notice requirements for termination. Under Article 17 of the Directive the agent is entitled to a certain indemnity after termination of the contract, provided that he requests it in writing within one year of the termination of the contract. The agent will be entitled to an indemnity which corresponds to the amount of business he brought the principal. The indemnity can be lost if the agent is guilty of culpable behaviour. Finally, the agent can seek damages if, for example, he has not be able to amortise the investments he has undertaken pursuant to the principal's advice.

5.1.7 The ICC Model Agency Contract

Scope of application – This ICC Model Contract is meant specifically to apply to international contracts with self-employed commercial agents for the sale of goods. Agency contracts for *services*, for example, or with agents who are not self-employed (e.g., "salaried commercial representatives"), do not come under the specific scope of this contract, although it may still be used as a source of inspiration. Similarly, "buying agents" or "purchasing agents" who procure goods for a principal, generate a different set of considerations and the ICC Model is not ideal for these situations.

Agents as employees – In the case of agents who may be considered *employees* of a particular principal, national labour law may override the provisions of the ICC Model Contract. The simplest way to avoid this problem is for principals to contract only with agents which have the legal status of a company or corporation or other "legal person".

.1.8 Key clauses in agency contracts

The following is an examination of the specific clauses found in agency contracts, and is largely based on the clauses of the ICC Model Agency Contract. For a more detailed study of these clauses, consult the very thorough article-by-article review provided in the *Commentary to the ICC Model Contract*, written by the drafting team of the ICC Model Contracts. The level of detail included here is intended to give some idea of the amount of careful thought required for the preparation of a well-made international commercial contract. Because many of the legal aspects of the distributorship contract overlap or coincide with those discussed in the section on agency contracts, our discussion of distributorship contracts is somewhat briefer.

1) *Territory and Products*[1] – A precise definition of the products is essential because the obligations set out in the contract may apply only to products which are clearly covered by the contract. Agents commonly desire the right to distribute as many as possible of the principal's current and future products, whereas principals may wish to restrict the agent to only certain products. The contract products can be described specifically or generally. A specific listing is more precise but can result in a contract which must be updated too frequently to accord with a periodically changing product line. An overly general description may bring goods into the contract which the principal would have preferred to distribute through another agent or himself.

The ICC Model's compromise solution is to provide that the principal must inform the agent of his intention to put new products on the market and to discuss with the agent the possibility of including them in the contract. By providing an impetus for negotiation, it allows the parties come to agreement without being constrained by a rigid rule.

The contractual Territory should also be described precisely. Generally, this Territory is that area where the agent can realistically promote sales, although in some cases a wider Territory may be granted as a form of incentive (additional territories may be permitted, for example, on a non-exclusive basis).

2) *Good Faith and Fair Dealing*[2] – This type of clause sets forth the parties' commitment to abide by standards of decency, fairness and reasonableness in the agency relationship.

3) *Agent's functions*[3] – This type of clause states the duty of the agent to actively and competently promote the contract goods, and to follow reasonable directions made by the principal. The ICC Model works on the assumption that the agent is independent and not an employee of the principal. This distinction can be significant, because in many countries an employee's contract cannot be submitted to arbitration, which would defeat one of the essential premises of the ICC Model.

The ICC Model also include a provision that the agent has no express authority to bind the principal toward third parties, nor to vary the terms and conditions of the principal's standard sales contract. Note, however, that the principal cannot completely remove the possibility that the agent will act with "apparent" authority, the only solution being practical supervision and vigilance.

Note further that there may be tax consequences to allowing an agent to enter into contracts which bind the principal. Such acts may be considered for tax purposes as sufficient to indicate a "permanent establishment" of the principal in the given jurisdiction.

4) *Acceptance of orders by the Principal* [4] – It is important for the agent to contractually oblige the principal to inform the agent rapidly and in good faith whether an order has been accepted or rejected. The principal should not arbitrarily refuse orders. A principal unhappy with an agent but lacking objective or contractual justification for terminating the contract, might be tempted to "freeze" the agent out of business by arbitrarily refusing orders. Under the ICC Model, such "freezing out" would constitute a breach of contract.

5) *Undertaking not to compete*[5] – The agent must not sell products which compete with those of the principal. It may not always be easy to determine exactly what constitutes a "competing product", so it may be advisable to provide for a precise definition of "competing products".

Under the ICC Model, the agent is free to represent non-competing products, provided that he informs the principal in advance. He does not have to inform the principal if the products are so obviously non-competitive that it would be unreasonable to expect him to do so. However, an exception to this latter rule is made for the products of a competitor of the principal. If an agent worked for competing principals this could easily give rise to conflicts of interest, which could impair the necessary trust between principal and agent.

6) *Sales organisation*[6] – A good agency contract will balance the principal's right to set standards of quality with the agent's freedom to design his own internal organisation:

Servicing or warehousing – If these are an important competitive feature in a particular sector, the principal should contractually provide for minimum service standards or warehousing capacity. The parties should determine whether the stock should be owned by the agent (which may entail changing the legal status to that of distributor) or by the principal (in which case it would be consignment stock).

Consignment agreements – A consignment agreement should make clear which of the parties will be liable for the cost of storage and maintenance of the stock. Specific clauses should cover handling, safeguarding, insurance, and procedures for inventorying the stock.

In some countries special laws apply to consignments, making recognition of the principal's ownership of the stock conditional on the stock being appropriately *identified* and even stored physically apart from other goods. This is especially important in the event of the insolvency of the agent, in which case the agent's creditors may seize the agent's stock. The principal must have precisely followed the legal provisions in order to be able to assert control over the goods.

Stock owned by the agent – The parties may want the agent to hold stock on his account, so that he is able to rapidly effect delivery. This raises issues of whether or not the relationship is really one of principal and exclusive distributor. In the European Union this raises the question of whether competition and cartel regulations may apply. A presumption of a distributorship may also arise if the agent is contractually required to effect after-sales servicing activities free of charge, without receiving any compensation from the principal.

After-sales service – If service is under the principal's guarantee, it is common for it to be free (to the agent as well as to the ultimate customer) and in some way reimbursed by the principal. Also, if the after-sales service is judged as "necessary", the agent can ask the principal for compensation for costs. After-sales service may in some cases be a cost or burden for the agent, but in other cases it can be a primary source of revenue. For example, it would appear that in the elevator business the agent may earn more from the service contract than the sale contract.

The parties should calculate the probable costs associated with after-sales service, and then decide whether these costs should be covered by the agent's commission, or whether extra compensation will be granted for service. The parties should specify whether the agent will be required to stock spare parts.

Advertising – Agents usually are not responsible for advertising, but the principal may wish to allow it in particular cases. The agent's knowledge of the local market may enable him to suggest necessary adaptations to the principal's advertising materials. Sometimes the agent is reimbursed for a percentage of advertising costs incurred, as an incentive for the agent to invest in the product, and as an encouragement to use his best efforts to sell the product.

Fairs and exhibitions – Presence at trade fairs and exhibitions may be important. If so, the parties should develop a team approach with shared responsibilities.

7) *Guaranteed Minimum Target*[7] – Under the formulation of the ICC Model, the parties can set either a *sales target* or a *guaranteed minimum target*. An ordinary sales target is a "soft" target, indicating what the parties believe is possible, but fixing no direct consequence from a failure to reach the target. Especially in new markets with no previous experience with the principal's product, it may be unreasonable to set a guaranteed minimum target. A guaranteed minimum target is a "hard" minimum. It can be calculated in terms of money, amount of products sold, or percentage of the general sales target. Failure to reach the target constitutes a breach of contract allowing the principal to terminate the contract. However, the principal might take steps less drastic than terminating the contract, i.e., eliminating the agent's exclusivity, or reduce the size of the agent's territory.

The agent may, therefore, wish to negotiate for a clause excusing non-attainment of the minimum when such failure was caused by conditions beyond his control (such as an economic decline, new import restrictions, the arrival of new competitors, etc.)

Since it may be difficult to estimate a suitable minimum target, the parties may provide an alternative incentive, by requiring the agent to spend a minimum amount of money on advertising, sales promotions and participation in trade fairs. Under this option, the agent is given an incentive to recover his investment, but he does not bear the risk of termination of the contract based on limited sales, which may be beyond his control.

8) *Sub-agents* [8] – Either the matter will be completely left up to the agent ("Alternative A" in the ICC Model), or the principal will require that the agent, for example, notify her before the engagement of any sub-agent ("Alternative B" in the ICC Model). The employment of sub-agents is most commonly left to the agent, because of the basic principle that the agent is independent and should be free to organise his activities. However, in some cases the principal may have entered into the agency contract specifically because of the personal reputation of a particular agent. In this case the principal may justifiably refuse to allow the agent to delegate his responsibilities to a sub-agent.

9) *Principal to be kept informed* [9] – The agent should report back to the principal on market conditions, and answer any reasonable request for information from the principal. Under the ICC Model, the agent must also keep the principal informed on regulations such as those involving labelling and technical specifications.

10) *Financial Responsibility* [10] – The agent must generally take a certain level of care in checking the solvency of potential customers. Although, under the ICC Model, the agent is not required to perform an exhaustive credit check on the potential customers, he must not pass on an order to the principal if he has any reason to doubt the solvency of the customer. If the principal wants the agent to perform a credit check on all new customers, then this should be included in the contract.

Del Credere Contracts – The ICC Model spells out the possibility of a *del credere* contract, under which the agent agrees to reimburse the principal for any loss the principal may suffer from non-payment by the customer. Because the potential exposure of the agent under such an agreement is great, these agreements are frequently subject to certain legal limitations on the extent to which the agent must indemnify the principal. There are two basic possibilities:

i) 100% reimbursement – the agent agrees to reimburse the principal for 100% of the loss he may suffer, in which case it may be advisable for the agent to limit this exposure to certain types of business or certain sectors; under this option, the parties will usually agree on an increased commission for the agent; or

ii) limited percentage reimbursement – the parties limit the agent's exposure to a certain percentage of the loss (i.e., 15%) suffered by the principal; the primary goal under this option is to provide a strong incentive for the agent to do a thorough job in verifying the credit of potential customers.

Because the del credere clause can have a large financial impact on the agent, the ICC Model requires that the Del Credere Annex be signed by *both* parties. Since many national laws limit the agent's power to subject himself to del credere exposure, parties should seek to arrive at a balanced solution which does not impose undue liability on the agent (a rule of thumb is to limit the percentage to that of the agent's commission).

11) *Principal's trademarks and symbols*[11] – Both principal and agent have an interest in protecting the principal's intellectual property rights in the contract products: infringement will cost both parties money. Thus, agency contracts often require the principal to protect his intellectual property interests in trademarks, trade names and corporate symbols (although this is not the ICC approach). Similarly, the agent is often contractually required to share the obligation of protecting such property, as by initiating legal procedures – though this is not required under the ICC Model.

In the absence of any contractual provisions on intellectual property, an unscrupulous agent might be able to register the principal's trade names or symbols under his own name, and retain the rights to these names after the termination of the contract. The consequences could be serious if the principal had allowed the agent to use the principal's name or symbols in the agent's corporate name – after termination of the contract the principal might not be able to prevent the agent from continuing to use a name which could easily be confused with the principal's.

The ICC Model therefore expressly prohibits the agent from registering the principal's marks in his own name. After the termination of the contract, the agent must immediately and clearly stop associating himself with the principal's trademarks. The agent must also inform the principal of any possible infringements of the principal's trademarks. However, since a defence of these trademarks may be quite expensive and prove unsuccessful, *there is no obligation in the ICC Model for either party to undertake such a defence.*

12) *Complaints by customers*[12] – Under the ICC Model, the agent has no authority to commit the principal to take back allegedly defective goods or to compensate the buyer for any alleged breach. In many cases, however, the principal and agent will agree on the need to quickly respond to customer complaints. If it is anticipated that such a quick response will be necessary, the principal should give the agent specific written authorisation to respond to the complaints.

13) *Exclusivity*[13] – Agency agreements may provide for total exclusivity in the territory to the agent, or for no exclusivity whatsoever. Generally, the principal will grant exclusivity only if he is convinced that the agent will do a good job of promoting the goods throughout the territory. Many agents will refuse to undertake investments in promoting the principal's products in the territory unless assured of exclusivity.

The ICC Model seeks to strike a balance. The agent is granted exclusivity in the territory, with the exception that the principal himself can make sales into the territory (provided that he informs the agent and pays the agent's commission on these sales). If the principal already has large customers or prospects in the territory, there is not much reason for him to grant full commission to the agent on sales made to these parties. Therefore, the ICC Model provides for an Annex in which these customers can be listed, and allows the principal to pay reduced commission for these sales. Where the agent is in a strong negotiating position, he may obtain full exclusivity: even if a customer within the territory contacts the principal directly and without intervention by the agent, the principal must pay commission to the agent.

14) *Agent to be kept informed*[14] – The agent should be kept continually informed on developments involving the products, their technical features and their competitive position against the prices and technical characteristics of rival products. The agent should also be fully briefed on the principal's operations, because clients may ask for details. For example, the agent should know the principal's financial status, growth projections, factory specifications, number of employees, capital reserves, research plans, export strategy, etc. Ideally, the agent will have a permanently accessible interlocutor at the principal's home office.

The ICC Model's clause does not prevent the principal from carrying on business according to his own strategic interests. He may decide to rank the territory as a low priority in terms of marketing or promotional investments. However, he may not act so as to harm the interests of the agent, as by refusing to make deliveries when a credit-worthy customer places an order, or by making late deliveries or deliveries of defective products.

15) *Commission*[15] – The agent's commission is usually expressed as a percentage of the value of sales made during the life of the contract. The commission may be a simple set percentage, or there may be a variable commission depending on the size of a particular sale or on the total volume of sales.

Under the ICC Model, the agent is entitled to a commission an all sales made in the territory, even if the agent did not actually do any of the work required to approach a particular customer. This provision was drafted so as to accord with Art. 7.2 of the European Directive on Agency.

Exceptions to the rule are allowed for (entitlement of agent is to payment of a reduced commission):

- sales made by the principal himself
- orders placed outside the territory, but owing to the agent's work, or placed within the territory, but not owing to the agent's efforts
- sales on reduced price terms
- commissions where the customer turns out to be insolvent but the principal is reimbursed for her loss by insurance

The above rules avoid the problem of two agents from different national territories claiming commission for the same sale, by encouraging agents to try to make sales even if it appears that the ultimate order will be placed from outside the territory. Agents are often willing to make sales at reduced prices even if it means giving up part of the commission; the ICC Model therefore allows for such a practice if expressly agreed to by the parties.

The agent will not be reimbursed for any expenses incurred in fulfilling the contract (such as telephone or travel expenses). It is expected that the commission paid will allow the agent to cover these expenses and still earn some profit. However, the ICC Model allows the parties to provide otherwise with a specific agreement in writing.

16) *Method of calculating commission and payment* [16] – The calculation of the commission payable to the agent is not unfrequently the source of disagreement between the parties. The ICC Model seeks to set out a clear scheme by calculating the commission on the net amount of the invoice. An alternative would be to agree on a fixed lump-sum commission per item sold.

Since the calculation is based on the net invoice price, any reductions granted by the agent to the customer will reduce the commission owed. If the principal grants any additional price reductions after sending the invoice, such as a discount for payments made in cash, these will not affect the commission. Additional expenses for packaging, carriage, or taxes, are excluded from the calculation when they appear separately on the invoice, which is generally the case. However, if the additional expenses and taxes are included in the net invoice price, they must included in calculating the commission.

Time of payment of commission – If the agent has been given the authority to represent the principal, then it may be reasonable to allow him to claim the commission as soon as the customer has agreed to place an order. If the agent lacks the authority to bind the principal, several options are possible – the commission may become payable when:

- the order is placed (very favourable for the agent – he may even claim commission on orders ultimately rejected by the principal)
- the order is accepted by the principal; here the commission will remain due even if the order is ultimately not executed or the customer fails to pay;
- the goods are delivered by the principal
- the customer pays for the goods (most favourable for the principal)

The ICC Model has chosen the latter of the above possibilities – commission is payable when the principal receives payment from customer for the good. The agent is allowed partial payment only in proportion to partial payments made by the buyer. The commission must be paid not later than the last day of the month following the quarter in which it became due (this rule is required under the EC Directive).

17) *Unconcluded business* [17] – The ICC Model clause strikes a balance as regards allocating liability for the principal's failure to conclude a contract with a customer. If the principal does not conclude the sale because, for example, of insolvency of the buyer, strikes or natural disasters or other factors beyond her control, he will not have to pay commission. If the non-performance, however, is the principal's fault, then the commission will still be owed to the agent.

18) *Term of the Contract* [18] – The ICC Model provides for two alternatives:

- a contract for an *indefinite* period or (which can be terminated at any time upon sufficient notice by either of the parties); or
- a contract for a *fixed* period which is automatically renewable for successive one year periods (which can be terminated at the end of the fixed period, provide sufficient notice has been given).

In either case, if the contract has lasted *less than five years*, a minimum of *four months' notice* is required by either party to terminate the contract; if the contract has lasted *more than five years*, the minimum notice is *six months*.

Typically, the principal and agent will have opposing perspectives as regards the term of the contract. The agent, called upon to invest time and energy in marketing the principal's products, wants to be assured of a long duration. The principal, on the other hand, would like to be free to move to another system of distribution, as by opening a subsidiary himself, and therefore prefers a shorter term. A common compromise is for parties to agree to an indefinite term but to specifically enumerate the conditions under which each party is allowed to terminate the contract. The parties should always keep in mind that the applicable national law may require certain minimum conditions concerning termination, rendering invalid any contractual provisions to the contrary.

19) *Unfinished business*[19] – Under the ICC Model, if the agent's efforts result in orders being placed before the termination of the contract but only concluded after termination, a commission shall be payable to the agent. In the case of the agent's efforts resulting in orders placed *after* the termination of the contract, the agent must inform the principal in writing of the pending nature of these negotiations in order to receive the commission.

20) *Earlier termination*[20] – Notwithstanding the basic termination provisions, an earlier termination is possible if either of the parties is guilty of a substantial breach of contract. Moreover, the parties may indicate specific conditions which they would consider as constituting a substantial breach; certain specific situations automatically give rise to the termination right: bankruptcy, liquidation, receivership, etc.

21) *Indemnity in case of termination*[21] - In many countries there is a legal right on behalf of the agent to claim compensation for the goodwill that the agent has built up for the principal in the event of termination of the contract. Therefore, the ICC Model provides for two possible alternatives:

i) A termination indemnity equal to a maximum of one year of an agent's average remuneration.

ii) No indemnity. However, in many jurisdictions it will not be possible to choose the second alternative.

Clearly, agents will prefer to stipulate an indemnity in the contract, whereas principals will be reluctant to agree. However, the principal should be aware that regardless of the contract drafting, national law in certain countries (particularly in Latin America and the Middle East) imposes certain restrictions on principals and protection for agents. Even where an indemnity is made available by law, an agent generally cannot benefit from the indemnity if in fact the principal has not derived any substantial revenues from customers introduced by the agent.

22) *Arbitration – Applicable law*[22] – In the ICC Model, dispute-resolution is by conciliation and arbitration under the rules of the International Chamber of Commerce. Arbitration was chosen because arbitration proceedings are not public, are less formal, and are often faster and cheaper than litigation in state courts.

Two alternatives are provided in the event that the arbitrators are not able to find the solution by looking to explicit contractual provisions. Under the first alternative, the arbitrators will refer to the lex mercatoria, which are the principles of law generally recognised in international trade as applicable to agency contracts. The second alternative is to specifically make the contract subject to a particular national law.

If the agent is established in a country where mandatory legal rules are in force with respect to agency contracts, these mandatory rules will be applied regardless of the choice of lex mercatoria as the legal foundation for dispute-resolution.

23) *Previous agreements; modifications in writing*[23] – The ICC Model is presumed to supersede all previous agreements between the parties. Modifications to the contract must be in writing. The remaining two articles of the ICC Model are a prohibition on assignment of the agency obligations and a rule as to the authentic text of the contract.

5.2 Distributorship contracts – the ICC Model Distributorship Contract

5.2.1 Characteristics of exclusive distributorship contracts

The *ICC Model Distributorship Contract* refers to "exclusivity" of representation. In practice, a distinction is sometimes made between what is referred to as a "sole" distributorship and an "exclusive" one, to the effect that with a "sole" distributorship the principal himself may make sales into the territory, whereas with an "exclusive" distributorship not even the principal may compete with the distributor in the territory. However, this distinction is not always supported by the law.

Because the distributorship contract contains many of the same elements as the agency contract, we will not repeat the same detailed analysis here as above. However, the following points concerning the characteristics of the distributorship relation should be noted.

Generally speaking, a sole distributorship agreement provides that a seller grants a foreign party the sole trading rights within a particular territory with respect to the seller's goods. This agreement is commonly completed by a reciprocal provision that buyer will rely on seller as sole source of supply.

Note that the sole distribution agreement is not itself a contract of sale – rather, it sets out the framework for later individual contracts of sale between the manufacturer and distributor, and further sales to end customers. Where the contract includes exclusive buying provisions, and the buyer resides in either the European Union or the United States, which have strict competition laws, the parties should be careful to avoid violating the law.

Although distributors are often loosely referred to as agents, a sole distributor does not – as opposed to an agent – act on behalf of the principal in dealing with the end customer. Rather, the distributor resells the goods in his own name and his profit is derived from the difference between his buying price from the principal and his selling price to the customer, and this difference is in principles left to his discretion.

An important advantage of the distributor agreement for the exporter is that he does not have to worry about the credit-worthiness of the ultimate customers

– he only sells to the distributor, whose credit he will have fully investigated before signing onto the distributorship agreement.

5.2.2 Key clauses in distributorship agreements

a. **Territory** – The geographical extent of the territory should be precisely described. In some cases, the parties may wish to provide that when sales reach a certain level, the distributor will be entitled to a larger territory. The principal will often be required to pass on direct inquiries from consumers in the territory to the distributor, and the distributor may also be required to pass on enquiries from outside the territory to the principal. The principal will often require the distributor to keep lists of customers and to supply them to the principal. Within the European Union, a principal may not prohibit a distributor from accepting orders emanating from another exclusive distributor's territory. So long as the distributor does not actively solicit such customers, no further restrictions are allowable.

b. **Price** – The competition laws of many countries prohibit principals from requiring distributors to adhere to certain, fixed prices. Distributors must therefore be allowed freedom to set their own resale prices. Manufacturers may, however, provide suggested prices and price ranges.

   As for the price of the goods to the distributor, this provision is tricky in the same way as any other long-term supply contract. Obviously, the prices of most goods will vary according to economic or strategic developments. One solution is to peg the contract price to a publicly available market price on a specific date. Another solution is to grant the distributor a price equal to the best price quoted by the principal to any customer which is not a subsidiary or associated company of the principal. In order to avoid contravention of antitrust rules, the exporter should avoid trying to set the distributor's prices precisely or to control them.

c. **Sole buying or selling rights** – While it is common for the principal and distributor to exchange reciprocal agreements for sole buying and selling rights, this is not necessary. The principal may be wise to specifically provide that the distributor will undertake positive and energetic efforts to offer the principal's goods in the market. Otherwise, the distributor would be free to ignore the distributorship contract after having signed it, although he would be able to prevent the principal from selling into the territory through any other intermediary. Along these lines, the principal may wish to provide for a minimum target, giving the principal the option of terminating the contract if the orders placed by the distributor do not represent a minimum value during a trial period.

d. **Advertising; market information; protection of intellectual property** – The seller commonly requires the distributor to undertake certain minimum obligations with respect to the advertising of the goods, as well as to provide the principal with basic commercial and market information, and moreover to help protect the principal's intellectual property rights in trademarks or patents.

5.3 International Franchising

The basics: Franchising is a form of shared investment in the expansion and replication of successful business systems. International franchising allows franchisors to grow rapidly in foreign markets with minimum capital investments. "Unit" franchises confer the right to exploit a single operation, while "master franchises" and "area development" agreements confer the right to sub-develop and/or grant sub-franchises in a particular territory. Master franchises are particularly suitable internationally because they permit local supervision of networks. Franchising contracts can be complex and in some jurisdictions are subject to local laws for the protection of franchisees. The ICC is currently engaged in developing a model clauses for an international direct/unit franchising contract. Unidroit is currently preparing a Legal Guide to Master Franchise Agreements.

5.3.1 Introduction

Franchising is based on the attractive notion of replicating success. The origin of most franchises is in the development of a business system so efficient and competitive that it that has superior chances of succeeding in new territories. However, in order to grow rapidly, business networks need large infusions of capital. Rather than invest his own capital, the franchisor enters into agreements with (usually) local entrepreneurs – the franchisees. The franchisor grants to each franchisee the right to exploit all or part of the franchisor's business system, including trademarks, logo and distinctive signs, intellectual property, technical know-how and processes. In return, the franchisee usually makes a "front money" payment in order to enter the franchise network, invests a minimum amount in setting up and operating the business, pays the franchisor fees and royalties, and obeys the franchisor's standards for quality of services. The combination of the franchisor's reputation and expertise with the franchisee's capital, local knowledge and motivation, can result in explosive growth.

Salient examples are MacDonald's, Holiday Inn, Yves Rocher and Hertz, but there are countless others. Franchising has become one of the primary distribution channels for products and services in developed economies, where image and service reputation can determine market share. Franchising is found in industries as diverse as fast food chains, computer retail sales, real estate services, automobile rental and service stations, to name but a few. According to the International Franchise Association, more than one third of all retail sales in the United States are conducted through franchises, accounting for hundreds of millions of dollars in annual sales and hundreds of thousands of jobs. Even outside the top franchise markets of the United States, Canada and the United Kingdom, franchising is becoming one of the most popular methods for business expansion.

In addition to the advantages described above, franchising can offer cost savings from the decentralisation of management and financial controls. A further attraction for the franchisor is that franchisees are usually familiar with national labour, safety, health and technical standards. However, one of the corresponding risks for the franchisor is that the franchisee may eventually set up his own firm and become a competitor of the original franchise. Therefore, franchising contracts often contain special non-competition clauses.

Franchising, like agency, has in some countries raised political sensitivities. Some organisations have expressed concern that local franchisees, like agents, have little bargaining power against large franchisors and therefore require mandatory legal protection. Thus, in certain countries there are strict regulations dealing with such things as the amount of disclosure that must be made by franchisors when recruiting franchisees. It does happen that franchisees claim to have been "lured" into franchises by a franchisor's inflated, fraudulent statements as to likely returns on investment.

5.3.2 Different types of franchises and franchising structures

Product (or *trademark*) franchising involves granting the right to manufacture and/or market a product under a specific trademark to the franchisee. *Business format* franchising covers a complete system of doing business, including service concepts and operations, in addition to trademark and logo rights. In *production* (or *manufacturing*) franchises, the franchisee manufactures according to the franchisor's specifications and sells the goods under the franchisor's trademark. In a *service* franchise, the franchisee provides a service developed by the franchisor under the franchisor's service mark. Under a *distribution* franchise arrangement, the franchisor manufactures the product and sells it to the franchisee for resale to the final consumer.

The franchisor may structure a franchise network in terms of either *unit* or *territorial* franchising. In the case of unit franchising, the franchisor enters into an agreement directly with each franchisee. Under a territorial franchise, an entire geographical area is developed by a *master franchisee* or *area developer* responsible for a number of outlets.

International franchising is generally conducted in the following ways: 1) direct/unit franchises, 2) through franchisor's branch or subsidiary, 3) through a development agreement, 4) through a joint venture, 5) through master franchises. Unit franchising is most common in domestic markets – it facilitates a maximum of control by the franchisor over the individual outlets, with promotion of the franchise system and trademarks usually remaining in the hands of the franchisor. In an international context, however, a unit franchise approach runs counter to one of the underlying business principles of franchising – minimising costs via decentralisation. The costs of supervising an international national network from a single headquarters could prove onerous. In the international context, therefore, it is generally only advisable to franchise directly when the target country is geographically, culturally, linguistically and/or legally proximate to the franchisor's country.

Territorial franchises cover multiple outlets in a specified area and may be granted through either a franchise development agreement or a master franchise agreement. Under a typical development agreement, the developer/franchisee is required to open and operate a certain number of units in the assigned geographical area (usually a particular country) within an agreed time frame. The franchisor benefits from dealing with a manageable number of franchisees. Area developers usually have sufficient financial and human resources to manage the set-up and day-to-day operation of the business with a relatively high degree of independence from the franchisor. Training costs can also be reduced, because the franchisor only trains the developer; the developer in turn trains the unit franchisees.

Area developer agreements are also subject to corresponding risks. If the developer fails, all of the outlets in the territory will be affected. On the other hand, if the franchisee does extremely well, he may become uncomfortably indispensable to the franchisor, because the developer may represent so many outlets. Another possible problem is that area developers may employ salaried managers to run the individual shops (as opposed to highly-motivated unit franchisees).

Under master franchise agreements the franchisor grants the master franchisee (or sub-franchisor) the right to develop and operate franchise outlets on his own account, as well as – in some cases – the right to sub-franchise outlets to sub-franchisees. Some sub-franchisees may even be allowed to run several units, which may add to the complexity of the system. Decreased control over sub-franchisees is generally to be expected as a corollary to the increased decentralisation. Although master franchise agreement commonly include strict provisions regarding the supervision of the system, their enforcement may be difficult in certain countries.

A variety of other legal forms can be chosen for international franchise agreements. One option is to establish an overseas subsidiary in each target territory to act as franchisor. Under this system, the franchisor retains direct control over the foreign franchisees, but still benefits to some extent from local know-how. Alternatively, a joint venture may be set up by the franchisor and a local enterprise. Guidance from an experienced lawyer is essential.

Notes

[1] See *The ICC Model Agency Contract: A Commentary*, article 1 (commentary by Fabio Bortolotti).

[2] Id., article 2 (Ole Lando).

[3] Id., article 3 (Klaus Meyer Swantee).

[4] Id., article 4 (Didier Matray).

[5] Id., article 5 & Annex II (Didier Ferrier).

[6] Id., article 6 (Meyer Swantee).

[7] Id., article 7 & Annex III (Meyer Swantee).

[8] Id., article 8 (Meyer Swantee).

[9] Id., article 9 (Bortolotti).

[10] Id., article 10 (Bortolotti).

[11] Id., article 11 (Bortolotti).

[12] Id., article 12 (Lando).

[13] Id., article 13 (Ferrier).

[14] Id., art. 14 (Meyer Swantee).

[15] Id., art. 15 & Annex VI (Matray).

[16] Id., art. 16 (Matray).

[17] Id., art. 17 (Matray).

[18] Id., art. 18 (Meyer Swantee).

[19] Id., art. 19 (Matray).

[20] Id., art. 20 (Lando).

[21] Id., art. 21 (Meyer Swantee).

[22] Id., art. 22 (Lando).

[23] Id., art. 23 (Bortolotti).

Chapter Six

International Payment Options

The basics: There are a wide variety of payment methods available in international trade, each with particular advantages and disadvantages. In essence, if traders seek to assure a high level of payment security, then payment methods will be relatively more costly. Conversely, if payment security is not a priority, because the parties know or trust each other, then cheaper, simpler payment methods can be used.

The central risks in international trade are the exporter's risk of non-payment and the importer's risk that the goods shipped will not conform to the contract. Both of these risks may be reduced via the documentary safeguards provided by the documentary credit mechanism. However, since documentary credits involve relatively higher banking fees and more complex documentary procedures, this option is not always appropriate. Parties with long trading histories or residing in adjacent countries may be willing to make sales on open account or with payment in advance, payment modes which are easier and less expensive, but which do not similarly reduce risk.

Exporters should be aware that documentary credits require impeccable document-management on the part of the exporter.

In addition to payment-related risks and safeguards, other transaction risks can be reduced via effective credit investigations and management, exchange rate management, bank guarantees or suretyship bonds, and insurance.

Negotiable instruments (like bank drafts and bills of lading), which are at the heart of payment-security systems, can also be used by traders to raise interim finance or receive immediate, discounted payment.

6.1 Overview of payment, finance and security for international transactions

Export payment mechanisms such as the documentary credit and documentary collection, are flexible systems which can be used as 1) means of payment, 2) security mechanisms, and/or 3) finance devices.

1) *Payment means* – There are simple ways for the importer to effect payment, such as by bank draft or wire transfer, but in an international transaction these alone would leave either the exporter or importer entirely at risk (depending on whether payment was made before or after receipt of the goods). In international trade, bank cheques are uncommon. More common is to find payment effected when the importer (or his bank) accepts or pays the exporter's *draft* or *bill of exchange*. Drafts or bills of exchange are in themselves simply payment devices (and when used alone are referred to as *clean bills*). However, traders have found further protection by requiring the attachment of additional documents to the bills of exchange; these bundles of documents are then processed through

banks: hence, *documentary bills* (a bill of exchange with other documents – such as bill of lading and commercial invoice – attached).

2) *Security mechanism* – With documentary bills, the exporters' goods (represented by the bill of lading or other transport document) and the importer's payment (represented by the importer's acceptance or payment of the bill of exchange) are exchanged through a neutral third party, the bank. This removes that danger that either exporter or importer will unfairly end up with both goods and money. Documentary bills, which are used in both documentary credit and documentary collection operations, therefore represent a linkage of payment and security functions.

Note, in contrast, that standby credits and demand guarantees are meant to be used primarily as security instruments rather than payment devices. Thus, if an exporter agrees to grant the importer 90 days credit, backed by a standby credit, the standby credit is not meant to be the primary payment device. Rather, the exporter will submit invoices for payment to the importer at the appropriate time. Only should the importer fail to pay will the exporter seek recourse to the standby credit. Security devices will be looked at in detail in Chapter 8.

Each of the international payment options has different risk-reduction and documentary characteristics. Generally, the reduction of risk is purchased at the cost of greater documentary complexity and higher banking fees or service costs. Parties tend to choose the cheaper and simpler options when they have a great deal of confidence in each other, or when one of the parties has such a strong bargaining position that he is able to force the other to accept somewhat risky terms.

Both export seller and import buyer are exposed to risk. The seller faces the risk of non-payment, the buyer the risk of non-receipt of goods of contract quality in due time. These risks can be reduced or eliminated by selecting wisely amongst the various payment mechanisms.

3) *Finance device* – Finance, in contrast to payment, is related to the need to grant credit to the exporter or importer. Bills of exchange, either alone or in combination with documentary credit or collection operations, can be used as sources of finance. Essentially, importers want to be granted a credit period (from 30 up to 180 days or more), so that they can earn revenues from re-selling the goods before they have to repay the exporter. Exporters may be willing to grant such terms provided the importer (or the importer's bank) undertakes to pay at the end of the credit period, as by issuing a deferred payment letter of credit or accepting a term bill of exchange. Exporters are able to discount the accepted bills for ready payment. Discounting practices, such as "forfaiting", are covered along with factoring and other short-term finance devices in Chapter 7.

6.2 Credit management and export credit insurance

6.2.1 Credit management

Credit management begins with the firm's realisation that delayed payment, non-payment or difficulties with collection can become extremely costly. Proper credit management is one of the distinguishing characteristics between small, "amateurish" firms and their larger competitors – it is a mark of professionalism. Firms that have become aware of the importance of credit management seek to integrate it throughout the entire export process, from quotation to final receipt of payment. Sales personnel are not allowed to conclude contracts without a credit manager's approval of the payment method and terms. Customers are thoroughly investigated for credit-worthiness, and penalty schedules are established for customers who pay late or exceed their allotted credit limit.

Most professionally-managed enterprises have developed systems for dealing with domestic credit risk. However, it is not sufficient for the exporter simply to translate domestic procedures into the international arena. The exporter should set up specific systems for dealing with risks not found in domestic trade. International transactions by their nature involve countries with differing politico-economic environments, thus, the element of *country risk*. In addition, exporters should not assume that payment-linked security mechanisms which are effective in the home market will necessarily be effective abroad. Legal remedies, for example, may prove surprisingly weak or difficult to apply.

Although small exporters may wish to avoid these complexities by simply turning the entire process over to an export credit insurer, international factor or other service provider, a basic familiarity with the issues will allow the exporter to better oversee the work of these agents. Export credit management can be summarised as follows:

a. **Creation of an export credit management system and credit policy** – If the exporter has a domestic credit manager, he should set down on paper the specific additional steps that will be required for international transactions. These should be communicated to export marketing, sales and shipping personnel. Standard contracts and conditions of sale may need to be adjusted accordingly. It may be useful to consult with a specialised credit insurer, the trade finance department of a bank, or an export consultant or management company.

b. **Assessment of the risks associated with potential customers** – For many countries, ample credit information will be available, especially as regards larger customers. Highly detailed analyses are provided by credit ratings companies such as Dun & Bradstreet. At the very least a credit history or a reference from the customer's bank may be available. These services can be expensive, so the need for them should be balanced against the size of the sale and the payment mechanisms that the customer is willing to accept. For a buyer willing to pay cash in advance or by confirmed letter of credit, extensive credit checking may not be worth the expense (unless the goods are made to order or require specific preparation).

Despite the foregoing, the exporter's credit analysts should understand that other countries have different accounting systems and business practices. A comparatively high level of late payment or a low level of working capital may be considered acceptable in the importer's country, and the exporter who is too risk-averse may find himself shut out of these markets. In some of these cases, informal measures of credit-worthiness, such as general and personal impressions gained on business trips, may significantly supplement the data available to the credit analyst (although such informal indicators should never substitute for rigorous credit investigation).

c. **Choice of the appropriate payment mechanism or other security** – The exporter's credit policy should specify appropriate payment methods for different transactions amounts and customer risk profiles. If we look at these payment options from the point of view of the exporter's credit management policy, we can make the following observations:

1) *Cash in advance* – Obviously the safest for the exporter, this is generally unavailable in competitive markets. The importer may accept if granted a discount; such a discount may be calculated by adding the cost of interest over the credit period requested by the importer (i.e., 30, 60, 90 days) to the cost of credit insurance or credit management overhead that is foregone. A partial advance payment (e.g., 20-30%) may be more acceptable to the importer and therefore more realistic, but leaves the exporter exposed to risk on the balance.

Open account payment backed by a standby credit or demand guarantee can be as secure as cash in advance (and even more secure than partial cash in advance). Although the exporter grants the importer credit and expects payment by bank transfer or other similar means upon presentation of commercial invoices, the standby credit or demand guarantee is the best possible payment security. If the importer does not pay the invoice, the exporter can claim the amount of the standby credit or guarantee. The danger here, of course, is for the importer. An unscrupulous exporter could make an unfair or fraudulent claim under the standby credit.

2) *Letter of credit*– The next safest method for the exporter; because of its complex documentary nature, this can be relatively expensive in terms of banking fees; moreover, the exporter must have a rigorous document-preparation system in place so as to avoid the risk of non-payment due to non-conforming documents being presented to the bank.

3) *Documentary collection* – Not as safe as a letter of credit, but significantly cheaper; the seller must be willing to take the risk that the importer will not pay or accept the documents.

4) *Open account*– The least safe method, to be used when the importer is fully trusted and creditworthy. The exporter should consider the need for protection with credit insurance.

d. **Management of exchange rate risks**– The easiest way for the exporter to avoid exchange rate risk is to only accept payment in his own currency. However, in competitive markets exporters must often be prepared to accept payment in a foreign currency, thereby exposing themselves to exchange rate fluctuations.

The various mechanisms for dealing with exchange and currency risk are summarised in the last section of this chapter.

e. Installing document-processing systems – Export transactions today are based on the circulation of paper documents (in the near future, this movement of information will be transposed into the electronic sphere). When documents are processed behind schedule, or contain erroneous information, or are incomplete, the exporter risks delayed payment or non-payment. Export documentary systems should combine checklists of necessary documents with time-schedules for issuing or receiving them. Export software programmes can greatly simplify these tasks. Another alternative is to turn over certain document-processing responsibilities to a reputable freight forwarder or export management company. Specialised documentary credit consultants are available in some countries to take over a trader's documentary credit processes.

f. Obtaining export insurance – This is a basic safeguard which does not, however, cover all risks or for an unlimited time. Moreover, this protection comes at a price. It is explored in the section below.

g. Collection of overdue accounts – Late payment penalties may dissuade importers from tardiness in settling accounts, but if the exporter has not arranged for a payment security, he may need to implement a collection procedure. Of course, any legal recourse should be preceded by informal persuasion, such as by telephone calls and letters which contain an increasingly serious tone. The exporter may then wish to turn the account over to an international collection agent or factor. In large transactions, a legal action for non-payment may be commenced; for more detail on this latter course, see the section on international dispute resolution.

6.2.2 Export credit insurance

As we have seen in other sections, the major distinction between domestic sales and international ones is that the latter involve higher risk for a variety of reasons. Insurance companies are in the business of risk, so it is not surprising that insurers have seen the opportunity to provide essential services to the international trade market. Let us first consider the range of risks the exporter may wish to insure himself against:

Currency risks
- exchange rate fluctuations
- imposition of foreign exchange controls

Business risks
- the importer refuses to pay for whatever reason
- the importer goes bankrupt
- the exporter fails to adequately perform the contract
- the exporter or importer's performance is blocked by a force majeure event, such as a natural disaster

Political risks
- political force majeure event, such as revolution or outbreak of war
- confiscation or expropriation
- enactment of new regulations which prevent performance of the contract

a. **Insurance providers** – The basic dichotomy is between public and private insurers. Examples of well-known public insurers include the US Eximbank, Canada's Export Development Corporation, the UK Export Credits Guarantee Department, and France's COFACE. The provision of publicly-financed export insurance has in recent years been the object of international political sensitivity, because such insurance can be considered as an indirect export subsidy which can unfairly distort international markets. As a result, an international agreement has been implemented – the OECD Consensus on Export Credits – with rules on minimum interest rates and down payments and maximum lengths of credits. Especially with regard to short-term coverage, public sector insurers have been scaling down their operations in favour of private insurers. Public sector insurers, unlike private insurers, generally do not offer the exporter the ability to cover both domestic and international risks.

The provision of services by private insurers is frequently done through the intermediary of specialised credit insurance brokers. These brokers consult exporters on how to make the best choice from amongst the wealth of insurance services and policies available. In the event of a claim, the broker will assist the exporter in preparing necessary documentation and dealing with the insurance company.

Private credit insurers tend to offer many of the same services provided by the brokers. Credit insurers help exporters not only by reimbursing them for losses sustained from non-payment, but also by helping them set up proper credit management procedures. Insurers may provide exporters with credit data on prospective customers, suggest appropriate credit levels, and supply information on a foreign country's economic and political risk. Some insurers even offer collections services for overdue accounts.

b. **Types of policies** – Different kinds of insurance policies will provide protection against certain of the above risks. Export "credit insurance" is perhaps the most common variety, covering the exporter against non-payment or default by the importer. A "comprehensive policy" may cover the exporter against currency, business and political risks. Various combinations are possible depending on the specific risks the exporter wishes to cover. An example of a useful combined policy is one that covers both domestic and international credit risk.

Another basic distinction is between short- and long-term insurance. Although there is no formal dividing line, coverage for anything less than one to two years is generally considered short-term. Short-term insurance is often used in combination with other short-term financing devices to enable an exporter to maintain cash flow on the security of his insured receivables.

Exporters who wish to handle credit management by themselves (often the case with large companies) may nonetheless wish to take out a catastrophic loss or "excess of loss" policy. These policies provide total coverage for any losses in excess of a certain threshold, leaving the company to self-insure for losses below that amount.

c. Coverage – As with other forms of insurance, coverage extends only to risks specifically named in the policy. Thus, non-payment caused by the exporter's own default is normally excluded from coverage. This can lead to delays in the payment of a claim in cases where the importer alleges that the exporter is guilty of late delivery or of supplying goods which are not of contractually-specified quality. In such cases, the exporter may need to prove that he was not in default. Coverage of currency risk is exceptional, especially as the term of coverage increases, and may require a separate policy or premium.

The amount of coverage is commonly in the 90-95% range, although greater or lesser coverage may be possible in particular cases.

The cost of coverage is commonly in the range of from less than 1% to 2% of the contract price, plus a base fee and the insurer's minimum processing charges.

6.3 Documentary sales and payment: shipping documents

Because of the central role of documents in our discussion of payment mechanisms, we will briefly summarise the characteristics of the principal documents here:

6.3.1 The key documents

a. The Bill of Exchange

A *draft* or *bill of exchange* (*B/E*) is a negotiable instrument which represents an unconditional demand for payment. Together with the bill of lading, it forms the basis for documentary collections procedures; together with the exporter's commercial invoice (see below) it can be used to charge the importer for the goods. Bills of exchange are defined as follows: "An unconditional order in writing addressed by one person to another signed by the person giving it requiring the person to whom it is addressed to pay on demand or at a fixed or determinable future time a sum certain in money to or to the order of a specified person or bearer."

Thus, the draft is written by the *drawer* (export seller) to the *drawee* (import buyer), requiring payment of a fixed amount at a specific time. A draft payable upon presentation is called a *sight draft*, while a draft payable at a future time is called a *usance* (or *time*) *draft*. The draft is legally *accepted* when a bank or the buyer writes "accepted", the date, and a signature on the face of a time draft. A draft accepted by a bank is called a *banker's acceptance*, while a draft accepted by a buyer is called a *trade acceptance*.

When the seller attaches the bill of lading or other transport document to a bill of exchange, the bill of exchange is called a *documentary bill*. By doing this, the seller ensures that the buyer will not obtain any rights to the goods (via the bill of lading) before having accepted or paid the bill of exchange. Since they are negotiable, drafts may be transferred by endorsement to a third party, who may become a *holder in due course*.

b. The Bill of Lading

> **A venerable definition of the bill of lading...**
> *"A cargo at sea while in the hands of the carrier is necessarily incapable of physical delivery. During this period of transit and voyage, the bill of lading...is universally recognized as its symbol, and the endorsement and delivery of the bill of lading operates as a symbolical delivery of the cargo. Property in the goods passes by such endorsement and delivery of the bill of lading...just as under similar circumstances the property would pass by an actual delivery of the goods...[T]he bill of lading is...a key which in the hands of the rightful owner is intended to unlock the door of the warehouse, floating or fixed, in which the goods may chance to be."*
>
> – Lord Justice Bowen, Sanders Brothers v. Maclean & Co. (1883)

The bill of lading (commonly referred to in the trade as the "B/L") is a central document in the traditional export transaction, linking the contract of sale, the documentary payment contracts, and the contract of carriage. We shall briefly summarize here the function of the classic B/L, the marine (or ocean) bill of lading, which provides the documentary basis for traditional maritime shipments. For a fuller discussion of the bill of lading, see Chapter 9.

The *marine bill of lading* serves three basic functions:

1) The B/L – at any rate a B/L made out "to order" represents control over – or "stands for" – the goods. It is sometimes said that the B/L is a document of "title" – a phrase which may give the inaccurate impression that the party who holds the bill of lading also *owns* the goods. As we shall see in chapter 9, the holder of the bill can exercise control over the goods vis-a-vis the carrier: whether she owns the goods or not will depend on the contract of sale.

2) The B/L *evidences the contract of carriage* – The B/L must contain the terms of the contract of carriage, either explicitly or by reference to another document. Under documentary shipment sales the seller must procure and transfer to the buyer a contract of carriage on "usual" or reasonable terms. Provided, therefore, that the B/L contains no "unusual" term, it will represent the contract of carriage called for by the contract of sale.

3) The B/L is *a receipt* – The B/L is a receipt which evidences the delivery of the goods for shipment. As such, it describes the goods and states that in a certain quantity and in apparent good order they have been loaded on board. If there is a notation that the goods have been in any way damaged, this will be made on the face of the B/L. At that point, the B/L may no longer be acceptable for presentation under a documentary credit.

A B/L may be issued in either negotiable form (often called an "*order bill of lading*") or non-negotiable form (a "*straight bill of lading*").

Perhaps the key issue as regards bills of lading in the payment context is their value to the banks as security for the credit amount. This security value will vary depending on whether or not the bill is a negotiable one – in which case possession of it has money value, because the bill can be auctioned off – or whether it is a non-negotiable "waybill"-type document, in which case it may have virtually no security value to the bank, unless the bank is named as consignee and steps are taken to ensure that this designation is irrevocable.

c. **The commercial invoice** – This document is prepared by the exporter and includes: identification and addresses of the seller and buyer, a listing and description of the goods (including prices, discounts and quantities), an invoice number, packaging details, marks and numbers, shipping details, and the date and reference number of the buyer's order. *Because other documents (such as the documentary credit) will be checked against the commercial invoice, it is of the utmost importance that it be correct and exact in all particulars. An inexact invoice can be fatal to a letter of credit transaction.* The buyer will often need the information in the invoice in order to comply with import licenses, customs duties and exchange restrictions. Because of these needs, the buyer will often request an advance form of commercial invoice, called the *pro forma invoice*.

d. **Insurance documents** – With documentary sales under such trade terms as CIF and CIP Incoterms 1990, the seller must procure and pay for insurance for the benefit of the buyer. A letter of credit application will necessarily reflect this insurance obligation, and an insurance document will have to be presented by the seller in order to receive payment. Depending on the case, the document required may be an *insurance policy* (or facultative policy, for single consignments), an *open contract* (for continuous or repeated shipments), or a *certificate of insurance* (indicating cover under an open contract). The Institute of London Underwriters Clauses specify the coverage required under Incoterms 1990; they are generally attached to policies, and indicate precisely the risks covered and exclusions from coverage.

e. **Official certificates and licences** – The most important of these is the *certificate of origin*, which evidences the origin of the goods and is usually prepared by the seller's local Chamber of Commerce. *Inspection certificates*, which certify the quality of the goods, are commonly prepared by private inspection agencies; two of the most famous are SGS (Switzerland) and Bureau Veritas (France).

EXPORT DOCUMENTS – DRAFT (BILL OF EXCHANGE)

Exchange for US$100,00⁻   Austin, May 18, 1997

At sight of the bill of exchange pay to the order of ourselves
One hundred thousand and 00/000 US dollars

Drawn under Banco Mexicano, Mexico, D.F., Documentary Credit N°.12345

Value received and charge same to account of

TO: Banco Mexicano S.A.,
           Ave. Insurgentes 1910
           Mexico, D.F., Mexico
                                          _____
                                          Acme Exports, Inc.

UNCITRAL bill of exchange format

Austin, May 18, 1997

US$100,000

At sixty days after sight for values received,
pay against this bill of echange to the order
of ourselves

the sum of US dollars one
hundred thousand

effective payment to be made in US dollars
only without deduction for and free of any tax,
import levy or duty

present or future of any nature under the laws
of the United States or any political
subdivision thereof or therein.

This bill of exchange is
payable at
The First Bank of Texas in Austin

Drawn on The First Bank of Texas,
Austin

Accepted ....

                    _____
                    For and on behalf of
                    Acme Exports, Inc.
                    Austin, Texas

EXPORT DOCUMENTS – BILL OF LADING

Hapag-Lloyd Aktiengesellschaft, Hamburg/Bremen	MULTIMODAL TRANSPORT OR PORT TO PORT SHIPMENT	PAGE 2

SHIPPER:

VOYAGE-NO.

B/L-NO.

SHIPPER'S REFERENCE

CARRIER:

STATUS*:

CONSIGNEE OR ORDER:

Hapag-Lloyd

NOTIFY ADDRESS (Carrier not responsible for failure to notify; see clause 20 [1] hereof):

Place of Receipt:

PRECARRYING VESSEL:

Place of Delivery:

OCEAN VESSEL(S):

PORT OF LOADING:

PORT OF DISCHARGE:

PORT(S) OF TRANSHIPMENT:

Container Nos, Seal Nos; Marks and Nos.	Number and kind of packages; description of goods	Gross weight	Measurement

Bill of Lading ORIGINAL

SHIPPED ON BOARD

DATE:

NVOCC-F.M.C.-NO.:

Shipper's declared value:
(see clause 7(1))

Above Particulars as declared by shipper:
Without responsibility or warranty as to correctness by carrier (see clause 11(1) and (2))

Total No. of Containers received by the Carrier:	Packages received by the Carrier:

Movement:

RECEIVED by the Carrier from the Shipper in apparent good order and condition (unless otherwise noted herein) the total number or quantity of Containers or other packages or units indicated in the box opposite entitled ""Total No. of Containers/Packages received by the Carrier" for Carriage subject to all the terms and conditions hereof (INCLUDING THE TERMS AND CONDITIONS ON THE REVERSE HEREOF AND THE TERMS AND CONDITIONS OF THE CARRIER'S APPLICABLE TARIFF) from the Place of Receipt or the Port of Loading, whichever is applicable, to the Port of Discharge or the Place of Delivery, whichever is applicable. One original Bill of Lading, duly endorsed, must be surrendered by the Merchant to the Carrier in exchange for the Goods or a delivery order. In accepting this Bill of Lading the Merchant expressly accepts and agrees to all its terms and conditions whether printed, stamped or written, or otherwise incorporated, notwithstanding the non-signing of this Bill of Lading by the Merchant.

IN WITNESS WHEREOF the number of original Bills of Lading stated below all of this tenor and date has been signed, one of which being accomplished the others to stand void.

Freight and Charges:	Prepaid	Collect
Origin Land Freight / Transp. Add'l		
Origin THC / LCL Charge		
Sea Freight		
Destination THC / LCL Charge		
Destination Land Freight / Transp. Add'l		

Freight payable at:

Place and date of issue:

Number of original Bs/L:

Commodity Code:

Appropriate columns to be marked with "X"

*e.g. owner of the cargo, freight forwarder, NVOCC or other classification

90112361

EXPORT DOCUMENTS – FIATA BILL OF LADING

Consignor

Emblem of National Association

FBL

NEGOTIABLE FIATA MULTIMODAL TRANSPORT BILL OF LADING
issued subject to UNCTAD/ICC Rules for Multimodal Transport Documents (ICC Publication 481).

ICC

Consigned to order of

Notify address

Place of receipt

Ocean vessel

Port of loading

Port of discharge

Place of delivery

Marks and numbers

Number and kind of packages

Description of goods

Gross weight

Measurement

according to the declaration of the consignor

Declaration of interest of the consignor in timely delivery (Clause 6.2.)

Declared value for ad valorem rate according to the declaration of the consignor (Clauses 7 and 8)

The goods and instructions are accepted and dealt with subject to the Standard Conditions printed overleaf.

Taken in charge in apparent good order and condition, unless otherwise noted herein, at the place of receipt for transport and delivery as mentioned above.

One of these Multimodal Transport Bills of Lading must be surrendered duly endorsed in exchange for the goods. In Witness whereof the original Multimodal Transport Bills of Lading all of this tenor and date have been signed in the number stated below, one of which being accomplished the other(s) to be void.

Freight amount	Freight payable at	Place and date of issue
Cargo insurance through the undersigned ☐ not covered ☐ Covered according to attached Policy	Number of Original FBL's	Stamp and signature
For delivery of goods please apply to:		

Text authorized by FIATA. Copyright reserved. © FIATA Zurich Switzerland 6.92

EXPORT DOCUMENTS – COMMERCIAL INVOICE

SHIPPER/EXPORTER Glotz Industries 1492 Columbus Blvd. Fort Wayne, IN 12345-6789	**COMMERCIAL INVOICE NO.** TO-02 / **DATE** July/16/96

SHIPPER/EXPORTER	COMMERCIAL INVOICE NO.	DATE
Glotz Industries 1492 Columbus Blvd. Fort Wayne, IN 12345-6789	TO-02	July/16/96

CUSTOMER PURCHASE ORDER NO. 193   **B/L, AWB NO.** AA 2977321

COUNTRY OF ORIGIN USA   **DATE OF EXPORT** July/16/96

CONSIGNEE
Widgets by Otto
Rudiger Paschold Strasse
Baden-Baden, Germany

TERMS
Sale: FCA Chicago (O'Hare Airport)
Payment: Net 30 days

EXPORT REFERENCES
Currency: U. S. Dollars

NOTIFY
Zoll Clearance
6 Haberkamp Strasse
Stuttgart, Germany

FORWARDING AGENT
A. N. Deringer
29320 Goddard Rd.
Romulus, MI 48174

AIR/OCEAN PORT OF EMBARKATION
Chicago

EXPORTING CARRIER/ROUTE
Air Everywhere Flt 102 Frankfurt

Terms of sale and terms of payment are governed by Incoterms 1990 (ICC 460), UCP 500 for letters of credit, and URC 522 for documentary collections.

PKGS.	QUANTITY	NET WT. (Kilos)	GROSS WT. (Kilos)	DESCRIPTION OF MERCHANDISE	UNIT PRICE	TOTAL VALUE
5	50 ea	153.7	160.8	Blue Widgets (HS# 123456)	$ 5.00	$ 250.00
				TOTAL EXW FORT WAYNE, IN		$ 250.00

PACKAGE MARKS:
Otto
Baden-Baden
1/5 - 5/5
MADE WITH PRIDE IN USA

MISC. CHARGES (Packing, Insurance, etc.)	
Pre-Carriage	$ 34.50
FCA Chicago **INVOICE TOTAL**	$ 284.50

CERTIFICATIONS

We certify that this invoice is true and correct, and that the origin of these goods is the United States of America. These goods licensed by the U.S. for ultimate destination Germany. Diversion contrary to U.S. law is prohibited. License G-Dest.

AUTHORIZED SIGNATURE

EXPORT DOCUMENTS – INSURANCE CERTIFICATE

GERLING-KONZERN
ALLGEMEINE VERSICHERUNGS-AKTIENGESELLSCHAFT
Otto-Beck-Str. 36
D-68165 Mannheim

Certificate of Insurance
Versicherungs-Zertifikat

Date of Issue/Ausfertigungstag
20.03.1996

Insurance cover is granted to/ Versicherungsschutz besteht gegenüber:	Cover No./Vertrags-Nr. 28-434854

Certificate No./Zertifikat Nr.
2

to order of
Smith & Co.
P.O.Box 650

Number of Originals/Anzahl der Originale
337

Mogaro/Tanzania

Sum Insured/Versicherungssumme
16.940,-- US-$ US-Dollars sixteen
thousand nine hundred forty------

~~for account of whom it may concern/fur Rechnung, wen es angeht~~

In case of loss or damage exceeding 2.000 DM immediately contact/Bei Schäden über 2.000 DM sofort benachrichtigen:

Toplis and Harding (Tanzania) Ltd
P.O.Box 799
1 st Floor Dsm Bookshop Bldg.
Indira Gandhi Street
Dar es Saalam/Tansania

Tel. (51) 25508
Fax   (51) 39881

Insured Voyage/Versicherte Reise

Place of commencement of insurance/Ort des Beginns der Versicherung
Ladenburg/Germany

Means of transport/Transportmittel truck, rail	Oversea vessel/Seeschiff M/S "Nedlloyd Asia"
Port of loading/Verladehafen Bremen	Port of destination/Bestimmungshafen Dar es Salam

Place of termination of insurance/Ort des Endes der Versicherung
Mogaro/Tanzania

Insured Goods (Marks, Nos; number; kind of packages)/**Versicherte Güter** (Markierung, Nr.; Anzahl; Art der Packstücke)

Marks:	**Goods:**
MUSTERMAN BARIUM GMBH	oone 20' container
STRONTOUM CARBONAT 'A'	STRONTIUM CARBONATE A TYPE
MADE IN GERMANY = EINECS-NO: 216	ORIGIN GERMANY, CREDIT NUMBER M02
EINECS-NO: 216-643-7 = H-O	gross: 17,710 to Net: 17,500 to

Conditions (to be followed overleaf)/**Bedingungen** (Fortsetzung umseitig)

1. German General Rules of Marine Insurance (ADS). Special Conditions for Cargo (ADS Cargo 1973-Edition 1984)/
   Allgemeine Deutsche Seeversicherungsbedingungen (ADS). Besondere Bestimmungen für die Güterversicherung
   (ADS Güterversicherung 1973 in der Fassung 1984).
2. Conditions of the above mentioned Cover/Bedingungen des oben genannten Vertrages.
3. Types of Cover, Conditions or Clauses (as printed overleaf)/Deckungsformen, Bedingungen oder Klauseln (wie umseitig)

13	16	17	--	--	--

Premium paid/Prämie bezahlt

4. In addition/Ferner

including rain and fresh water damages as in the above mentioned
conditions and clauses. Claims are payable in US-Dollars.

GERLING-KONZERN
ALLGEMEINE VERSICHERUNGS-AKTIENGESELLSCHAFT

Reineke   ppa. Dr. Herold

TR 8/1 - 10. 95 - 20"

EXPORT DOCUMENTS – INSPECTION/QUALITY CERTIFICATE

SGS SGS Société Générale de Surveillance S.A.

1, place des Alpes
Case Postale 2152
CH-1211 Genève 1
Tél. : (41-22) 739.91.11
Fax : (41-22) 732.35.22
Tlx : 422140

CERTIFICATE OF
QUALITY / CONDITION

Certificate No. : 1401 /   054295

Goods described as	: "ROMANIAN MILLING WHEAT IN BULK".
Vessel	: M/V "SIRENE".
Quantity	: 4,200.160 MT AS PER B/L dated 05.03.96.
Port of loading	: CONSTANTZA, Romania.
Port of discharge	: IZMIR, Turkey.
Notify	: XPORTS TRADE CO. ANKARA / TURKEY.

We hereby certify that our correspondents SGS ROMANIA S.A. were present during loading of above defined marchandise. They report as follows :

SAMPLING :

Increment samples were uniformly and systematically drawn throughout loading; the sampling material so obtained was then well mixed and reduced to average samples. One of these average samples was submitted to an independant Laboratory for analyses. Results are as follows :

QUALITY :

	SPECIFICATIONS	ACTUAL FOUND
Test weight	Min 77 KG/HL	77.10 KG/HL
Moisture	Max 14 %	13.10 %
Foreign matter	Max 1 %	0.60 %
Other grains	Max 1 %	0.15 %

CONDITION :

Based on visual examination of an average sample drawn at time of loading, the goods are deemed to be free from live insects.

This certificate reflects the findings determined at time and place of intervention by our correspondents in Romania, SGS ROMANIA S.A., only.

Geneva, 8th March 1996   SGS Société Générale de Surveillance S.A.

EXPORT DOCUMENTS – CERTIFICATE OF ORIGIN

(C) SITPRO 1992

CERTIFICATE OF ORIGIN

Seller (name, address, VAT reg. no.)		
SB SmithKline Beecham International SB House, Great West Road, Brentford, Middlesex, TW8 9BD. Telephone: 0181 560 5151 FAX: 0181 975 4481 VAT No. GB 493 9256 01		

Invoice number		Sheet no.
00017989 / 027951	00076163	1
Invoice date (tax point)	Seller's reference	
13OCT95		
Buyer's reference	Other reference	

Consignee	VAT no.
MAURITIUS PHARMACEUTICAL MANUFACTURING CO. LTD. P.O. BOX 685 BELL VILLAGE PORT LOUIS, MAURITIUS	

Buyer (if not consignee)	VAT no.
MAURITIUS PHARMACEUTICAL MANUFACTURING CO. LTD. P.O. BOX 685 BELL VILLAGE PORT LOUIS, MAURITIUS	

UNISON NO 207

Country of origin of goods	Country of destination
UNITED KINGDOM	MAURITIUS

Terms of delivery and payment

CIP - PORT LOUIS
180 SIGHT BILLS OF EXCHANGE

Vessel/flight no. and date	Port/airport of loading
MSC ROSA M	FELIXSTOWE
Port/airport of discharge	Place of delivery
PORT LOUIS	MAURITIUS

VESSEL: MSC ROSA M
ETS: 24.10.95
ETA: 20.11.95
REF: MLCLF 471 1526

Shipping marks; container number	No. and kind of packages; description of goods	Commodity code	Total gross wt (kg)	Total cube (m3)
FULLY ADDRESSED	11 KEGS PHARMACEUTICALS		387	0.748
MPM/139/VA/PS	74022 SB	Total net weight (kg) 320		

Item/packages	Gross/net/cube	Description	Quantity	Unit price	Amount
		Invoice Line Item Total GBP			XXXXXXXXXXX
			Invoice total GBP		XXXXXXX
			U.K. POUND STG		

Name of signatory
LISA ABEL
Place and date of issue
BRENTFORD, MIDDX   11OCT95
Signature

V501   SmithKline Beecham p.l.c. Registered in London 2337958. Registered Office. New Horizons Court, Brentford, Middlesex, TW8 9EP

Export Trade Connections, SITPRO approved licensee No 10

6.4 Method of operation of the basic payment mechanisms

Open Account
Cash in Advance
Collection
Documentary collection
Clean collection
Letter of Credit (see §6.5)

6.4.1 Payment on Open Account

With open account payments the seller sends the goods directly to the buyer, transmits an invoice and other shipping documents, and then awaits payment; i.e., the importer "buys now, pays later". These are sometimes called sales "on credit", because the seller extends credit without documentary security for the buyer's indebtedness. Open account sales are fairly common in domestic sales, but are less common in international transactions because they substantially increase the risk for the seller. An export seller should only agree to open account terms if he has absolute confidence in the import buyer as well as in the stability of the buyer's country and its import regulations. An additional source of security is a stable market in the particular goods, because in unstable markets a sudden drop in prices will often motivate importers to try to escape their contracts.

For the importer, of course, open account terms are quite advantageous, as there is no need to pay for the goods until they have been received and inspected. An importer may even be able to sell the goods and use the proceeds to pay the exporter's commercial invoice when it arrives.

6.4.2 Payment in Advance

As we have seen, payment on open account is used when the trading partners have the utmost confidence in each other. At the other extreme, when the exporter has serious doubts about the creditworthiness of the importer (or doubts about the stability of the importer's country), the exporter may demand *cash in advance*. Here, the seller takes no risk whatsoever. However, the importer is obviously at serious risk, and should never consider a cash in advance payment unless full information on the reputation of the seller is available. If advance cash payments are made at all, they are usually only partial payments.

A variation on cash in advance is for an advance payment to be made via some form of documentary instrument, such as under a "red clause" letter of credit.

6.4.3 Collection – Documentary Collection / Clean Collection

While cash in advance represents the ideal option for the exporter, and open account payments represent the ideal for the importer, the next two payment mechanisms we will consider are compromises which offer benefits to both sides: the documentary collection and the documentary credit.

The *documentary collection* must first be distinguished from the *clean collection*, which is essentially nothing more than an open account payment made via bill of exchange. A documentary collection allows an exporter to retain control of the goods until he has received payment or an assurance of receiving payment. Generally, the exporter ships the goods and then assembles the relevant commercial documents, such as the invoice and the document of title (bill of lading), and then turns them over, along with a draft, to a bank acting as an agent for the exporter. The bank will only release the document of title to the importer if the importer pays against the draft or accepts the obligation to do so at a future time. There are two possibilities:

1) *D/P – "Cash against documents"* – The importer *pays* the draft in order to receive the document of title to the goods; hence this is referred to by banks as *documents against payment* or *D/P* (or *sight D/P*).

2) *D/A – "Documents against acceptance"* – Here, the importer *accepts* the draft in order to receive the documents of title to the goods. By accepting the draft, the importer acknowledges an unconditional legal obligation to pay according to the terms of the draft.

The exporter's instructions to present a draft for acceptance or payment will be transmitted through a series of banks. Usually, this will involve at least the exporter's bank (here called the *remitting bank*) and a bank in the importer's country (called the *collecting* or *presenting* bank, because it *presents* the relevant documents for *collection* to the drawee). This somewhat long information-chain makes it crucial that the exporter's initial instructions be precise and complete. To this end, the remitting bank will generally request the exporter to fill out a *collection form* (also called a *lodgment form*), which enables the exporter to easily indicate the instructions the exporter wishes the banks to follow. On the basis of this information, the bank prepares a *collection order* which will accompany the documentary collection as it is transmitted to the collecting bank. The banking practice relating to collection arrangements is standardised in the ICC's Uniform Rules for Collections.

a. **Advantages and disadvantages** – Advantages of collections for the exporter are that they are relatively easy and inexpensive, and that control over the transport documents is maintained until the exporter receives assurance of payment. The advantage for the importer is that there is no obligation to pay before having had an opportunity to inspect the documents and in some cases (as by an examination in a bonded warehouse) the goods themselves.

Disadvantages for the exporter are that collections expose the seller to several risks: the risk that the importer will not accept the goods shipped, the credit risk of the importer, the political risk of the importer's country, and the risk that the shipment may fail to clear customs. The prudent exporter will, therefore, have obtained a credit report on the importer as well as an evaluation of country risk. Another disadvantage for the exporter is that collection can be relatively slow. However, the exporter's bank may be willing to provide finance to cover the period during which the exporter is waiting for the funds to clear.

The importer takes only the risk under a D/P collection that the goods shipped may not be as indicated on the invoice and bill of lading, but this risk can generally not be avoided unless the importer requires an inspection certificate as part of the documentation. The banks assume no risks for documentary collections (other than that of their own negligence in following directions). This is one reason why collections are generally significantly cheaper, in terms of bank fees, than documentary credits.

During negotiations a documentary collection may be suggested as a helpful compromise. In terms of relative advantages for exporter and importer, it lies mid-way between the sale on open account (advantageous for the importer) and the letter of credit (advantageous for the exporter). Thus, an exporter will prefer the documentary collection as an alternative to a sale on open account proposed by the importer. The importer will prefer a documentary collection as an alternative to a letter of credit proposed by the exporter.

6.5 Documentary credits (letters of credit): An in-depth look

The basics: Documentary credits (also called letters of credit) facilitate international payments, providing security for both export seller and import buyer. The seller is assured of payment upon production of constructive evidence of shipment of the contract merchandise, and the buyer is assured that the bank will not pay unless the seller has met documentary requirements complying with the buyer's instructions. International letter of credit practice is governed by a set of rules produced by the ICC, commonly known as the UCP 500 (Uniform Customs and Practice for Documentary Credits).

6.5.1 Introduction

Documentary credits (also called letters of credit or "L/C's") substantially reduce risks for both exporter and importer. Not surprisingly, therefore, the letter of credit is the classic form of international export payment, especially in trade between distant partners. The letter of credit is essentially a document issued by the importer's bank which undertakes to pay the exporter upon due compliance with documentary requirements. Hence, the term *"documentary credit"* – payment, acceptance or negotiation of the credit is made upon presentation by the seller of *all stipulated documents*. These documents (e.g., bill of lading, invoice, inspection certificate) provide a basic level of proof that the right merchandise has been properly sent to the importer – although, of course, there is always the chance that the documents may prove inaccurate or even fraudulent.

Although there are endless variations on the letter of credit, as we shall see below, a typical procedure is as follows. The process begins when the exporter and importer agree on a contract of sale. Typically, it is the exporter who insists on payment by letter of credit – because the exporter does not want to take a credit risk, and cannot get sufficient information on the creditworthiness of the buyer so as to grant another form of payment.

The importer then initiates the letter of credit mechanism by going to her bank and requesting to *open* a letter of credit. The importer's bank issues the documentary credit (and is hence called the "issuing bank"), under which it agrees to pay according to the importer's instructions. The credit is then sent to the exporter or to a bank in the exporter's country (depending on the type of credit).

Commonly, under the sales contract and/or credit application the exporter's bank (or another bank in the exporter's country) will be requested to *confirm* the documentary credit, thereby committing itself to pay under the terms of the credit. Exporters may insist on confirmed credits when they want to have a trusted local paymaster.

If the exporter agrees with the terms of the credit, the exporter then proceeds to ship the goods. After shipment, the exporter goes to the bank nominated in the credit to effect payment and presents the documents that the importer has asked for. The exporter usually also presents a *bill of exchange* or *bank draft*, a document representing the bank's payment obligation (see document definitions above).

The bank examines the documents carefully to ensure that they correspond exactly with the terms of the credit. If the documents do not conform to the letter of credit, the bank observes a documentary *discrepancy*, notifies the exporter, and refuses to pay the credit. The exporter may then either correct the documents or obtain a waiver of their discrepancy from the importer.

There are benefits for both sides from the banks' examination of the documents. For the buyer, clearly, because payment will only be made against documents in conformity with the precise terms and conditions of the credit. But the exporter may also benefit from an early examination of the documents, since this allows for a possibility of quickly correcting any discrepancy. With documentary collections, discrepancies may remain undetected until much later, when the documents are checked by the buyers themselves.

6.5.2 Rules for Letters of Credit: the UCP 500

International letter of credit practice has been standardised by ICC rules known as the Uniform Customs and Practice for Documentary Credits ("UCP 500"). The UCP is sometimes cited as the foremost example of how international business self-regulation can be more efficient than treaties, government regulation or case law. Indeed, legal commentators have called the UCP the most successful act of commercial harmonisation in the history of world trade.

Letter of credit law developed primarily in the United Kingdom in the 19th century, and since WW1, also extensively in United States courts, as well as in other national courts and legal systems around the world. But, as can be seen elsewhere in international trade, purely legal solutions are insufficient in an international business context, because trading partners do not want the burden of having to predict the reasoning of judges and tribunals in distant countries.

Thus, there was a need for international standard rules for letter of credit practice, rules which could be updated in light of changing banking practices. The first adopted version of the UCP dates from 1929; the 1933 revision of this text gained broad acceptance in Europe. The next revision was adopted in 1951 and brought the UCP to truly global scope, being used by banks in Asia, Africa, Latin America, the United States and Europe. The 1962 revision provided a major breakthrough, gaining the acceptance of the influential UK and Commonwealth banking community. Further revisions, adding technical refinements and improvements, were released in 1974 and 1983. The currently valid version, UCP 500, entered into effect on 1 January 1994.

The UCP is a more flexible set of rules than any national or international legislation. When the United Nations drafts an international treaty or convention, the entire process, if one includes ratification by the signatory countries, can take decades. The UCP, in contrast, is not binding law, but applies because banks voluntarily incorporate the UCP into the contracts upon which the letter of credit is based. In essence, the UCP is the codification of actual business practices, based on the experiences of trade banks, exporters and importers. Periodic revisions have allowed the UCP to keep in step with advances in banking practice. As a result, the UCP arguably provides a more practical procedural framework than could an international law or treaty.

With regard to the legal effect around the world of the ICC's rules documentary credits, the basic rule is that the UCP rules are creatures of contract, and thus apply principally when they have been voluntarily incorporated by the parties. Thus, documentary credit application forms generally contain a statement to the effect that the credit will be subject to the UCP 500 – this is considered legally to represent the parties' willingness to submit interpretation of the credit to the rules of the UCP.

After more than 60 years of existence, the UCP has achieved such universal effect that in some countries the UCP is recognised as having the force of law, or at least that of a trade custom. However, in other countries, such as the UK, the UCP does not have formal legislative status, and will only apply when the parties specifically incorporate them into the documentary credit by explicitly invoking the UCP on the credit application forms. In the United States, the Uniform Commercial Code governs the use of letters of credit, but the UCP is considered to govern when the parties have specifically incorporated the UCP or when the UCP is the customary trade practice.

Even where the UCP is applicable, the somewhat general provisions of the UCP cannot cover all cases. As a result, national courts are often asked to interpret certain provisions. The Banking Commission of the ICC also regularly issues interpretations of provisions of the UCP based on questions received by the ICC, and these opinions are collected and published by the ICC every few years and can be a valuable aide for practitioners.

Although it is beyond the scope of this text to go in detail through the numerous refinements and improvements included in UCP 500, the most important ones deserve brief mention here:

• A credit is now deemed to be *irrevocable* when the credit is silent on whether it is revocable or irrevocable (this reversed the position under UCP 400).

• The bank examining the documents will have a reasonable time not to exceed *seven banking days* following the day of receipt of the documents to decide whether or not to take up the documents or reject them and inform the beneficiary to that effect (the previous position under UCP 400 did not give a precise maximum time limit for examination of documents). However, note that courts may rule that in particular cases a "reasonable" time is much shorter than seven days.

• Transport documents – *Articles 23–30* – These provisions have been fundamentally reworked, so that each type of transport document now is covered by a separate article, thereby rendering the respective requirements for each type of document somewhat clearer. There has been some criticism from transport circles that UCP 500 went too far in specifying the requirements for transport documents.

• International banking standard – Article 13 (a) sets forth the rule that the compliance of documents with the terms of the credit will be judged according to *international standard banking practice.*

6.5.3 Basic Concepts and Terminology

a. **The parties** – In documentary credits, the seller/exporter is alternatively referred to as:

Beneficiary – Because it is the seller who receives payment from the letter of credit.
Shipper – Because the seller ships the goods.
Consignor – Again, because the seller ships the goods, sometimes referred to as "consignment" in international transport.

The buyer/importer is alternatively referred to as:

Opener – Because the importer "opens" the credit to begin the process.
Applicant – Because the importer must begin the process by submitting a credit "application" to a bank.
Account party – Because the importer's application to open a credit creates an "account" relationship with the bank, and is supervised by an account officer.

b. **The banks and their roles:**

1) *Issuing* (or "opening") bank – The bank which receives the importer's application and agrees to "issue" the credit. The issuing bank is commonly, but not necessarily, located in the importer's country. By issuing the credit, the bank is making an irrevocable undertaking to pay the beneficiary the value of the draft and/or other documents, provided that the terms and conditions of the credit are complied with.

2) *Nominated* bank – The bank which is stipulated in a credit as authorised to pay, issue a deferred payment undertaking or accept drafts. Unless a credit expressly states that it is available only with the issuing bank, it should nominate some other bank. If the credit is of the "freely negotiable" variety, any bank qualifies as a nominated bank. A nominated bank is not normally bound to pay under the credit, unless it has added its confirmation to the credit and become a *confirming bank* (see below).

3) *Advising* bank – The bank which notifies or "advises" the exporter that a credit has been opened in the exporter's favour. By advising a credit, the bank is only acting as a conduit for the issuing bank; the advising bank does not take any further risk, and only has the responsibility of taking reasonable care that the credit is an authentic one. The advising bank is commonly, but not necessarily, located in the exporter's country. An advising bank will frequently perform one or more of the functions of confirming, negotiating, or paying, which are defined below.

4) *Confirming* bank – The bank (normally also the advising bank) which adds its own irrevocable undertaking (known as "confirmation") in addition to that

given by the issuing bank. The confirmation allows the exporter to be paid by a bank in the exporter's own country, or by a bank which the exporter otherwise trusts. The confirming bank irrevocably commits itself to paying the exporter upon presentation of conforming documents. As with the role of paying bank, the bank accepting the role of confirming bank exposes itself to the risk that it will fail to detect a discrepancy in the documents.

5) *Paying* (or "paying agent") bank – The bank which reviews the documents presented by the exporter and, if they conform to the terms and conditions of the credit, arranges payment to the exporter. A paying bank's main risk is of paying against documents that turn out to contain discrepancies, in which case it may not be able to recover the funds from the issuing bank. However, a bank acting as paying agent may refuse to pay the exporter if the issuing bank's account is not sufficient to cover the draft (this applies where the bank has not added its confirmation to the letter of credit).

6) *Negotiating* bank – The bank which examines the documents presented by the exporter, then "negotiates" the credit (i.e., in the case of a usance draft, purchases the draft from the exporter at a discount from the face value). This *negotiation*, or purchase, is usually done "with recourse", which means that if the issuing bank fails to reimburse the negotiating bank, the negotiating bank will recover the funds advanced to the exporter. This distinguishes the negotiating function from the confirming function. When a confirming bank pays the exporter, it is "without recourse", which means that even if no reimbursement is received from the issuing bank, the confirming bank cannot recover the funds from the exporter.

c. **Types of letters of credit (to some extent also dealt with in definitions of banks):**

1) *Irrevocable/revocable* – An irrevocable letter of credit cannot be amended or cancelled without the consent of all parties. This essential undertaking allows the exporter to procure the goods or prepare them for shipment with the assurance that payment will be received if the stipulated documents are presented. A revocable letter of credit provides little if any security for the exporter, and is consequently unusual. The UCP 500 provides that credits will be deemed irrevocable unless explicitly stated as revocable (this reversed the previous position under the UCP 400).

2) *Confirmed* – As stated in the definition of confirming bank above, a credit is confirmed when a bank (usually the advising bank in the exporter's country) adds its own irrevocable undertaking at the request of the issuing bank in addition to that of the issuing bank. Generally, this assures the exporter of payment by a local bank or one which is trusted more than the issuing bank.

3) *Sight/Usance* – Credits may provide for payment at *sight* (immediately) or for payment at a specified time in the future – a *usance* credit.

4) *Revolving* – If the importer is a regular customer of the exporter, the parties may wish to arrange for a *revolving* credit. Under a typical revolving credit, the

bank issues a credit for a certain maximum sum which is automatically renewed at certain intervals. Revolving credits save the parties from the administrative tasks of having to repeatedly re-apply and re-issue similar credits. Although revolving credits do have expiry dates, they tend to be valid much longer than normal credits.

5) *Red clause* – A *red clause* credit allows pre-shipment advances to be made to the exporter at the risk and expense of the applicant. Under a red clause credit the bank will honour the exporter's sight drafts up to a specified percentage of the total credit against production of certain preliminary documents. Originally, the clauses specifying a red clause credit were actually printed or typed in red ink, hence the name. Obviously, such credits should only be used when the importer has great trust in the exporter.

6) *Transferable* – *Transferable* credits are used in "middleman" situations, where an export merchant or agent plays the role of an intermediary between a supplier and the importer. The middleman-beneficiary transfers all or a portion of its rights to a supplier-beneficiary (called the "second beneficiary" in the UCP). The middleman may not wish to reveal the identity of the ultimate supplier, and may keep this information from the importer by substituting the middleman's invoice for the ultimate supplier's invoice. The various permutations of transferable credits can become exceedingly complex, so that importers should proceed with some caution. In particular, the importer may accept the risk that the ultimate source of the contract goods remains unknown; therefore, it is difficult for the importer to be assured of the ultimate supplier's reputation and reliability.

7) *Back-to-back* – Under a back-to-back credit, the middleman-beneficiary uses the letter of credit as security for a second, separate credit in favour of the ultimate supplier. Whereas under a transferable credit the importer must request the transferable credit in the application, under a back-to-back credit the importer may be ignorant of the back-to-back arrangement. Although the middleman may, therefore, wish to use a back-to-back credit if it wishes to conceal its recourse to an ultimate supplier, the middleman takes an additional risk in doing so. With the back-to-back procedure, the middleman must repay the bank for any valid payment to the ultimate supplier under the second letter of credit regardless of whether or not the middleman receives payment under the first letter of credit. This is a major risk area for banks, which are very cautious as regards back-to-back credits.

8) *Standby* – The standby credit is to be distinguished from the above-defined letters of credit in that the primary function of the standby is to serve as a security or guarantee rather than as a payment mechanism. Under a typical standby, the beneficiary will claim payment in the event that the contract partner has failed to perform or fulfil certain obligations. Standby credit practice has largely developed in the United States, where banking law long forbid banks to issue guarantees (recent changes in the law, however, do not seem to have significantly changed bankers' reliance on the standby). From a legal point of view, standby's are virtually indistinguishable from bank guarantees. In practice, however, standbys appear to be used for a much broader spectrum of uses. Although

standby credits are specifically referred to in the UCP 500, the majority of the articles have no direct bearing on the issuance or handling of this type of credit. Note that standby's may also be issued subject to the ICC Uniform Rules on Demand Guarantees (see Chapter 8). A draft set of uniform rules for international standby practice is currently being formulated by the Institute of International Banking Law and Practice.

6.5.4 Example: procedure for an irrevocable, confirmed credit

Note: The documentary credit process described below covers the specific case of a *confirmed, irrevocable* letter of credit. Note that not all credits are confirmed (nor irrevocable), so that the procedure below is not meant to apply to all cases (thus, the example does not apply to cases where a credit is only *advised* and not confirmed).

a. **The sale contract** – The sale contract should clearly specify that payment will be by confirmed irrevocable letter of credit if the exporter wishes to insist on this highly secure form of payment. The sale contract is sometimes referred to as the *underlying contract* in relation to the documentary credit operation. As will be discussed later, it is a fundamental principle that the documentary credit is independent and autonomous of the contract of sale, meaning that disputes under the contract of sale cannot normally prevent payment under the credit. However, *the credit must be opened in accordance with the conditions specified in the contract of sale.*

The sale contract may or may not provide additional details or conditions with respect to the credit (as, for example, the time of payment, the documents to be presented, etc.). The export seller will normally insist on a confirmed credit whenever he is less than fully confident in the credit risk of the issuing bank, or when he fears that there may be political or foreign exchange risks associated with the buyer's country.

b. **The credit application** – Assuming that the parties have agreed in the sales contract as to the terms of the documentary credit, the importer (the *applicant*) will apply for the credit at her bank. The *credit application*, when accepted, constitutes a contract between the importer-applicant and her bank (the issuing bank). The bank agrees to issue the documentary credit and the buyer agrees to reimburse the bank for payments made under the credit. Since the bank will open a credit which follows the instructions given by the importer, it is up to the importer to make sure that these instructions do not contradict the contract of sale (if there is a contradiction, the importer will be *in breach* of the contract of sale).

Although the applicant must respect the terms of the contract of sale, it is quite common for the contract of sale to be silent on one or more terms and conditions. In such cases, the applicant may include additional details but the exporter-beneficiary will not be contractually bound to accept them when he reviews the credit.

In some cases the applicant will bring in the sales contract to his bank when she prepares the credit application. The issuing bank may be tempted to simply transpose the conditions of the contract into the credit. However, great care should be taken that the credit does not contain any *non-documentary conditions* – conditions which cannot be established by a specific document.

Amongst the minimum details that will be specified in the credit application are:

i) Time of payment – Specifying whether the credit will be payable at sight or under a usance draft;

ii) Date and place of expiry of the credit – These dates should give sufficient time for the beneficiary to prepare and ship the goods;

iii) Latest date for shipment and presentation of documents – As above, these time limits should be reasonable in light of circumstances to allow the beneficiary to perform his obligations; in any event, should the credit be silent on the time allowable for presentation of documents after the date of the transport document, the UCP specifies a maximum period of 21 days;

iv) Beneficiary – the beneficiaries' name and address must be exactly and completely spelled out;

v) Type of credit – i.e., irrevocable/revocable, confirmed, transferable, etc.

vi) Amount – In some cases, due to uncertainty as to the exact quantities to be shipped or the freight rate, the sales contract will only have contained an approximate price. The credit may, therefore, specify an amount which is "about" or «approximately" a certain sum, in which case a 10% variation will be allowable; alternatively, the credit may specify a maximum amount through the use of such words as "up to";

vii) Shipment details – These will specify, inter alia, whether partial shipments or transhipments are allowable. Unless the applicant has strong reasons for disallowing partial shipments, it is better to allow them, as they provide flexibility for the beneficiary. If the goods are of a hazardous or bulky nature which may require carriage on deck, the credit should specifically allow for bills of lading indicating that such carriage has occurred or may occur;

viii) Goods – It is important that the goods *not* be described in *excessive detail*, which can give rise to disputes later when documents are presented; rather, as is stated in the UCP, the description of the goods should be general and with just sufficient detail to identify the contract goods. It is advisable for applicants to identify the contract by its reference number; applicants may also wish to require that the beneficiary provide a certificate to the effect that all conditions of the contract have been complied with. In no case should contractual documents (such as pro forma invoices or technical specifications sheets) be attached to the letter of credit, as these multiply the opportunities for confusion and mistakes;

ix) Documents – The documentary requirements are of the utmost importance and should be carefully thought through by the applicant, as it is likely they will undergo close scrutiny by the beneficiary when the credit is received. In general, applicants should be discouraged from asking for an excessive number of documents or from insisting on full sets of originals when single documents or photocopies will do. The prudent beneficiary will understand that as the number of documentary requirements increases so does the possibility that a document will contain a discrepancy and therefore block payment under the credit.

The importer makes the credit application by filling in a standard form provided by the bank. On occasion, these forms are based on models proposed by the ICC (see ICC Publication N° 516, New Standard Documentary Credit Forms for the UCP 500). The application form has been designed to correspond to the model form for the credit itself, thereby greatly facilitating the transfer of information from the application to the credit.

c. **Issuance of the credit** – The issuing bank will decide whether or not to issue the credit after considering the importer's creditworthiness. From the bank's point of view, the documentary credit amounts to a borrowing request by the importer for the time period dating from the opening of the credit to its expiry date.

The bank issues a documentary credit in favour of the exporter-beneficiary under which the bank agrees to pay the beneficiary provided that the beneficiary presents documents which conform to the terms and conditions of the credit. It is said that this undertaking constitutes the third "contract" of the documentary credit mechanism (although, strictly, under some systems of law it is not a true contract owing to the unilateral nature of the undertaking) – the first contract being the contract of sale between the exporter and buyer, and the second contract being the one formed by the credit application, whereby the bank agrees to issue the credit for a fee and the applicant agrees to reimburse the bank for payments made under the credit).

d. **Confirmation** – When the credit application specifies a confirmed credit, the issuing bank will request that another bank, usually in the beneficiary's country, *confirm* the credit. By confirming the credit, the confirming bank adds its irrevocable obligation to that of the issuing bank. The exporter is thus assured of a reliable paymaster in his own country.

The confirming bank's decision to confirm will involve a credit analysis of the issuing bank's credit risk as well as the relevant political and foreign exchange risks. Having confirmed the credit, the confirming bank must pay the beneficiary upon presentation of conforming documents, regardless of the issuing bank's ability to reimburse the confirming bank.

The confirming bank advises the confirmed credit to the beneficiary. The confirming bank's undertaking to pay now constitutes the fourth contract in the chain.

e. **Receipt and review of credit by seller-beneficiary** – When the exporter receives the letter of credit, it is *strongly recommended* that he *immediately* review it, carefully checking it against the terms of the contract in light of the anticipated circumstances of the shipment.

A disturbingly high percentage of documentary credit transactions encounter difficulties upon first presentation of documents (as many as 50% - 90%, depending upon the country). One of the reasons for this problem is that sellers so often neglect to review the credit when they receive it. An immediate review allows sellers to detect in due time any inconsistencies with the contract of sale or with their intended means of preparing or shipping the goods.

If the exporter, upon reviewing the credit, realises that it would be impractical or impossible to comply with its terms, he should immediately notify the importer and request that the credit be *amended*. The exporter should verify that the

The stages of a documentary credit operation

The case of a confirmed, irrevocable documentary credit:

A. The sale contract; credit application

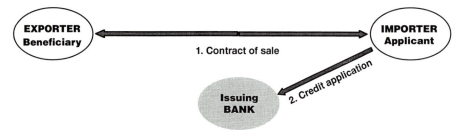

In documentary credit terminology, the Exporter is called the "Beneficiary", and the Importer is called the "Applicant". Generally, the parties will have concluded a contract of sale with a payment provision stipulating payment by documentary credit. The importer then proceeds to her bank and submits a credit application, which should be in conformity with the contract of sale.

B. Issuance of the credit; confirmation

Provided the bank approves the credit application, it will issue the credit and request that a confirming bank add its own irrevocable commitment to pay under the terms of the credit.

C. Advice of credit; review by beneficiary

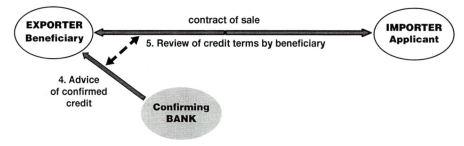

Once the Exporter-Beneficiary has received the written notification of the credit from the confirming bank, he should carefully review the provisions of the credit, comparing these with the provision of the contract of sale, and further making sure that he will be in a position to furnish all stipulated documents in due time.

D. Shipment; shipping documents; presentation of documents

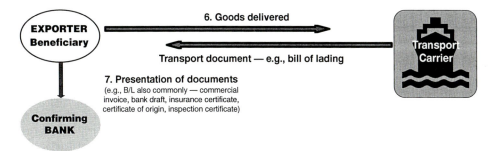

The Exporter-Beneficary, having delivered the goods to the transport carrier, receives a transport document which, together with the other stipulated documents, is presented to the Confirming Bank for payment.

E. Bank examination of documents; payment; reimbursement

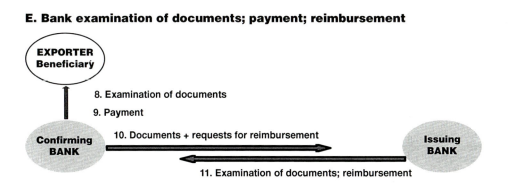

The Confirming Bank will closely examine the documents to see if they contain "discrepancies" or conflicts with the credit provisions; if not, the Confirming Bank will pay and will forward the documents to the Issuing Bank, along with a request for reimbursement. The Issuing Bank will also examine the documents and, if it also finds that there are no discrepancies, will reimburse the Confirming Bank.

F. Release of documents; obtaining delivery of goods

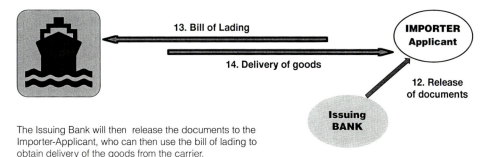

The Issuing Bank will then release the documents to the Importer-Applicant, who can then use the bill of lading to obtain delivery of the goods from the carrier.

credit is actually amended and that he is notified of the amendment – it is unfortunately not unheard of for the exporter and importer to agree to an amendment but neglect to inform the issuing bank, thereby permitting a troublesome discrepancy to arise later.

f. Shipment of goods and presentation of documents – In order to be paid under the credit, the exporter must prepare the goods for shipment in due time, and must assemble all the necessary documents. The exporter is well-advised to check the documents himself against the documentary credit specifications before presenting them to the bank.

It is highly recommended that the beneficiary present the documents as early as possible, and at the very least, more than seven working days prior the expiration of the credit. This is because the bank will take a certain amount of time to check the documents (a period which cannot exceed seven working days under the UCP 500) and, in the event the bank detects a discrepancy which can be corrected, the beneficiary will want to have enough time to correct the discrepancy and re-present the documents before the expiry of the credit.

After shipment, the beneficiary presents the documents (and a draft, in those common cases where the credit calls for a draft) to the confirming bank.

g. Examination of documents by confirming bank – The confirming bank will carefully check the documents presented by the beneficiary against those specified in the letter of credit. The bank will note any *discrepancies* (differences between the documents presented and the terms of the credit), or will observe that the documents are *conforming* (that they correspond to the requirements of the credit).

Under the UCP, the bank must conduct its examination of the documents within a reasonable time not to exceed seven banking days following the day of receipt of the documents (this is equally true for the Issuing Bank, Confirming Bank and/or Nominated Bank). The bank must notify the beneficiary of a decision to refuse the documents by telecommunications or other expeditious means, in no event later than the maximum period specified above.

If the documents are found to be conforming, the bank will pay, accept or negotiate the credit, according to its terms. A confirming bank's payment to the beneficiary is *without recourse*, which means that the confirming bank cannot recover the funds from the beneficiary, regardless of the issuing bank's subsequent decision to not reimburse the confirming bank (there may be an exception to this rule in some jurisdictions, with the effect that a bank can recover the funds if it can prove fraud by the already paid beneficiary).

If the documents are discrepant, the exporter may be able to correct the documents if there is still time remaining before the expiration of the credit, and provided that the discrepancies are of a nature that permits correction. Obviously, some kinds of discrepancies cannot be corrected (transport document not as per credit, inspection certificate indicating flawed merchandise, etc.), regardless of the time frame. Should the beneficiary be unable for whatever reason to correct the documents, he may still approach the applicant for a waiver of the discrepancy (the approach may be made directly or via the advising or confirming bank). An applicant may be willing to grant a waiver, especially if the discrepancy appears to be an insignificant one and there are strong commercial reasons for going through with the deal. Unfortunately, however, it is sometimes reported that applicants use discrepancies as an opportunity to bargain for discounts from exporters; all the more reason for beneficiaries to prepare the presentation of documents with great care.

h. **Issuing bank review; release of the documents to the buyer** – The issuing bank will also review the documents, which it has received from the confirming bank (or, in other cases, the negotiating bank). If, in the judgement of the issuing bank, the documents are discrepant and the confirming bank has made an error in paying under the credit, the issuing bank can recover the funds which it has been debited by the confirming bank. Under article 13 of UCP 500, the issuing bank must take no more than seven banking days to conduct its examination of the documents and take up or reject them.

   If the issuing bank's review indicates that the documents were in fact conforming, then it will debit the account of the applicant and release the documents to her. The documents (particularly the document entitling control of the goods, such as the marine bill of lading), will allow the importer to collect the goods from the carrier. However, the importer is also entitled to conduct her own review of the documents. It is possible that the importer may discover a discrepancy which has been missed or ignored by the banks. In such a case, the buyer can refuse to reimburse the bank and can herself reject the documents. An importer may scrutinize the documents with particular care in cases when the market price for the goods has fallen drastically and it makes commercial sense to escape the transaction if possible. This is why banks conduct such painstaking examinations of the documents – a bank which has paid against discrepant documents may find that it must simply absorb the loss.

6.5.5 The two fundamental principles of documentary credit practice

1) the *independence* of the credit from the underlying contract and,
2) the requirement that documents *strictly comply* with the terms of the credit.

a. **Independence of the documentary credit from the underlying contract** – The documentary credit is completely independent of the underlying contract. If the exporter fulfils the documentary obligations, payment must be effected according to the terms of the credit, regardless of disputes connected to the underlying contract.

   It is essential that all parties remain confident that issuing or confirming banks will respect their payment commitments. The payment obligation of an issuing bank is separate and autonomous from the underlying export contract. Thus, the exporter's breach of a contract condition (i.e., with respect to quantity, quality, delivery date, etc.) is not sufficient to entitle the importer to instruct her bank to stop payment under the credit. The principle exception to this rule has to do with fraud. A bank which receives a clear notification or proof of fraud committed by the beneficiary is not only entitled, but obliged, to withold payment. However, banks are not required to investigate mere suspicions of fraud.

   Courts are quite reluctant to grant injunctions ordering a bank to withold payment, so clear indications of fraud are generally necessary. Since letter of credit practice has arisen to some extent to avoid risks related to the lack of knowledge or trust between the two trading partners, it is essential that both parties trust the banks. Letters of credit could not function if the parties lacked confidence that the banks would honour their obligations regardless of arguments submitted by the parties. Judges have referred to letters of credit as the "life blood" of international commerce. If banks were allowed to refuse to pay letters of credit whenever trading parties had a dispute, the vital flow of international commerce would soon be blocked.

In some cases, the issuing bank's officers may be obliged to resist pressure from the applicant to bend the principle of absolute neutrality and independence. However, it is unfortunately quite possible for a seller to send bad merchandise (so long as this does not amount to a clear fraud) and yet present good documents. That is one of the reasons that an inspection certificate is so frequently called for. If the importer learns that she may receive an inadequate or late shipment, she may sue for damages for breach or contract.

b. Strict compliance – The terms of the letter of credit must be strictly adhered to: this is known as the doctrine of *strict compliance*. What this means in everyday practice is that documents presented under the credit must conform very precisely with the terms of the credit.

A court's view of strict compliance...

"There is no room for documents which are almost the same, or which will do just as well."

    – Equitable Trust Co. of New York v. Dawson Partners Ltd (1927) 27 Ll L Rep 49.

The great majority of letter of credit disputes relate to the issue of discrepancy in the documents, and bankers' decisions as to discrepancies must be based on this doctrine of strict compliance.

In the letter of credit process, the issuing bank acts as an agent of the importer, and as an agent the bank must strictly follow the instructions of the account party.

Example: Strict compliance and falling markets...

An importer contracts for a large shipment of coffee for $200 per bag. Then, the coffee market crashes and by the time shipment arrives the price of coffee has dropped to $100 per bag.

The exporter presents the documents required under the credit, and the bank must normally pay under the credit. However, it is clear that the importer has a strong incentive to refuse to reimburse the bank if it turns out that the documents accepted by the bank were not in fact conforming.

Thus, if the bank makes a mistake and has not strictly followed the instructions given by the importer, the importer may elect to sue to avoid reimbursing the bank. Moreover, if the exporter fails to respect precisely all documentary requirements under the credit (no matter how seemingly trivial), the importer can refuse to authorise an amendment of the credit, and thereby avoiding paying the exporter. Although this might seem unethical, in some cases the importer might feel it is the only way to avoid going through with a commercially disastrous deal. Of course, the exporter may still have some legal rights to payment under the contract, but as we have seen in Chapter 3, legal redress can be expensive and risky.

Thus, both exporters and the respective banks must take care that the documents are *exactly* correct. Exporters sometimes complain that banks go to excessive lengths to make sure that the documents are exactly correct, even down to the spelling of unimportant words. But it should be understood that if the bank pays against even a minor discrepancy, it may find itself faced with an applicant who refuses to reimburse it for that payment. An additional justification for banks' punctiliousness in checking for discrepancies is that banks cannot be expected to be expert in all areas of business. What is clearly a trivial discrepancy to an exporter may not be so clear to the bank. Thus, a bank cannot be expected to know that two different technical words actually mean the same thing.

In one celebrated legal case[1], the letter of credit application specified that the contractual goods were a certain kind of nuts, which were called "Coromandel groundnuts". The bill of lading referred to them, however, as "Machine-shelled groundnut kernels". In reality, these were basically the same kind of nuts, but the bank refused to pay the credit. The court upheld the bank's decision on the grounds that bankers are not required to be experts in the terminology of nuts, nor in the terminology of any of the thousands of trade sectors in which dealings letters of credit are issued. In many legal cases where a bank rejected a credit because of such apparently small discrepancies in the wording on required documents, the bank was found to have acted correctly by courts of law. Unfortunately, it is difficult to derive any universal principle as to just how "big" or "small" an error must be in order to count as a discrepancy. The significance of misspelling and mis-numbering, for example, is an endless source of dispute. As a general rule, exporters should be careful to ensure that spelling and description in the commercial invoice are absolutely perfect and in conformity with the credit.

There is always the possibility that the importer will waive any discrepancies in the documents presented, and this is likely whenever the importer still wants the goods. Thus, a waiver is quite probable if the market is rising and the goods have increased in value, or whenever the buyer desperately needs the goods to fulfil another contract. In any event, the importer must make the decision whether or not to waive discrepancies quickly, so as to avoid exceeding the time limits for review.

5.5.6 CHECKLIST: Golden Rules for Letter of Credit Practice

For the exporter/seller

Before beginning to use credits: make sure that you have implemented a rigorous document-management and verification system. Small errors can be extremely costly. Ideally, try to tailor the documentary credit to your commercial context by specifying in the contract of sale precisely the type of credit that you require.

• Carefully evaluate the credit as soon as you receive it – request the buyer to amend the credit if you think you may have any difficulty in complying with its terms.

• Prepare the exact documents called for in the credit – do not volunteer unnecessary information.

• Verify – does the credit call for the requested documents, e.g.:
a Marine Insurance <u>Certificate</u>, or
a Marine Insurance <u>Policy</u> ?

• Present the documents <u>well before</u> the relevant time limits.

• Make sure corrections are <u>authenticated by the issuer</u>.

• Make sure your company is properly listed as the intended beneficiary.

• If possible, ensure that one person in your company is given central responsibility for controlling, co-ordinating, and verifying the progress of the letter of credit.

For the buyer/opener/credit applicant

• Do not include excessive detail; avoid complex, technical specifications.

• Make sure that the credit exactly reflects the contract.

• Do not include non-documentary provisions; for example, any inspection must be evidenced by a document; quality should be evidenced by a certificate.

• Do not call for documents the seller cannot provide; i.e., a marine on board bill of lading when combined or containerised transport will be used.

• Request the issuing bank for advice or assistance in case of any doubt.

• Seriously consider whether you are willing to grant a credit without requiring an inspection certificate. Although many exporters are reluctant to provide such certificates, they are the buyer's best assurance that the goods which were shipped met the contract quality requirements. One compromise is for the buyer to pay for the inspection.

The banks

• Assist the applicant to avoid problems with transport documents, especially if combined transport is called for –
is transhipment prohibited?
is a multi-modal document authorised?
is the place of dispatch specified, or a port?

• Counsel inexperienced buyers on the value of inspection certificates.

• Periodically review the wording of the credit application form; ensure that it conforms with Incoterms 1990, UCP 500; check it against the model forms provided by the ICC.

• Do not exceed a reasonable time for review of documents, even if the applicant is requested to waive possible discrepancies. Understand that the UCP specifies a maximum reasonable time of 7 days, but that courts in particular countries may enforce a substantially shorter period.

• As issuing bank, do not unilaterally alter the Incoterm suggested by the applicant if this Incoterm is already incorporated in a sales contract; rather, suggest to the applicant the advisability of contacting the counterparty to have the contract modified before issuing the credit.

6.6 Managing currency and exchange rate risks

The basics: All firms involved in international trade must face the challenge of managing currency and exchange rate risk. Given the existence of volatility in exchange markets, firms that fail to plan for exchange rate risk are exposing themselves to financial disaster.

Exchange rate risks are necessarily linked to profit opportunities: wherever money can be lost if the exchange rate moves one way, money will certainly be gained if the exchange rate moves the other way. Thus, firms can profit from exchange rate fluctuations as much as they can lose from them.

Beginning and small exporters may prefer simply to avoid exchange rate risk altogether, thereby giving up the possibility of profiting from fluctuations. The most common risk management techniques for simply avoiding exchange rate risk are: 1) insisting that the contractual currency of payment be one's own currency, and, should that fail, 2) using *forward* or *option* contracts to *hedge* against exposure. Larger or more experienced firms may wish to take advantage of the opportunities for profits from exchange rate fluctuations. Once a firm's foreign exchange exposure grows to a certain level, it generally becomes advisable to assign currency management to a single, highly specialized person or department. This will allow the firm to apply a wider range of currency management techniques, which can even generate significant revenues for the firm.

It is generally said that foreign exchange risks fall into three categories: transaction risk, translation risk and economic risk:

6.6.1 Transaction risk

When an international sales transaction involves parties from countries whose currencies are not fixed or pegged, an element of uncertainty is necessarily present. Transaction risk refers to the risk for each of the counterparties that the exchange rate will move in a disadvantageous direction in between the time the price is agreed in the contract and the time payment is made or received. Both parties are always initially exposed to transaction risk.

Example: An American exporter selling to Germany finds himself compelled to quote a price in Deutsche marks. The contract specifies delivery within 30 days, payment 90 days after receipt of commercial invoice. The contract price is one million DM, and on the date of the signing of the contract this is equal to $500,000 (USD).

Both parties are exposed to *transaction risk*:

1) If the dollar weakens against the DM in between the time the contract is signed and the time payment is required, the exporter will benefit, because the DM eventually received will buy more dollars than were expected when the contract was negotiated (e.g., the 1M DM might ultimately yield $550,000).

2) If the dollar strengthens against the DM, the 1M DM received by the exporter will buy fewer dollars and the exporter will have lost (e.g., the 1M DM finally received by the exporter might, after being exchanged into dollars, yield only $450,000).

A conservative or inexperienced exporter will be primarily concerned with avoiding a loss, rather than with potential gain. Therefore, he may wish to use a *forward hedge,* a foreign exchange contract which locks in the exchange rate in force on the day of the signing of the export contract. The hedge is a contract between the exporter and a bank or intermediary on a foreign exchange market. In the above example, the exporter will conclude a contract to buy $500,000 in exchange for 1M DM on or after the date payment is due from the importer (in reality, the exporter will receive less than the 500,000 USD, because the bank or other party to the foreign exchange contract will charge a commission, for example, 0.9% ($4500 USD), leaving the exporter $495, 500.

The $4500 paid to the bank or foreign exchange dealer can be looked at as a sort of insurance policy against currency fluctuation. No matter what happens, the exporter is assured of receiving $495,500. He has given up the possibility of gain that would ensue if the dollar weakened, but he has received in exchange the assurance that he will not lose if the dollar strengthens.

6.6.2 Translation risk (also known as balance-sheet exposure)

Translation risk is derived from the periodic nature of accounting report practices. A company will periodically need to state on its balance sheet, in a particular reporting currency, assets and liabilities which may be denominated in another currency. In between two reporting periods, the relative values of the two currencies may have changed. To some extent, the exposure to translation risk can be said to be a strategic risk factor, which should be taken into consideration when weighing the potential costs and benefits associated with a foreign investment decision.

6.6.3 Economic risk

Economic risk is the risk of currency fluctuations over the long term, and is thus also of a strategic order. It arises from a company's commitment over time to a particular set of counterparties and their currencies. Note that this risk can not be avoided through simple hedging techniques. For example, an exporter may wish to transfer transaction risk to the importer by requiring payment in the exporter's currency. However, over a period of years, if the exporter relies to a great deal on that particular market, he will inevitably be affected by substantial exchange rate fluctuations between the two base currencies.

Notes

[1] J.H. Rayner & Co. Ltd. v. Hambros Bank Ltd (1943) KB 37.

Chapter Seven

Short-term Trade Finance: Factoring and Forfaiting

The basics: Both exporters and importers may need short-term financing in order to operate continuously without having to stop and wait for the funds they expect from particular transactions. Cash fuels the engines of trading companies, and a steady flow is essential to keep the motors running. Cash flow problems may in some cases be avoided via the use of short-term finance techniques. When there is some security that the trader will receive funds from trading partners, intermediaries step in on the strength of that security to provide funds. This enables the trader to bridge the time gap between investment and recoupment of profits. Amongst the most common trade finance devices are factoring, forfaiting, discounting of bills of exchange, and letter of credit finance.

7.1 The various forms of short-term trade finance

When an exporter has delivered goods on a contract in which he has been forced to grant credit terms to the importer, he is faced with a gap between the time he has performed the contract and the time he will be paid for it. This may be a problem if that exporter needs to pay off his own suppliers, or if he has the opportunity to make further deals but needs to buy materials in order to perform subsequent contracts. On the one hand, the exporter needs cash, and on the other hand, he is in possession of "accounts receivable" – obligations on the part of his trading partners to make payments to him at specified times in the future. Depending on the legal/financial security of the accounts receivable obligations (i.e., mere contracts, promissory notes, bills of exchange or confirmed letters of credit), the exporter may obtain financing through a variety of different systems.

The easiest, but most limited, solution is for the exporter to rely on overdraft or credit lines with his bank. In essence, the exporter just borrows the funds he needs as he needs them. However, high interest rates make this an expensive alternative which is not suitable for a large volume of transactions. If the export sale is made via a mechanism involving bank draft or bill of exchange, such as a documentary collection or letter of credit, the exporter can obtain cash by having his bank negotiate or discount the bill. The bank may alternatively be willing to make an 80% or 90% advance against the bill and other shipping documents. The exporter should distinguish between a payment "with recourse" (the bank may charge the exporter if the bill goes unpaid) or "without recourse" (the exporter can retain the finance sums regardless of whether the bank eventually obtains payment under the bill). In the case of confirmed letters of credit and avalised bills of exchange there is not much risk of the bank failing to obtain payment, so financing is generally without recourse.

"Forfaiting" is a variation on the above schemes which is generally used only for larger contracts (e.g., above $50,000-$100,000), under which the exporter sells the bill of exchange to a third party. Factoring is a broader concept than forfaiting (and may include forfaiting), in which specialised firms offer a range of financing and risk management services to exporters. These two concepts are further explored below.

Like the exporter, the importer may require interim financing. For example, an importer who pays in advance or upon delivery of the goods is faced with a gap between the time she has paid for the goods and the time that this investment is recouped when the goods are sold for a profit. The importer may be able to increase the total number of her transactions if she can obtain an advance upon the revenue she expects from the imported goods, using the advanced funds to pay for further import shipments. The importer may obtain this financing by using a straightforward loan or overdraft facility, but as explained above, this is an expensive and limited option. Often, the importer will pledge the bill of lading to the goods to her bank in exchange for the advanced sums. If the importer subsequently needs to take back the bill of lading to physically obtain the goods, she may contractually guarantee return of the bill of lading to the bank, such as by a "letter of trust" or similar device.

7.2 Factoring

It has been claimed that the origins of factoring date from more than four thousand years ago, when the ancient Mesopatamians exchanged their receivables for cash.[1] "Factoring" is a broad term, covering diverse services offered either separately or in combination by factoring companies (called "*factors*"). The range of basic services offered includes credit risk assessment and protection, collection of overdue accounts, administration of sales accounting ledgers, and financing. An attempt to reach a standard definition of factoring by UNIDROIT (the International Institute for the Unification of Private Trade Law), concluded that any arrangement which contained at least two of the above services could be considered factoring.

Factoring services are generally called into play by the exporter's need to manage a continuous flow of low average-value invoices to foreign customers. The factor steps in to provide the exporter with one or all of the following facilities:

1) Advance cash payment by the factor to the exporter against sale or assignment of the exporter's receivables.

2) Elimination of the credit risk that the importer may fail to pay.

3) Collection of funds from the importer.

Exporters tend to turn to factors when other means of short-term trade finance are unavailable or inappropriate. Thus, an exporter may be faced with the type of cash-flow problems indicated above, but find that the services offered by banks are too expensive or are based only on negotiable instruments (i.e., bills of exchange) which do not cover a large part of the exporter's accounts receivables. Moreover, in addition to the financing services which banks also offer, factors can provide overall management of the export accounting process. Thus, just as small exporters can virtually sub-contract the entire transport function to freight forwarders, they can also turn over the whole financial side to factors.

Factoring arrangements can be generally divided into two-factor and single-factor schemes. Under a two-factor system, the exporter enters into a contract with a factor in the exporter's country, called the export factor. The export factor in turn will establish an agreement with a correspondent factor in the importer's country, called the import factor. The two factors may belong to the same company or may simply establish a contractual relationship.

The import factor will prove especially helpful in performing a credit check on a prospective customer in the importing country. When the exporter has delivered the goods or otherwise performed under the contract, he will issue an invoice to the importer, with a copy to the export factor. The export factor will then make an immediate partial cash payment (commonly up to 80%) available to the exporter. The two factors together will then completely take over the remaining financial and administrative responsibilities. The import factor will chase any overdue accounts and even resort to legal action if necessary. The import factor's knowledge of the importer's local language and customs can make the factor very effective in pursuing recalcitrant payers.

Single-factor or "direct export" factoring functions in much the same way as above, except that there is no import factor. In cases where there are long or well-established relationships between the exporter and importer, an import factor's expertise in credit-checking or collections may not be perceived as necessary. Clearly, single-factor systems will tend to be cheaper and will also be more exposed to certain risks.

When the exporter is considering making use of the factor's credit protection services, the question arises as to the complementarity of factoring and credit insurance. Factors and credit insurers provide differing benefits depending on the characteristics of the exporter and the transactions concerned. Thus, the factor will often provide a higher level of credit protection (e.g., 100% as opposed to 90%), but will be slower and more exhaustive in conducting its credit evaluation of the prospective customer. The factor's fees are correspondingly higher than those of the credit insurer. In general, beginning exporters may prefer to rely on factors, because of the additional level of service; experienced exporters, with a good understanding of the risks inherent in particular transactions, may prefer the lower cost of credit insurance premiums.

In certain contexts an exporter will not wish importers to know that he is making use of a factor's services, and will require "undisclosed" factoring – the factoring is not revealed to the customer. One reason for this is that customers may make certain negative assumptions about the financial status of a company which uses factoring. The key form of undisclosed factoring is "invoice discounting". Under this type of factoring the factor provides financing against the exporters invoices, but does not provide credit management or accountancy services.

There are four large international groupings of factoring companies. Each of these groups seeks to adhere to standard operational principles, which avoids some of the problems arising from the differing national legal frameworks which govern factoring.

7.3 Forfaiting

Forfaiting is related to factoring in that it provides exporters with a source of trade finance, but there are several important distinctions. First of all, while factoring deals primarily with low-value short-term accounts receivable (e.g., less than $10,000 average invoice, 90-120 day payment terms), forfaiting tends to involve higher-value short-, medium- and long-term obligations (e.g., more than $50,000-$100,000, up to and above 180 day payment terms). Thus, while factoring contracts tend to involve coverage of a stream of small invoices, forfaiting generally involves a sequence of single, independent transactions.

Since forfaiting only involves the financing related to individual transactions, it does not comprise the additional credit protection and accounting services offered by factoring. Finance payment and costs are different as well. With forfaiting, payment is made on the full value of the invoice price, minus the charge for discounting the bill of exchange. Although there is no discount with factoring, the exporter will only receive a partial advance payment (e.g., 80%) prior to settlement by the customer, and will pay interest on the advanced sum.

In essence, forfaiting can be summarised as the purchase by the forfaiter of an exporter's receivables which are based on negotiable instruments such as bills of exchange and promissory notes. Thus, the exporter sells a document containing the importer's definite obligation to pay at some future date. Since there will be a ready and liquid market for these bills only if they are "avalised" or guaranteed by a bank, such as the importer's bank, forfaiting is generally limited to bills supported by an aval or bank guarantee.

One of the central benefits to the exporter of forfaiting is that the forfaiter purchases the bills on a non-recourse basis. Thus, even if importer or his bank defaults on payment of the bill, the forfaiter cannot recover the payment to the exporter. The forfaiter therefore assumes both commercial and political risk. Should war break out or the importer's government suddenly impose exchange controls, the forfaiter may not be able to recover payment from the importer or the importer's bank. Interest and currency rate risks on the payment are also assumed by the forfaiter.

Another advantage of forfaiting is that the exporter is quoted a fixed rate for payment against the bill. The discount rate will depend on a variety of elements, including the date of maturity and other risk factors. However, the size of the discount may make the forfaiting option appear relatively expensive (the exporter should remember how much risk is being assumed by the forfaiter). In any event, the cost calculations related to a forfaiting deal can be quite complex and the exporter would be well-advised to seek expert advice. A disadvantage of forfaiting is that strict documentary requirements must be adhered to, which involves obtaining the importer's participation in obtaining the necessary bank guarantee or aval. The importer may be reluctant, for example, to instruct her bank to grant an aval which will count against the importer's credit lines, or to pay a fee for obtaining the aval.

Notes

[1] EXPORT FACTORING AND FORFAITING, Horst Ulrich Jaeger, in "The Law of International Trade Finance" (1989), p. 278).

Chapter Eight
Security for International Transactions

> **The basics:** Many international transactions involve the use of security devices, commonly referred to as *"guarantees"* or *"bonds"*, designed to protect one of the parties from a breach by its counterparty. Of course, a basic framework of legal security is already provided in the contract underlying the transaction, and additional security can be provided via documentary payment systems such as that of the documentary credit. However, in an international context the judicial enforcement of contractual rights can be slow and expensive, and documentary credits are sometimes felt to provide primary protection for the exporter, leaving the importer at the risk that the exporter will walk away from the contract. International traders, therefore, and particularly importers and employers of foreign contractors, have sought additional means of assuring the performance of their counterparties.

There are two basic kinds of guarantees/bonds in international trade:

1) *demand* guarantees – these represent "instant cash" for the beneficiary – which only has to make a "demand";

2) *suretyship* guarantees – these guarantees are conditional – the beneficiary must *prove* that he is entitled to the money, as by providing a court judgement.

Parties who remain in unsecured positions or who do not build adequate documentary safeguards into the transaction are particularly exposed to *international fraud*. The ICC's Commercial Crime Services provide a variety of publications, information and consulting services to help traders avoid becoming victims of fraud.

8.1 Guarantees and bonds

Historically, the earliest form of international commercial guarantee was the cash deposit. If one party failed to perform under the contract (e.g., the buyer failed to pay for or accept the contract goods, or the supplier failed to provide the contract goods), that party forfeited the deposit. The cash deposit system has many drawbacks. First, the trader must completely immobilise the deposit capital throughout the life of the guarantee. The trader loses the interest the deposit-money could have earned if invested. Moreover, cash deposits can be easily commingled with the counterparty's own funds, creating the risk that the counterparty would be tempted to use the deposited moneys for his own purposes.

These drawbacks were largely overcome with the advent of a system whereby a bank or other financial institution issued a guarantee or bond to the importer in lieu of the cash deposit. Such a guarantee can be "as good as" cash to the importer or other beneficiary in the event of a default, but is much cheaper for the exporter or other counter party.

The different kinds of guarantee mechanism available are variously referred to as "bonds", "guarantees", "indemnities", "standby letters of credit", "bank guarantees", "suretyship guarantees", "surety undertakings", etc. These security mechanisms may be provided by banks, insurance companies, specialised surety companies, or other financial services firms. It has been reported that there are a growing number of guarantees issued by individuals, including inter alia officers in limited liability companies personally guaranteeing the debts of the company. The variety of products and providers is further complicated because different terminology is used in different countries, market sectors, and legal systems.

As we shall see below, the ICC has developed three sets of rules to standardise guarantee practice:

- the *ICC Rules for Contract Guarantees* ("URCG 325" – first published in 1978), which are primarily intended for bank guarantees requiring documentary proof of default (these rules attempt to prevent unfair calls by beneficiaries by requiring the beneficiary's demand to be accompanied by a court judgement or arbitral award).

- the *ICC Rules for Demand Guarantees* ("URDG 458" – first published in 1991), which apply to demand guarantees; and,

- the *ICC Rules for Contract Bonds* ("URCB 524" – first published in 1992), which apply to conditional or suretyship guarantees;

Note also the :

- *ICC Model Guarantee Forms*: the ICC has developed model sets of forms for the URCG and URDG (ICC Pub. N°s 406, 503).

It should be further noted that the United Nations Commission on Trade Law (Uncitral) has recently developed a Convention applicable to independent undertakings such as bank guarantees, which if adopted by a sufficient number of countries will bring harmonisation to the legal framework underlying guarantee practice.

Guarantee/bond terminology: in the discussion below, the terms "demand guarantee" and "suretyship guarantee" will be used to describe two basic but distinct categories of guarantee or bond. However, note that although the word "guarantee" is used here as a general term, there is a lack of international standardisation as regards terminology. Although some legal systems distinguish between "guarantees", "bonds", "undertakings" and "indemnities", these terms are often used as synonyms in the everyday language of international traders. It may therefore be necessary to examine the particular characteristics and nature of the guarantee obligation in order to properly classify the guarantee.

8.1.1 The parties

a. **Beneficiary** – The party that receives the benefit of the guarantee in the event of non-performance by the other party. In practice, this is often the buyer or importer. In large construction contracts, the beneficiary is often a government entity.

b. **Principal / "Account Party"** – The commercial party that issues or directs the issue of the guarantee. Typical examples of principals/account parties include construction companies which guarantee that a construction project will be completed, or large exporters which guarantee that they will re-pay any sums advanced by the importer if the goods are not properly shipped.

c. **Guarantor** – The bank, insurance company or surety company which issues the guarantee on the instructions of the principal, and is responsible for payment of a determined or determinable sum under the guarantee according to its conditions.

8.1.2 Types of guarantee/bond

a. **Demand vs. Suretyship** – Two main categories of guarantee are *demand* and *suretyship*. The term "suretyship" is used as an expedient, for lack of a universally accepted term. Some insurance companies prefer terms such as "accessory bond", while legal experts may prefer "conditional" guarantee.

b. **Demand Guarantees** – Under a demand guarantee, the guarantor must pay on *first demand* by the beneficiary. The key concept is that the beneficiary only has to demand the guarantee; there is no need to prove that the principal has actually defaulted on a contractual obligation. The purpose is to provide the beneficiary with a speedy and absolutely certain monetary guarantee. Conceptually, thus, demand guarantees are a substitute for that more ancient system of security, the cash deposit. As a cash substitute, demand guarantees provide readily accessible, trouble-free security for the beneficiary. In most cases, the only documentary requirement for payment is that the beneficiary make a *written demand.*

Clearly, the principal takes the risk that the beneficiary will *unjustifiably* make the demand (as with the cash deposit, where the beneficiary could unjustifiably keep the cash). This is sometimes referred to as the problem of the *unfair call.* Although under most legal systems outright fraud or dishonesty by the beneficiary will enable the principal to avoid paying under the guarantee, these legal exceptions vary from country to country and are in any event often difficult to prove. As a result, prudent traders seek to avoid granting demand guarantees. In fact, demand guarantees are most commonly used when the beneficiary has great bargaining power and is able to impose the demand guarantee as a "take it or leave it" option. This has often been the case in major construction projects, where many contractors compete for a single contract. When a trader is forced to grant a demand guarantee, the only practical protection against an unfair call may be to obtain insurance against such an eventuality (although there are some procedural safeguards provided, for example, in article 20 of the URDG). Export insurers in some countries will provide insurance against unfair calls, provided that the commercial context meets certain requirements. The cost of this insurance can then be factored into the exporter's price tender.

Another difficulty inherent in the demand guarantee is that of setting an assured expiry date for the guarantee. Although guarantees are subject to an expiry date as a matter of routine, in practice the beneficiary may be able to force an extension of the validity period with a so-called "extend or pay" or "pay or extend" demand. The principal has no more protection available against such a demand than against an unfair call. In the absence of established fraud enabling the guarantor to refuse payment, the principal will have little practical alternative but to agree to the extension (note again, however, that some protection is provided in the procedural safeguards of the URDG). In some countries, the "pay or extend" practice is not at all uncommon, and can result in repeated forced extensions of the guarantee period.

However, it is certainly possible that a call for an extension may have some legitimate commercial purpose. Thus, such a call can serve as a second chance granted to the contractor by the employer to perform according to contractual obligations. In such cases, it would be unfair to deprive the employer of recourse to a "pay or extend" statement.

From a legal perspective, demand guarantees are said to be *independent* undertakings. The obligation runs directly from the guarantor to the beneficiary and becomes binding upon the guarantor once issued, regardless of the principal's subsequent ability or inability to reimburse the guarantor. Thus, the insolvency of the principal will not free the guarantor from its obligation to pay under the guarantee. The payment obligation is unaffected by the state of affairs under the underlying contract. Even if the principal should claim that the demand is in bad faith because the principal is not in fact in default under the underlying contract, the guarantor will still have to pay against the beneficiary's demand (so long as there is no established fraud on behalf of the beneficiary).

Although a demand guarantee can be fixed for any percentage of the value of the underlying contract, because of its unconditional nature it is rare for principals to agree to demand guarantees for more than a small fraction of the total contract value, e.g., in the 5% to 10% range.

The ICC has sought to standardise demand guarantee practice through its *ICC Uniform Rules for Demand Guarantees* ("URDG"), which were adopted in 1991. The URDG grew out of the perceived failure of an earlier set of rules (the *ICC Uniform Rules for Contract Guarantees* – "URCG") to gain market acceptance. The URCG represented an attempt to provide an alternative to the strict demand guarantee, in view of the danger of unfair calls. Thus, the URCG required the beneficiary's demand for payment to be accompanied by a court judgement or arbitral award establishing the fact of default. The approach of the URCG ran counter to the market reality of the frequently superior bargaining power of beneficiaries. Despite its drawbacks, the demand guarantee continued to be widely used internationally and is now clearly here to stay. Employers/importers who are in the stronger bargaining position may see no reason to agree to the kind of conditional guarantee covered by the URCG's provisions. Of course, the URCG may still be used for those contexts where the exporter-principal has been able to negotiate a conditional guarantee to be issued by a bank.

The URDG thus reflect the market reality of the continued broad use of demand guarantees. As with the UCP, the URDG apply when they have been incorporated by a specific reference (as by a mention at the bottom of a bank's guarantee application form). The scope of the URDG is limited to demand guarantees which are themselves in writing and which provide for payment on written demand. Although, technically, standby letters of credit are legally indistinguishable from demand guarantees and therefore fall within the scope of the URDG, the Introduction to the URDG observes that standby credit banking practice is more akin to documentary credit practice than it is to demand guarantee practice, and it is therefore expected that standby credits will continue to be issued subject to the UCP for documentary credits.

Article 2 (b) of the URDG enumerates the three basic principles of demand guarantee law:

- the independence of the guarantee from the underlying transaction;

- the documentary nature of the guarantee; and

- the limitation of the guarantor's duty to review the written demand to an examination of whether the demand and any accompanying documents conform *on their face* to the terms of the guarantee (this is further spelled out in article 9).

Article 20 of the URDG sets forth the formal requirements for a demand. Significantly, not only must the demand be in writing and in conformity with the express terms of the guarantee, *it must also be supported by a statement of breach by the beneficiary.* This statement must set forth the nature of the breach. Note that the statement of breach does not have to be provided by a neutral third party (unless expressly stipulated in the guarantee), such as an independent engineer or arbitrator — the beneficiary's own statement is acceptable. The intent of this provision is to discourage unjustified recourse to the guarantee, without going so far as to fundamentally alter the "on demand" nature of the guarantee. The drafters of the URDG felt that this provision would give pause to a beneficiary who might have the intention of making an unfair call, because he would first have to make a deliberately false statement of breach. However, wary of making the URDG unacceptable to beneficiaries, the drafters included a provision allowing the parties to *exclude* the requirement of a statement of breach; any such exclusion must be explicitly made within the terms of the guarantee.

c. **Suretyship or conditional guarantees (e.g., insurance bonds)** – Under a *suretyship* or *conditional* guarantee, the obligation of the guarantor is triggered by the *actual default* or contractual breach of the principal, as evidenced in a document such as a court judgement or arbitral award against the principal. Thus, in order to claim under a conditional guarantee, the beneficiary must first be able to *prove* in documentary fashion that the principal has failed to meet its contractual obligations.

In contrast to demand guarantees, conditional guarantees are said to be *secondary* or *accessory* obligations, because the guarantor's obligations are dependent on the principal's actual default in performance of the underlying contract. Moreover, the guarantor is only obliged to pay (or to perform the principal's obligations) to the extent of the principal's liability. The guarantor, in a sense, "steps into the shoes" of the principal, in order to fulfil the principal's obligations. Consequently, the guarantor may make use of any defences available to the principal.

Conditional guarantees eliminate the problem of unfair calls and are therefore, from the principal's point of view, preferable to demand guarantees. Since a principal is assured under a conditional guarantee that there will be no payment or performance by the guarantor unless there is a proven default, the principal may be willing to stipulate that the conditional guarantee cover a larger percentage of the total contract value. Thus, it is not unusual for conditional guarantees to be set at 30% or 40% of the contract value. Because of this relatively higher percentage of coverage, a conditional guarantee may be attractive to the beneficiary as well. It is moreover possible to use the two forms of guarantee in tandem on the same contract, the demand guarantee for a small percentage and the conditional guarantee for a larger percentage of the contract value.

As stated above, the ICC has issued two sets of rules which apply to conditional guarantees, one of which was drafted primarily for guarantees issued by insurance and specialised surety companies, while the other is more general in application but was designed primarily with banks in mind as guarantors:

- *ICC Uniform Rules for Contract Bonds* (1992) – for the insurance industry; and

- *ICC Uniform Rules for Contract Guarantees* (1978) – for conditional bank guarantees.

A potential disadvantage of the conditional guarantee for the beneficiary is that it may take quite some time to obtain the court judgement or arbitral reward specified in the guarantee as triggering the guarantor's obligation. In the interest of assuring a quick remedy for the beneficiary, the *ICC Uniform Rules for Contract Bonds* provide for the possibility of alternative documentary measures. Thus, the parties may agree that the guarantee obligation will be triggered by presentation of a "certificate of default" issued by an independent architect, engineer or ICC pre-arbitral referee. Another alternative is that the guarantor, upon its own investigation, may issue a certificate of default.

Because conditional guarantees require the guarantor to become involved in the factual details of alleged defaults by the principals, banks have traditionally been reluctant to issue them. From the banks' perspective, demand guarantees are preferable because their operation is simple and straightforward for the bank. Insurance companies, which have great experience in the investigation of the contingencies surrounding defaults, are more willing to issue conditional guarantees. Surety companies are in the market niche specialised in the management of conditional guarantees. However, there are no hard and fast rules; insurance companies and other firms may also be willing to issue demand guarantees, and banks may issue conditional guarantees.

8.1.3 Main uses of guarantees

a. **Performance Bonds/Guarantees** – These guarantees cover the risk that the exporter or contractor will fail to adequately perform the contract, or fail to perform in due time. The guarantee amount is generally a stated percentage of the contract price, commonly up to 10%.

A demand guarantee operation

Sometimes referred to loosely as a "bank guarantee", the guarantee on first demand is an essential and basic security device for international transactions.

I. Underlying commercial transaction

As part of an international commercial transaction, an importer may require an exporter to issue a demand guarantee (in such a case, the **EXPORTER** is the **principal** and the **IMPORTER** the **beneficiary**).

2. Issuance of the guarantee

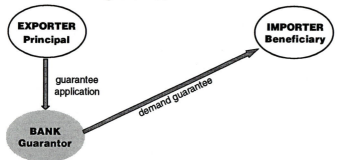

The exporter requests his bank to issue the guarantee in favour of the importer beneficiary.

3. The demand

The importer, should she feel justified in doing so, will made a written demand for payment under the guarantee. Regardless of any allegations by the principal that the demand is unjustified under the contractual provisions of the underlying transaction, the bank must pay (unless there is proof of fraud by the beneficiary): the guarantee is said to be independent of the underlying transaction.

b. **Bid (or Tender) Bonds/Guarantees** – These guarantees are used to secure performance in contracts awarded by competitive bidding. Typically, a governmental entity will solicit competitive tenders or bids for a procurement or construction contract; the tenderers will be required to issue a guarantee in favour of the governmental entity. The purpose of the guarantee is to ensure that the bidder chosen by the beneficiary actually accepts and signs the contract according to the terms of the bid (and also that the bidder provides a performance bond if one is required). Failure to take up the contract will result in payment of the guarantee amount, which is commonly set at from 2% to 5% of the contract value.

c. **Advance Payment or Repayment Bonds/Guarantees** – These guarantees are intended to ensure that the beneficiary's advance payments be returned in case of non-performance by the principal. Typically, an importer who allows an exporter to draw a cash advance will require that exporter to issue a repayment guarantee in the event that the exporter does not actually ship the contract goods in due time.

d. **Retention Bonds/Guarantees** – These guarantees are commonly used in contracts involving goods and services. For example, the employer in a construction project may negotiate to retain a certain percentage of the contract price as a sort of insurance against defects which are not immediately apparent. Rather than lose the use of the retained funds, the contractor will prefer to issue a retention guarantee for payment of a specified sum in the event that building defects are eventually discovered.

e. **Maintenance (or warranty) Bonds/Guarantees** – These guarantees typically secure the warranty obligations of equipment suppliers throughout the period of the supplier's liability for defects.

8.1.4 Demand guarantee operation and procedure – direct vs. indirect

a. **Direct (three-party) Guarantee** – Three-party guarantees, which involve the principal, the beneficiary, and a guarantor (a bank or other trusted third party). Typically, the exporter-principal will instruct its bank to issue the demand guarantee in favour of the importer-beneficiary. The bank will require the principal to enter into a reimbursement contract (called a "counter-indemnity"), obliging the principal to repay any sums paid out under the guarantee to the beneficiary. If the beneficiary believes that the principal has failed to fulfil the contract, the beneficiary will present a written demand for payment to guarantor. The guarantor will pay regardless of any information it may receive concerning the underlying contract. The guarantor will then claim reimbursement from the principal under the counter-indemnity.

b. **Indirect (four-party) Guarantee** – This guarantee is similar to the direct guarantee except that a bank in the beneficiary's country is added to the guarantee-chain. Here, the principal's bank instructs a bank in the beneficiary's country to issue the guarantee in favour of the beneficiary. The principal's bank must itself agree to reimburse the beneficiary's bank via a "counter-guarantee". In some countries the local banking authorities may issue administrative rules which have the practical effect of requiring that demand guarantees be in the indirect form. The indirect structure poses certain disadvantages for the principal. First of all, since two banks are involved the charges will be higher. Second, the guarantee issued by the bank in the beneficiary's country may be subject to the law of the beneficiary's country. The application of local law may preclude certain defences against fraudulent or abusive calls which might be available under the law of the principal's country.

Chapter Nine

International Transport

The basics: Transport in international transactions has a direct impact on such key sale contract elements as price, speed of delivery and the risk of loss or damage. While large traders may have well-staffed logistics departments, smaller traders often rely on international freight forwarders. It is essential that the freight forwarder receive all possible relevant information about the sale contract, and that the directions to the freight forwarder be as precise as possible, especially with regard to such items as place of pickup, place of delivery, costs for handling and loading, and amount of required packaging.

The choice of sea, air, or ground transport may appear to be dictated by the type of product, destination or buyer, but exporters should take care not to underestimate the competitiveness of alternative means. Air freight can be surprisingly competitive if one factors in cost-savings related to lower insurance rates and the increased speed and security of shipment.

Each of the main transport methods has a corresponding legal and documentary framework with which traders must be familiar. Above all, traders should seek to ensure that transport considerations are integrated into overall export management, with sufficient communication between sales, marketing, purchasing and logistics personnel.

9.1 Transport management

Choosing the optimal mode of transport can mean the difference between export success and failure. Consequently, some form of systematic evaluation of the different transport modes available is advisable; this discipline is sometimes called "physical distribution management" or "logistics analysis". Small traders may prefer to delegate this analysis to a freight forwarder, but the trader should have sufficient in-house understanding of transport to be able to supervise and evaluate the performance of forwarders. Regardless of company size or type of management structure chosen, traders must take into consideration the following basic elements of transport management:

a. **The Fundamental Cost Principle: Volume Discounts** – It is a universal commercial principle that merchants will accept lower prices for large purchases; in doing so, they maximise total revenue. Thus, transport service providers often charge lower freight rates (or offer rebates or discounts) for *large* or *regular* cargo shipments. The implication for exporters and importers is that they should seek, whenever possible, to ship larger volumes. This can be done by various means, including:

- consolidating several different sales into a single shipment;

- arranging for "door to door" shipment; and,

- organising shippers' clubs or councils for collective bargaining of freight rates.

Another possibility is to contract with an intermediary who acts as a wholesaler or distributor of transport services. For example, a forwarder, logistics firm or broker, can contract at a discount for the bulk purchase of transport services from a large carrier, and then offer attractive rates to small individual exporters and importers.

b. **Transport costs' impact on the price of goods** – Transport costs may account for a significant part of the total cost of the product, especially in the case of commodities or relatively low-value products. The price which the exporter quotes to the importer is inevitably linked to the particular *Incoterm* chosen and how much of the corresponding transport required must be covered by the exporter. Small and beginning exporters may prefer to choose the Ex Works Incoterm (EXW), under which all transport responsibilities are entirely the buyer's affair, or FCA or FOB, which place the cost of international transport on the buyer.

However, in choosing Incoterms which place few transport obligations on the seller, such as EXW, FCA or FOB, the exporter may neglect an important profit centre. Instead, the exporter could manage the transport operation himself and charge a commission to the buyer for services rendered. An exporter who can competently negotiate and oversee the transport chain can earn money by quoting prices CIF, CIP or DDU/DDP, handling the transport himself, and billing the buyer a commission for these services.

Optimal transport economy will logically result when either the exporter or importer wholly undertakes the transport obligations. This is because the total amount of transport services purchased will be larger, since it will not be divided between two parties. Since a basic transport principle is that larger shipment volumes command proportionately lower prices, it would seem that the choice of Incoterms at either "extreme" of the range would result in economies. These terms are Ex Works or FCA on the one hand (buyer is responsible for transport), and DDU or DDP on the other (seller is responsible for transport). In fact, in many countries DDU and DDP have become increasingly popular with exporters.

c. **Speed of Delivery** – In many markets, speed of delivery is a crucial competitive factor. In addition to speed, traders must pay attention to reliability: how common are late or delayed shipments? Since delays may result when a shipment is transferred from one transport provider to another, this is another reason for exporters to consider managing the entire transport chain. For some parties, reliability may prove to be a higher priority than speed. Regardless of which party is at fault for a delayed shipment, the exporter may risk breaching a contractual deadline or otherwise losing the customer by projecting an image of unreliability.

Long transit times also increase total costs owing to the payment of interest rates on working capital throughout the period the goods are inaccessible. For this reason, air transport is sometimes a surprisingly competitive alternative to sea transport. In some cases, shippers may wish to take advantage of deferred air freight rates – rates for shipments under which the shipper accepts that his cargo is a low priority and that transport will consequently be somewhat longer.

d. Stock and inventory management – In recent years many companies have identified stock and inventory management as a means for cutting costs and increasing efficiency. A prime example is in Japan's renowned "just-in-time" (JIT) manufacturing systems, which can virtually eliminate the need for a manufacturer to maintain large warehouses at the factory, because all necessary supplies are delivered daily. JIT systems are now common around the world.

Stock reduction depends on sophisticated transport management, generally involving a higher frequency of shipments of lower unit volume. The increased transport costs may well be offset by increased efficiencies from smaller warehouses, fewer obsolescent parts and more rapid customer service. JIT systems are often based on sophisticated electronic data interchange (EDI) networks which link the manufacturer to its suppliers.

e. Packaging – Packing and packaging costs vary substantially according to the mode of transport. Improper or insufficient packaging results in a higher rate of damage to goods in transit. Consequently, traders should take care not to evaluate different modes of transport purely according to freight rates. A transport mode with cheap freight may require a more expensive packaging and/or have a high frequency of lost or damaged goods. Thus, door-to-door shipments by full container load, which require minimal packaging, are often very competitive even against alternatives with apparently cheaper freight rates.

If the importer is arranging for transport, he should inform the exporter as early as possible of the nature of that transport, and particularly as it may alter the type or amount of packaging required.

f. Customs – The various transport modes entail different procedures for customs clearance, which may have an incidence on transit time. Thus, the simplified customs procedures available for air and postal shipments, and under certain regimes for road and rail shipments, can increase the competitiveness of these modes as against sea transport.

g. Payment systems – Certain payment systems will influence the mode of shipment. Thus, payments by documentary credit may in certain cases require the presentation of an *on board marine bill of lading*. If the seller stipulates, in the sales contract for example, a different transport document requirement under the credit, such as for a *multimodal transport document* or an *air waybill*, it may be possible for the exporter to trigger the payment mechanism at a much earlier date, because the transport document will be received as soon as the goods are delivered into the transport chain.

h. Collaboration vs. Competition – Whenever possible, shippers in a particular sector should consider forming collaborative groups enabling them to jointly negotiate lower rates and better service from transport providers. Often, competitive postures prevent shippers from working together, which can lower the international competitiveness of the entire sector vis-a-vis other countries.

9.2 International treaties and conventions

There are several different international treaties that apply to the various modes of transport. These are of interest to shippers and consignees because they state the extent and limitations of the carrier's liability for goods which are lost or damaged. In particular, the professional trader will be familiar with the following treaties:

a. Sea transport

• **The Hague Rules** (1924) – The International Convention for the Unification of Certain Rules relating to Bills of Lading (also known as the Brussels Convention). Signed by approximately 80 contracting countries, this treaty was subsequently criticised for setting liability limits for shipowners too low and for providing a multitude of exemptions and exclusions from liability. The Hague Rules apply to goods carried by sea under a bill of lading drawn up in one of the contracting countries.

• **The Hague-Visby Rules** (1968) – A Protocol amending the Hague Rules, and referred to as the Hague-Visby Rules, was signed in Brussels in 1968 and has to date been ratified by 32 of the countries which have signed on to the Hague Rules. The Hague-Visby Rules generally raised the exposure to liability of the shipowners.

• **Hamburg Rules** (1978) – The UN Convention on the Carriage of Goods by Sea, signed in Hamburg in 1978, was intended to remedy some of the defects of the rules produced by the earlier two Conventions. The Hamburg Rules have found little favour in shipping circles, and although they went into force in 1992, many of the major trading nations have not signed the treaty, and there is some doubt as to whether it will be signed by enough of the trading powers to provide truly global harmonisation.

b. Air Transport

• **Warsaw System** (1929) – The international treaty governing international air transport is the Warsaw Convention, signed in 1929 and subsequently supplemented by the Hague Protocol (1929), Guadalajara Supplementary Convention (1961), Guatemala City Protocol (1971) and the Montreal Protocol (1975). This Convention has been virtually universally adopted.

c. Rail Transport

• **COTIF** (1980) – Since rail transport does not link the continents, as do sea and air transport, it should not be surprising that rail transport lacks a global, multilateral set of legal rules by which to operate. Nonetheless, in Europe at least, and in certain contiguous countries linked to the European rail network, rail transport is governed by the 1980 Convention concerning International Carriage by Rail (COTIF), which entered into force in 1985 and applies in approximately 35 countries.

d. Road Transport

• **CMR** (1956) – The situation in road transport is similar to that of rail transport. Approximately 25 countries – mostly European – have signed the Convention on the Contract for the International Carriage of Goods by Road.

e. Multimodal Transport

• **UN Convention on the International Multimodal Transport of Goods** (1980) – This Convention will enter into force when it has been signed by 30 countries.

9.3 The UNCTAD/ICC Rules for Multimodal Transport Documents

Given the absence of an international treaty effectively covering multimodal transport, freight forwarders have sought to establish and abide by standard rules and documents which would put documents issued by freight forwarders on a similar footing with those issued directly be sea carriers. The UNCTAD/ICC Rules for a Multimodal Transport Document, effective January 1, 1992, evidence a movement towards the liability regime of the Hamburg Rules, and a rejection of the loophole-filled approach of the Hague-Visby Rules. The UNCTAD/ICC Rules eventually were reflected in a standard industry document, the FIATA Multimodal Transport Bill of Lading. Through the wide use by freight forwarders of this document, it would seem that the UNCTAD/ICC Rules will have a certain level of international applicability in the foreseeable future. The UNCTAD/ICC Rules were meant to replace the prior ICC Uniform Rules for a Combined Transport Bill of Lading.

9.4 Carrier's Liability

As can be seen from the above, there are a number of different legal conventions that can define the extent of the carrier's duties and liabilities in the international carriage of goods. Adding to the complexity of the matter, these treaties do not all have global coverage.

While the rules related to carrier liability can go into fine detail, the following general principles are useful:

• **Money limit to liability claim** – Under each of the conventions, there is a monetary maximum that can be claimed for loss of a cargo, and this is usually expressed in terms of a fixed amount of money per unit of weight or per package.

• **Carrier's responsibility** – Under the Hague and Hague-Visby Rules, the carrier must exercise "*due diligence*" as regards the seaworthiness of the vessel, its state of fitness for handling the goods, and proper loading, storage or discharging procedures.

• **Carrier's immunities** – Again, under the Hague and Hague-Visby Rules, there are a long list of carrier's exemptions from liability, including:

– *force majeure or fortuitous* acts, such as earthquakes, tidal waves, fires, perils of the sea, wars, strikes, accidents;

– *defects in the goods/packaging* causing the damage – if the goods or packaging contain a defect which itself causes the damage, the carrier is exempt;

– *negligence of employees* – the carrier is not liable for the negligence in the navigation or operation of the vessel by the master, pilot or crew.

– *procedural limitations* – Normally, any action against a carrier must be brought within a certain time-limit, defined by the applicable conventions or law. A buyer receiving visibly damaged goods should make an immediate written, specific notation on the delivery note. This note should be immediately be addressed to the carrier or his agent as well as the insurer.

The extent of these carrier's immunities and protections should make it clear why it is so important for international traders to obtain sufficient insurance coverage.

9.5 Charter parties

a. **Introductory** – A buyer or seller may wish to transport certain merchandise by chartering, or hiring, an entire vessel or part of a vessel. The contract for the lease of the vessel is known as the *charter party*. Charters are generally classified as:

– *voyage charters* – the shipowner runs the ship and crew; the charterer merely "hires" the ship, or part of it, for one voyage;

– *time charters* – the shipowner runs the ship and crew, but the charterer handles sales and bookings of the cargo;

– *bare boat* – the charterer runs the ship and crew.

The charterer may himself sub-charter the vessel. Whether or not he does, bills of lading for goods shipped on the chartered vessel will be issued to particular shippers, who may or may not themselves be sub-charterers. These bills of lading are said to be issued "subject" to the charter party. In essence, the charterer becomes a commercial intermediary between the shipowner and the ultimate receiver of the bill of lading. The holder of the bill of lading in such cases needs to know who to sue if the goods are delivered in damaged condition or have been lost.

b. **Requirement of tender of charter party along with bill of lading** – Whether or not a bill of lading is an ordinary one or is one which is subject to a charter party and incorporates terms of the charter party can be of major significance for buyers as well as for the banks involved. As a result, under CIF Incoterms the seller in such a case is required to *tender* a copy of the charter party along with the bill of lading. Such a tender enables the buyers to compare the contract of carriage with the contract of sale to see if they are in conformity. For example, if the contract of sale specified delivery in the port of Marseilles, but the charter party actually only obligated the shipowner to go as far as Barcelona, then the buyer who had not seen the charter party would not have known of the inconsistency of the two contracts. Under CIF Incoterms, the seller would have had to tender both contracts at the same time, enabling the buyer to compare the two documents in due time.

Note that the UCP 500 did *not* set a requirement of tender of the charter party along with any bill of lading that refers to it, although if the letter of credit expressly calls for such tender, then the exporter must tender the charter party with the bill of lading for payment.

c. **Distinction between bill of lading and charter party** – The charter party contract is *only* a contract of carriage, and is thus distinct from a bill of lading, which is also a *receipt* for the goods and to some extent a *document of title*. A charter party is merely a contract between the *shipowner* and the *charterer,* setting forth the price of the freight and the other conditions of hire. Charter party contracts cannot, therefore, be endorsed and negotiated as are bills of lading.

In many jurisdictions charter parties are allowed greater freedom of contracting than is available for bills of lading, which may be governed by one of the international treaties. Thus, a shipowner may contract with a charterer under terms of lower shipowner's liability than would be possible with an ordinary shipper under a bill of lading.

There may be two kinds of bill of lading in charter parties: the shipowner's bill of lading to the charterer, for the whole of the goods received on board, and the charterer's separate bills covering parts of the shipment.

The fact that a particular bill of lading is issued in connection with a charter party has a definite impact on the interests of the cargo-owner, at least by making his rights much more complicated to ascertain. Thus, the purchaser or endorsee of a bill of lading issued under a charter party will have to ask himself certain questions, as for example:

- whom to sue – if the goods are damaged or lost, who should the buyer sue – the shipowner or the charterer? under which contract will the suit be made, the charter party or the bill of lading?

- acceptability – are bills of lading referring to charter parties acceptable under the terms of shipment sales and letters of credit?

d. **Incorporating the terms of the charter party into the B/L; arbitration clauses** – The bills of lading issued by the charterer may seek to "incorporate" the terms of the charter party contract. It is understandable that the charterer would want the two contracts to accord with each other, so that he would not to expose himself to any liability beyond that entailed in the charter party.

If the charterer transfers the bill of lading received from the shipowner to a third party, the contract between the shipowner and the third party will be covered by the bill of lading.

If the bill of lading incorporates a charter party, and if, for example, the charter party specifies that dispute resolution will be by arbitration, then any litigation by a third party buyer against the shipowner would have to be dismissed, because the appropriate forum would be an arbitral one.

However, to incorporate the terms of a charterparty, the bill of lading must do so conspicuously and clearly, and in any event the terms of the charter party must not contradict the bill of lading itself, nor the provisions of any international convention applicable to the bill of lading.

9.6 Freight forwarders

9.6.1 Introductory

An essential member of the international trade community, the freight forwarder generally acts as an agent for the exporter or importer in shipping cargo internationally. Like travel agents – but dealing with cargo rather than passengers – freight forwarders use their knowledge of varying freight rates to offer the customer the best "package deal".

Amongst the many additional services offered by the freight forwarder are the handling of export and customs documentation, insurance, and port and terminal charges. Small exporters will therefore often consult with their freight forwarder before quoting a price in a tender for a particular international transaction.

Traders should understand that the terms "freight forwarder" and "forwarding agent" are generic terms and that there are a variety of specialised functions within the profession. Some forwarders offer a wide range of these functions whereas others restrict themselves to a single speciality or particular geographical coverage. These various functions are summarised below. In addition, it is important for traders to understand that forwarders may act as either *agents* or *principals*, with differing legal consequences.

Freight forwarders as Agents or Principals – A freight forwarder acts as an *agent* when he performs functions on behalf of, and under the instructions of, the principal (the trader or carrier). As an agent, the forwarder may procure the services of third parties who will perform the packing, storage, transport, handling and customs clearance of the goods. The agent thus acts as an intermediary, "introducing", in a manner of speaking, the principal to the service providers. The principal then enters into direct contractual relations with the service providers. Consequently, the forwarder is generally *not liable* for the errors or breaches of the service providers. As with other agents, the forwarder owes the principal various duties, including the duty to inform and the duty of diligence (see Chapter 5 on agency law).

When the forwarder acts as a *principal*, he contracts directly with the exporter or importer (the "customer"). The customer will deal only with the forwarder, who will issue a single bill to the customer for the total amount of services rendered. As a principal, the forwarder is generally *liable* for the errors or breaches of the sub-contracted service providers.

It is also possible for a forwarder to enter into "hybrid" arrangements, acting as agent for certain functions and as a principal for others.

9.6.2 Different functions and types of forwarders

a. Consolidators/NVOCC (Non-Vessel Operating Common Carriers) – This function involves grouping or assembling diverse shipments from various customer so as to make up full container loads, thus obtaining lower freight rates. Some consolidators offer regular shipments on seagoing vessels which they do not own; these are referred to as NVOCC's (Non-Vessel Operating Common Carriers).

b. Multimodal (or intermodal) Transport Operators (MTO's) – A multimodal transport operator offers "one-stop shopping" for traders. This enables traders to completely outsource or sub-contract their export logistics to a single service provider. Multimodal transport operators typically offer "door to door" transport, with coverage of all related functions such as insurance, customs, warehousing, etc.

c. Customs brokers – These parties act as the agents of exporters and importers in order to process customs declarations and other formalities and pay duties and taxes. Because they may be liable for very large payments of duties or fines, customs brokers are usually bonded by banks or insurance companies. Traders should take care to give precise directions and limits to customs brokers to avoid incurring liability in the event that an unexpectedly high tariff or fine makes it uneconomical to process a particular shipment.

d. Port (sea port, airport or cargo terminal) agent – This agent represents the shipper at the point where the goods are transferred from one transport mode (typically, from a truck or lorry) to another (as to a seagoing vessel or airplane).

e. Air freight agent (air waybill agent) – These agents process shipments for airlines and may have the authority to issue air waybills. Frequently, the air freight agent also handles customs clearance.

f. Road haulage brokers – Road transport is characterised in many countries by the proliferation of small service providers. Road haulage brokers act as intermediaries between road carriers and shippers and are usually paid by commission.

g. Loading Brokers – These brokers act as the agents of shipowners to obtain and process cargo shipments. Commonly, a freight forwarder will represent the shipper while a loading broker represents the shipowner, so that there are two intermediaries between the customer and the transport provider.

9.7 Shipping documents

9.7.1 Miscellaneous documents

The documents associated with international transport frequently also play a key role in the payment mechanism and the underlying sales contract.

Consequently, certain of these documents have been treated elsewhere in the sections on legal and payment aspects.

The most important transport document is the *bill of lading* (or one of its many variants); because of its central role, it will be presented in some detail. First, however, we will summarise some of the other documents commonly encountered.

a. **Commercial invoice** – This is essentially a bill for the goods sold. It should include all essential information concerning the sale, including a precise description of the goods, address and identity of exporter and importer, and delivery and payment details. In some countries, the customs authorities will use the invoice to calculate duties.

b. **Inspection certificate** – A certificate generally issued by a respected independent agency, it verifies that the quality, quantity or specifications of the goods shipped is in conformity with the sales contract.

c. **Certificate of origin** – A certificate, usually issued by a local Chamber of Commerce, establishing the country where the merchandise was produced or manufactured. This may be required, for example, for exports from developing countries to benefit from preferential tariff treatment.

d. **Insurance certificate** – Proof of type and amount of insurance coverage, generally required for payment by letter of credit (especially under CIF and CIP Incoterms).

e. **Packing list** – A highly-detailed list describing the weight, volume, content and packaging for each separate export package.

f. **Export license** – Some countries require all exporters to obtain an official government export license. Hazardous (e.g., toxic chemicals) or politically sensitive goods (e.g., weapons) often require special export licenses and may in addition be subject to quotas or ceilings.

g. **Consular invoice** – Some countries require an invoice on an official form for all imported goods; these invoices are generally purchased from that country's local consulate in the exporter's country.

9.7.2 The bill of lading

The bill of lading (the "B/L") is a central document in the traditional export transaction, linking the contract of sale, the documentary payment contracts, and the contract of carriage. We shall first consider the classic B/L, the marine (or ocean) bill of lading, which provides the documentary basis for traditional maritime shipments.

a. **The marine bill of lading** – The *marine bill of lading* is issued by the transport carrier (or its agent, such as a freight forwarder). This B/L serves 3 basic functions:

1) *The B/L represents the right to physical delivery of the goods* – Or, as is sometimes

said, the B/L "stands for" the goods. The legal holder of the B/L is solely entitled to take delivery of the goods. Moreover, the B/L is a "negotiable instrument", because the B/L itself can be sold or transferred ("negotiated"), thereby transferring control over the goods. The goods may thus be sold repeatedly even while they are in transit, by mere transfer of the B/L. The negotiable status of the B/L makes it useful to banks as a security device; a bank which has been pledged a B/L may be willing to extend credit or additional credit on the presumed collateral value of that B/L. Under an order B/L, the shipper consigns the shipment "to the order of" a named party, who may be shipper himself, the buyer or a bank, depending on the level of trust existing between the those parties and the banks involved in the financing of the letter of credit. The export seller can transfer the B/L by endorsing it and delivering it to the buyer or to a bank where payment is organised through the banking system.

2) *The B/L evidences the contract of carriage* – The B/L must contain the terms of the contract of carriage, either explicitly or by reference to another document. Under documentary shipment sales the seller must procure and transfer to the buyer a contract of carriage on "usual" or reasonable terms; as between the buyer and the carrier, the B/L is that necessary contract of carriage.

3) *The B/L is a receipt* – The B/L is a receipt which evidences the delivery of the goods for shipment. As such, it describes the goods and states that in a certain quantity and in apparent good order they have been loaded *on board*. If there is a notation that the goods have been in any way damaged, this will be made on the face of the B/L and it will no longer be considered "*clean*". In some cases, a carrier will issue a B/L as soon as the goods are received, but before they are loaded – this is a "received for shipment" B/L, which will not be acceptable for documentary sales until, after loading, it is converted by the carrier into a "clean on board" B/L (also called a "shipped" B/L).

i) *Uses and advantages of the clean on board B/L* – In light of the above, we can discern certain useful advantages of the *clean on board B/L* (a B/L which shows the goods have been loaded on board, and which is "clean" – e.g., which does not contain any markings or notations indicating damage to the goods). For the buyer, the clean on board B/L provides a valuable bundle of rights. It provides evidence that the seller has performed his contract obligations, by shipping goods which at least appear to conform to the contract of sale (otherwise, the buyer could hardly be expected to allow her bank to make payment against the B/L).

Moreover, the B/L gives the buyer important rights against the carrier of the goods:

• the right to *demand delivery* of the goods when they arrive in the port of discharge, and

• the right to *sue the carrier* for lost or damaged goods.

The B/L also allows the buyer to speculate on the market, selling the goods in transit by transferring the B/L via endorsement. Finally, the B/L allows the buyer (and the seller) to raise finance on the strength of the document's value as the key to the goods.

Because the B/L provides the above benefits to the buyer, it has corresponding benefits for the seller: the seller can get paid as soon as the goods are properly shipped, by presenting the B/L to an authorised bank. Thus, the *seller avoids the risk of non-payment*. The B/L generally benefits international trade, especially in commodities, by reducing risk and enabling markets to speculate on goods while they are in transit. Trade is also facilitated because banks are willing to extend credit on the strength of the value of the goods represented by the B/L.

ii) *Disadvantages of negotiable marine B/L* – Despite the foregoing, there are significant disadvantages associated with the use of the traditional negotiable marine B/L. The most common of these arises when the ship arrives at the port of discharge before the B/L. Today, with the vastly increased efficiency of marine shipment, particularly in the case of container vessels, a large cargo shipment may cross the Atlantic faster than the related documents. In the oil trade in particular, it is common for the cargo to arrive before the documents. Because the negotiable B/L is a document of title, a carrier takes a grave risk in delivering to anyone other than the holder of an original B/L. If a carrier does so, it is liable to the true holder for the value of the cargo wrongly delivered. The most common solution for this problem is for the receiver of the goods to obtain a bank guarantee or letter of indemnity which protects the shipowner from liability for delivery to wrong person.

Another disadvantage of the marine B/L is that is not well suited to multimodal or combined transport, where the ocean shipment is only one leg of a chain of transport operations. Frequently, the entire operation will consist of a land leg from the seller's premises to the port of shipment, a sea leg to the port of discharge, and then another land leg to the buyer's premises. Only a multimodal transport document or B/L (discussed below) can cover all three legs.

b. **Multimodal transport B/L** – The *multimodal transport B/L* has very similar characteristics to the marine B/L, except that the multimodal B/L is used for carriage whenever there are at least two different forms of transport. Although the multimodal B/L also serves as a receipt for delivery of the goods, it does not necessarily evidence that they have been shipped "on board" an ocean-going vessel. Receipt in this case may refer to receipt of a container in a container handling terminal.

c. **Non-negotiable bills and waybills** – A shipment sent under a *straight B/L* is consigned to a specific party, usually the importer. The consignee does not need an actual B/L to receive shipment; adequate identification will do. Unless the choice of consignee is made irrevocable, the shipper remains free to change the consignee any time before the importer pays or accepts the obligation to pay. For this reason, the straight B/L does not provide banks with the security of an order B/L for the purposes of documentary sales. Straight B/L's may be used when the exporter is confident that the importer will pay, as in open account contexts, or when importer has already paid, as with cash in advance sales.

Another variation on the non-negotiable B/L is the *sea waybill*. The sea waybill (which comes under a variety of different names, as for example, *data freight receipt*) serves as evidence of the contract of carriage and as a receipt for the goods, but is not a document of title. Consequently, it should not be used whenever the importer wishes to sell the goods in transit, or when the bank requires the bill to provide collateral security. The sea waybill can be advantageous in that an original is not required to take delivery. This is useful whenever it is likely that the goods will arrive in the port of destination before the relevant documents – a common occurrence in international trade, especially on short ocean routes.

For air shipments, the transport document is the *air waybill* (or "*AWB*"), for which the standard form is the IATA air waybill (International Air Transport Association). The air waybill is frequently issued by freight forwarders acting as agents of the air freight carrier. Generally, the seller chooses the forwarder and has it clear the goods for export. The AWB's that forwarders issue are known as "*house air waybills*" (*HAWB*), while the airlines themselves issue "*master air waybills*" (*MAWB*).

For rail shipments, the transport document is the *railway consignment note*. In Europe, this document is governed by the CIM Convention (Convention Internationale pour le transport des Marchandises par voie ferrée).

For road shipments, a *road consignment note* is used, governed in Europe by the CMR Convention (Convention internationale pour le transport des Marchandises par Route).

9.8 Sea transport

9.8.1 Overview of basic commercial practice

World-wide, maritime transport carries over 90% of international trade. Much of international transport law and practice, even with regard to other modes of transport, is derived from long-standing practices in the carriage of goods by sea. Traders should therefore have a basic familiarity with sea transport.

A typical process begins when the shipper (in CIF contracts, for example, this means the exporter) concludes a contract with the consignee (importer). The shipper contacts a freight forwarder to arrange the transport. The forwarder will make enquiries to determine the dates and places of sailing of suitable ships. Frequently the forwarder will do this by contacting loading brokers, who are agents of shipowners, and market the shipowners' available space.

Loading brokers handle logistics from the carrier's side. They advertise the dates of sailings, supervise loading, and consult with shipowner's cargo superintendent with regard to the stowage (packing of goods in the ship's hold). In practice, it is not uncommon for a single forwarding firm to act as both forwarding agent and loading broker, although these tasks are usually handled by separate departments.

Carriers' liability: the ocean (through) bill of lading compared with the combined transport document

1. Ocean (through) bill of lading

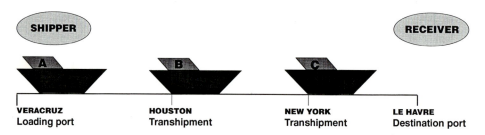

VERACRUZ	HOUSTON	NEW YORK	LE HAVRE
Loading port	Transhipment	Transhipment	Destination port

Under an ocean through bill of lading, each carrier is responsible for the period when it has charge of the goods. In this case carriers A, B and C are only responsible for the period in which the goods are under their respective control.

2. "Pure" through bill of lading

Here, the issuer of the bill of lading is responsible for the entire transit (e.g., carrier A).

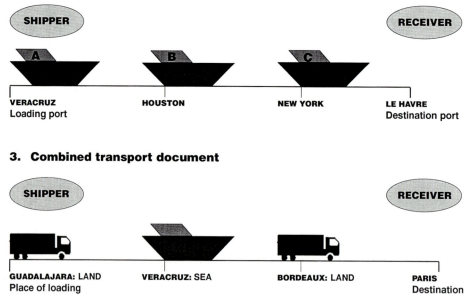

VERACRUZ	HOUSTON	NEW YORK	LE HAVRE
Loading port			Destination port

3. Combined transport document

GUADALAJARA: LAND	VERACRUZ: SEA	BORDEAUX: LAND	PARIS
Place of loading			Destination

With the combined transport document, the issuer is responsible for the entire transit, whether by sea, land or rail.

Commonly, the forwarder will reserve space on a particular vessel, then will appropriately fill in a set of pre-printed bills of lading (a "set" comprises from two to four identical originals). Most shipowners or carriers print their own bills of lading and make these freely available. The forwarder will indicate on the draft bill of lading all necessary information, including the identity of the consignee, a description of the goods which includes shipping marks (visible identification markings on the packages), and details regarding the payment of freight.

The shipper, with the forwarder's assistance, will make sure that the goods are either delivered alongside the ship or into the care of a port terminal, storage shed or warehouse. When the goods are delivered, the shipper will customarily receive a receipt document such as a *mate's receipt, dock receipt, cargo quay receipt* or *wharfinger's note.*

The shipowner will record the details of the goods received, as well as any important defects or damages, on the mate's receipt. This is important, because the bill of lading will be based on information from the mate's receipt. If the mate's receipt indicates damaged goods, then the shipowner will not issue a "clean" bill of lading, which as we have seen is generally necessary for the shipper to obtain payment under a letter of credit.

The shipowner will compare the details of the goods as loaded (recorded by the shipowner's clerks) with the draft bills of lading that the forwarder or shipper has provided. Provided the details match and the goods do not exhibit damage or defects, the shipowner will issue the completed and signed clean bills of lading. The information from the bills of lading is also recorded on a register carried by the ship itself, called the ship's manifest.

Once the goods have been loaded, and the shipper has in addition obtained a marine insurance policy (in CIF shipments, with buyer as policy-holder) and prepared a bank draft, the shipper is able to assemble a *set of shipping documents.* This bundle of documents serves as the hub of many international payment and finance mechanisms. Control over the goods can be freely transferred by endorsement of the bill of lading. Endorsement is effected when the party holding the bill of lading and wishing to make the transfer signs the back of the bill of lading. The signature may also be accompanied by directions to deliver to a specific person.

When the goods arrive at the port of destination the ship's master will deliver the goods to the first party who presents an *original* bill of lading. Commonly, the importer will present the bill of lading to the ship's agent, who will then issue a delivery order; the importer then uses the delivery order to obtain release of the goods.

It is not uncommon for the goods to arrive before the bills of lading have been processed through the payment system and received by the importer (the consignee). Since a delay in receiving the goods may result in penalties or storage charges, the consignee may ask his bank to issue a letter of indemnity ("LOI") to the shipowner, which will protect the shipowner in the event that he incurs liability for delivery to the wrong person. The shipowner will then release the goods against the letter of indemnity. In some sectors, such as the oil trade, this practice is extremely common.

9.8.2 Sea freight

a. **Conferences, tramps and outsiders** – *Conferences* are groups of shipping companies serving specific ocean routes and ports. They fix and publish common freight rates and adhere to quality standards and regular shipping schedules. Because they function much like cartels, which are prohibited by the antitrust or competition law of many countries, conferences have obtained specific exemptions to such laws.

Shipping companies which are not members of conferences are called *outsiders*. Outsiders are not obliged to adhere to conference freight rates nor observe their quality standards and shipping schedules. However, certain large outsiders are able match the quality and regularity offered by the conferences. Outsiders tend to offer lower freight rates than conference members.

Conference freight rates are normally not negotiable. However, conferences offer rebates to loyal customers, as well as discounts to freight forwarders. Rebates are calculated on either a deferred or immediate payment basis. Thus, the deferred rebate may be 10% (to be returned to the shipper if he remains loyal for a period of 6 months), or 9.5% payable immediately.

Tramps are vessels for hire. Their services are marketed through brokers and freight is negotiated on a case-by-case basis.

b. **Freight charges** – Freight is the price the carrier charges for carrying the goods to destination. The amount of freight is most commonly calculated according to the weight or volume (e.g., per ton or cubic meter), of the cargo, whichever is most favourable for the carrier. Commonly, the carrier will provide alternative freight rates based on a standard *ratio* between volume and weight. If the goods exceed the ratio of volume to weight, the freight is charged according to volume; otherwise, freight is charged according to weight. Other possibilities are for the freight to be calculated per unit or parcel, or relative to the value of the cargo.

c. **Surcharges (BAF and CAF)** – Sea carriers commonly levy certain surcharges on the basic freight. The most common surcharges are the Bunker Adjustment Factor (*BAF*), which allows the carrier to adjust freight according to fuel price fluctuations, and Currency Adjustment Factor (*CAF*), for fluctuations in the exchange rate of the currency in which the freight is quoted. While the basic freight is usually fixed for periods up to 6 months or 1 year, the CAF and BAF are subject to overnight revisions. Consequently, exporters should consider including price adaptation clauses in their sales contracts for CAF and BAF adjustments. Other common surcharges are levied for cargo which is exceptionally long or heavy.

d. **Freight Prepaid and Freight Collect** – Under CIF contracts the price includes carriage to the port of destination. The freight may either be prepaid by the seller or paid by the buyer on arrival under a "freight collect" bill of lading. Under freight collect terms the seller deducts the freight from the price on the commercial invoice.

e. **Cargo Handling** – Charges will commonly arise when goods arriving in the port area by truck or lorry are unloaded and transferred to storage sheds or brought alongside the ship. These charges are generally not included in the freight and will therefore be paid either by the exporter or importer according to the Incoterm selected (see section on Incoterms).

f. Liner terms – Before agreeing to a given freight rate, the shipper will want to know whether the loading and unloading of the goods is included in the freight. The answer will depend on the particular "liner term" offered by the shipping line. Again, since Incoterms such as FOB, CFR and CIF divide the costs and risks of loading at the ship's rail, it is important that the Incoterm chosen in the contract of sale accord with the liner term specified in the contract of carriage (see section on Incoterms). It is crucial that traders understand the distinction between liner terms, as part of the contract of carriage, and Incoterms, which are part of the contract of sale. Liner terms govern the contractual relations between *shipper* and *carrier*, whereas Incoterms govern the relationship between *seller* and *buyer*. The choice of particular liner terms within the contract of carriage does not decide the allocation of costs between seller and buyer, unless these have already been specifically allocated under the contract of sale.

Consequently, a trader who has the responsibility for carriage should look first to the contract of sale to see whether the chosen Incoterm sets a clear rule with regard to loading or unloading. The trader, acting as shipper, should then make sure when procuring a contract of carriage that any liner terms in it do not conflict with the contract of sale's Incoterm.

There are many variations for quoting liner term freight rates (see below as regards a new ICC attempt to introduce standard terminology). Commonly, however, particular liner terms correspond to freight which covers transport beginning and/or ending 1) on the quay, 2) under ship's tackle, and 3) on board the vessel. Each of these three variations can be found upon both loading and unloading (since these can be freely combined, there are at least nine basic variations; moreover, since port and conference customs vary widely, the practical number of variations is very high):

1) *ex quay*

  • loading – the carrier's responsibility extends to loading goods brought anywhere within the area alongside the ship. What exactly is meant by «alongside the ship» may vary according to port custom.

  • unloading – carrier's responsibility includes lowering the goods to the quay, sorting the goods into different consignments, and in some cases, storage under cover or in shed.

2) *under ship's tackle*

  • loading – the shipper must bring the goods directly under the crane or derrick which will hoist the goods on board; in particular, the goods must be taken out of any storage shed on the quay.

  • unloading – the carrier will unstow the goods and place them on the ship's deck; all other operations, including lowering the goods to the quay and sorting them, are for the shipper or consignee.

3) *on board* – also called "free in", "free out", or "free in and out" –

- loading – "free in" – the carrier only makes the ship available; the shipper must hoist the goods on board and stow them in the ship's hold.

- unloading – "free out" – the carrier only brings the ship alongside the quay; the shipper or consignee pay for having the goods unstowed and lowered to the quay.

- "free in and out" – under this variation, the carrier will handle only the stowing and unstowing of the goods.

g. **Stevedoring** – In many cases, private contractors called stevedores will take care of all cargo handling operations and will bill them, according to the particular shipment, to either the carrier, the shipper or the consignee. Stevedores will not normally split the charges between shipper and consignee. This has caused problems in the past with respect to the FOB, CFR and CIF Incoterms, which require that costs be divided at the ship's rail. This is one of the reasons that many shippers have moved away from these Incoterms to the corresponding newer Incoterms specifically developed for modern transport techniques, FCA, CPT and CIP.

9.8.3 Standard shipping terms – ICC Finland

The ICC Commission on Maritime Transport has undertaken a study to determine the feasibility of establishing standard shipping terms, which in essence would amount to a set of standard liner terms. This study is based on standard terms which are in actual practice in Finland, developed by ICC Finland. The purpose of the terms is to define the obligations of the contracting shipper and the carrier in marine transportation of break bulk goods. While it may be premature to question whether or not such terms can achieve wide or universal international usage, they are of interest for the light they shed on the basic range of shipping options.

> **Note** that each of these terms has both a loading and a discharging component. Thus, traders could agree on a combination of any of the two. For example, a contract could be concluded as follows: Loading – ICC Finland Gate Term; Discharge – ICC Finland Ship term.

a. **Gate term** – The term which imposes the least obligations on the contracting shipper: he merely delivers the goods on a means of transport to the unloading point. Discharging is by delivery on the loading bay of a warehouse, or loaded on to a further means of transport (Gate term, loaded).

b. **Warehouse term** – The contracting shipper delivers the goods in a warehouse in the port. At discharge, carrier delivers the goods to the consignees in a warehouse in the port of destination.

c. **Tackle term** – The contracting shipper delivers the goods to the carrier on the quay in the port of loading. In the port of discharge, the carrier delivers the goods to the consignee on the quay, unloaded from the vessel. The tackle term is meant for use with convention handling techniques, and should not be used with Ro-Ro transport.

d. Ship term (Free in) – The contracting shipper delivers the goods on board the vessel. At discharge, goods are delivered on board the vessel in the port of destination.

9.9 Containerised and multimodal transport

Although not all containerised transport is multimodal, and vice versa, they are so often inter-related that it is useful to consider these two concepts together. When, as is common in international trade, goods move from seller to buyer through two land legs and one sea leg, the advantages of using the container become evident. Not only is the container transferred with ease from one leg to the next, the risks of damage and theft are greatly reduced.

Containers are basically large boxes, 8 x 8 feet in cross-section, and either 10, 20 or 40 feet long. The first all-container ship came into operation in the Pacific in 1956. In 1965, the first container vessel docked in Europe. The spread of containerisation throughout the world over the next decades progressed with breathtaking speed. Today, each of the world's major ports handles millions of containers per year.

Container volumes are measured in *TEU*s (Twenty-foot Equivalent Units). The first container ships carried 500 TEU, with the most recent generation in the 3000-4000 TEU range. The standardisation of containers allows for great automation of loading and transhipment, so that port operations that used to take days are now measured in hours.

Shippers should always be careful to demand the *internal measurements* of the type of container they plan to use, so that the packaged or unitized goods can be prepared so as to properly fit the container.

9.9.1 Containers and Incoterms

In light of the tremendous importance of containerised shipment in international trade, the International Chamber of Commerce has seen fit to adapt its Incoterms to container traffic. Thus, it has introduced terms which are specifically appropriate to containerised and multimodal transport:

• *FCA* (Free Carrier), which can be thought of as the containerised/multimodal equivalent of FOB;

• *CPT* (Carriage Paid To), which can be thought of as the containerised/ multimodal equivalent of CFR; and

• *CIP* (Carriage and Insurance Paid to), which can be thought of as the con-tainerised/multimodal equivalent of CIF.

The importance of using these newer Incoterms is linked to questions of insurance cover and division of costs. Since container shipments are frequently taken over by the carrier at the shipper's premises or at container terminals which are remote from the port of departure, it does not make sense to divide the risk (and therefore, insurance coverage) at the ship's side, as is done under FOB, CFR and CIF.

If a shipper uses FOB or CIF for containerised shipments delivered early on to a transport terminal, he will have to be careful to provide for insurance cover from the point of handing over of the container to the ship's side. It may happen that the goods are damaged during this inland transit or while stored in container terminals, so that the shipper (who had only insured himself up to the point of delivery, the transport terminal) finds himself without possible recourse via an insurance claim.

Moreover, with regard to costs, the shipper who hands the goods over to the carrier at the shipper's premises prefers not to absorb the costs all the way to the ship's side, and therefore prefers FCA to FOB.

9.9.2 Overview of basic commercial procedure

As with traditional cargo shipments, container shipments are frequently arranged by freight forwarders. There is a basic distinction between shipments that fill a full container load *(FCL)* and shipments for less than a full container load *(LCL)*

a. **Full container loads – FCL –** In the case of FCL shipments, an empty container is taken out of a stack in a container park and sent to the exporter's premises, where it is stuffed with the goods. After the container has been stuffed, it is closed with the carrier's seal. Theft or pilferage of the goods in transit will normally be indicated by a broken seal.

b. **Less than full Container Loads – LCL –** In the case of LCL shipments, the exporter delivers the goods to a container terminal, where the cargo is grouped together with other cargo sufficient to stuff a container. At a terminal near the destination point, the cargo is unloaded from the container and broken down into separate consignments.

c. **Container freight –** There are two separate cost elements – the rental of the container, and the freight. Frequently, the rental of containers provided by the carrier is included in the freight. In other cases, however, the shipper will lease the container. Shippers are advised to take care as to the time period allowed under the lease contract, because these contracts often provide for liquidated damages in the case of containers returned late.

Container freight charged by shipping lines in conferences is generally linked to the type of goods shipped, whereas outsiders tend to charge a flat rate per box.

Containers are usually delivered in the port area to a terminal which charges a fixed amount for handling the container and moving it to the ship's side. At the port of departure the terminal charges are often referred to as *container service charges*, whereas at the port of destination the charges may be called *terminal handling charges*; in practice, the terms are employed *interchangeably.*

9.10 Air transport

9.10.1 Introductory

Air transport has profoundly accelerated the pace of international business. Not only can cargo shipments be moved in a fraction of the time required under sea transport, business executives and export documents can also reach remote destinations in a single day.

Indeed, international trade in certain kinds of merchandise would not exist were it not for the rapidity of air transport. Highly time-sensitive goods, such as newspapers and magazines, or highly perishable goods, such as fresh flowers or lobster, would not be available at all in many markets if it were not for air transport. The speed of air transport also reduces exposure to risk so substantially that goods of great value, such as jewellery, pharmaceuticals and medical supplies, prize livestock, art works or manuscripts, will usually move by air. Thus, air freight has been said to account for only 1% by weight, but 10% by value, of all goods transported. However, even with regard to products for which distribution is not so time-sensitive, air transport is deceptively competitive.

Although air freight rates are much higher than ocean rates, air shipments can provide savings with respect to other crucial costs:

1) *Insurance* – premiums are generally less than half those for sea transport (e.g., 0.3% of cargo value as opposed to 0.7%);

2) *Customs duties* – may be charged on gross weight, which is generally lower for air shipments (less packaging) than for sea shipments;

3) *Packaging* – much lighter and cheaper for air transport;

4) *Inventory costs* – in many cases air transport can greatly reduce and even eliminate the need for warehousing which would be necessary with sea transport; since warehousing costs include not only the leasing of warehouse space at either end of transit, but also related tax and insurance costs, as well as the cost of goods which become obsolescent while stored in the warehouse, this cost factor can be decisive in favour of air transport;

5) *Financing costs* – for shipments in which the buyer's payment obligation is triggered by delivery to the buyer's premises, the seller will receive payment much sooner with air transport.

Even in those cases where the cost of sea transport is lower, the seller may prefer to use air transport for competitive reasons. Thus, an export seller of spare parts may find that he cannot compete against domestic sellers unless he matches their delivery speeds, which can only be done with air transport.

9.10.2 Overview of air transport procedures

Air freight is either shipped:
- along with passenger's luggage in passenger planes,
- in hybrid aircraft with special compartments for cargo, known as "combi's", or
- in cargo aircraft.

Specialised cargo craft, such as the Boeing 747F freighter, can now carry payloads in excess of 100,000 kg., but combi's and passenger planes remain more profitable for airlines than cargo freighters. Thus, shippers have in the past complained that airlines did not pay enough attention to the cargo business. However, with some airlines today generating close to half of their revenues from cargo, shippers can now expect a competitive air freight market.

a. **Air transport and Incoterms** – In the past, many shippers quoted «FOB Airport» prices for air shipments. This caused many misunderstandings with respect to airport handling charges and extent of insurance coverage. Obviously, an airplane does not have a "ship's rail" and goods are not delivered "alongside the plane". Thus, the application of FOB principles derived from sea transport was not appropriate. Consequently, the ICC discontinued the FOB Airport term in its most recent revisions of Incoterms. The ICC recommends that shippers use the FCA Incoterm instead, with the specified point of delivery being the named air freight or consolidator's terminal.

b. **Freight forwarders/consolidators** – Air transport gave many freight forwarders an entire new line of business. Air carriers, through the International Air Transport Association (IATA), oversee a world-wide cargo agents' organisation, to which many forwarders adhere. Appointment as an IATA air cargo agent allows a forwarder to market air cargo services knowing that IATA airlines will carry the goods for a fixed price and with a commission for the forwarder. IATA agents must demonstrate certain financial and cargo-handling resources, and must agree to remit to the air carrier freight billings according to fixed schedules.

Air carriers may provide forwarders with air waybills (AWB's) featuring the airline's logo. As with other non-negotiable transport documents, the AWB is both a receipt for the goods and a contract of carriage. In some countries the AWB system is computerised and the air carriers only issue AWB numbers to the forwarders, leaving the forwarder to print out the AWB number and airline logo on a forms known as the Neutral AWB.

Forwarders acting as consolidators may issue AWB's in their own name as carriers, in which case their role can be likened to that of NVOCC's (Non-Vessel Operating Common Carriers) in sea transport. By consolidating – grouping – several consignments together, forwarders are able to obtain the lower freight rates offered by carriers for large shipments. In this, the air consolidators perform a groupage function like that of container shipping terminals. Consolidators may provide highly efficient warehouse services upon departure, and upon arrival may handle the notification of the consignee by telephone. In addition, consolidators often offer a door-to-door service, which includes customs clearance and insurance coverage.

c. **Cargo Handling** – Air cargo containers corresponding to the shape of the plane's cabin are known as *unit load devices (ULD's)*. There are various shapes and sizes of ULD's (some are called "*igloos*"), each designed to be stored in a different part of the airplane. Cargo is handled primarily by pushing or pulling of pallets and ULD's which move over systems of rollers. Since ULD's are usually stuffed in terminals at or near the airport, it is possible for cargo delivered to an air terminal to be shipped on a departing flight within two hours. The actual loading or unloading of cargo can take less than one hour.

d. **Guaranteed shipment time** – Some airlines offer guaranteed shipment times or dates, which eliminates the risk to the shipper that his cargo will be delayed as a result of being forced off a particular flight to make room for special high-priority items. Although the extent of the guarantee values from airline to airline, it is generally useful for the shipper to request one, in particular because some airlines make such guarantees at no extra charge.

e. **Hazardous goods** – Since shipments of hazardous goods can in some cases jeopardise the safety of the entire aircraft, regulations on restricted articles are strictly enforced. IATA publishes an annual update of such regulations. In many cases, cargo is allowed provided that it is appropriately packaged and "hazard" labels are affixed. Both shippers and forwarders must be quite careful in assuring that all declarations relating to potentially hazardous cargo are complete and correct; failure to do so can result in the application of heavy penalties.

f. **Air Freight** – Under IATA schedules, freight rates decrease according to the weight bracket of the shipment. The basic weight brackets are: 0-45 kg., 45-100 kg., 100-300 kg., 300-500 kg., 500 kg. – 1 ton, and above 1 ton. The benefits of *consolidation* are apparent. Rather than send five 25 kg. shipments on 5 separate flights over a period of days, it will be much cheaper to group the five shipments into one 100 kg. consignment. Preferential rates (sometimes called "corates") are available for certain commodities shipped in bulk.

As with sea freight, rates are also subject to a volume-weight ratio. Extremely light, low-density products will therefore pay freight based on a "theoretical weight" which is calculated as a fraction of their volume.

Cargo handling charges in airports can be relatively expensive. Shippers are therefore advised to have these specified in advance.

9.11 Road and rail transport

9.11.1 Road haulage

The total number of vehicles engaged in road haulage world-wide, more than *80 million*, dwarfs the number for any other transport method. The great advantage of international road haulage is that it offers the possibility of true door-to-door service with no transhipment whatsoever. Moreover, loading at point of departure and unloading at destination require relatively little in the way of specialised equipment – a loading platform and a steel sheet "bridge" are often all that is needed. Articulated vehicles (a lorry or truck which pulls a container-trailer) are particularly well-suited to *roll-on roll-off (Ro-Ro)* ships, which allow for safe and simple transfer from land to sea and back again to land. In addition to this great flexibility, road vehicles can carry as much as 45 tons, although national regulations may set a maximum limit.

As with sea and air transport, specialised forwarders offer consolidation services for road transport. Their services can involve grouping small consignments, warehousing, and integrating several modes of shipment so as to offer a door-to-door price. Sophisticated integrators today offer many computerised services, including monitoring of the progress of the shipment from departure to destination. In addition, many of these integrators offer express services featuring guaranteed delivery dates.

a. **Road haulage rates** – Rates vary widely from country to country. One reason for this is that labour rates for drivers will correspond to the prevailing wages in the particular country. As with sea and air transport, road freight is generally calculated by weight but subject to a volume-weight ratio. For road transport this ratio falls between the ratios for sea (1.33 to 1) and air transport (6 to 1), and is generally in the area of 3. Thus, if the volume in cubic meters is more than three times the weight in kg., freight will be set according to a "theoretical weight" in kg. calculated by dividing the total volume in cubic meters by three.

b. **TIR Carnet System – international customs carnet for road haulage** – The TIR (Transport International Routier) Carnet is very similar in function to the ATA Carnet discussed earlier, except that the TIR Carnet was created to allow trucks or lorries carrying international cargos to pass through intervening countries (provided they are signatories to the TIR Convention) without having to go through customs control procedures.

9.11.2 Rail transport

Just as road and air transport have boomed for half a century, rail transport has declined. As compared with road transport, rail transport is much less flexible in terms of the total number of shippers and consignees that can be directly reached, and loading is generally not so easy. Since different countries may use different rail widths or gauges, as well as different tunnel clearances, international consignments can be complicated and require transhipment.

However, for certain classes of shippers or cargo, rail remains the indicated transport choice. Railway wagons can carry cargo of tremendous weight. Certain special flat-bed rail trucks can carry up to 500 tons. Rail is thus often the preferred choice for bulk transport of industrial ore and liquids. Moreover, when both shipper and consignee have private rail sidings (direct connections from warehouses to rail lines) rail shipments can provide the most straightforward door-to-door service. Additional flexibility has resulted from the development of road-rail schemes, under which, for example, a road trailer arriving from a roll-on roll-off ship is placed on a rail wagon and transported to destination by rail.

Railway freight – In contrast to other modes of transport, freight is generally not subject to a volume-weight ratio. Railways generally offer two sets of rates for full wagons, one for express service and one for slow goods service. In terms of price per unit of weight, railway freight is quite competitive.

9.12 Cargo insurance

International trade shipments are almost without exception insured against damage or loss in transit by some form of cargo insurance. Depending on the Incoterm chosen and any express insurance provisions in the contract of sale, either the exporter or importer may have the primary responsibility to insure. In some cases, both parties will have the cargo insured to varying extents. The variety and complexity of possible permutations is such that no exporter or importer should do without the counsel of an insurance agent or broker.

Many small traders have insurance cover arranged by their freight forwarder. Alternatively, the trader may have a long-term "open" or "floating" cover with the insurance company, which will cover a number of shipments over a given period of time. In other cases, the trader will directly insure a particular shipment via a marine, aviation, or overland insurance policy. Despite their names, such insurance policies are generally not limited to insurance for only the marine, air, or land legs of transit, but can each be extended to cover the goods «warehouse to warehouse».

a. **Duty to insure vs. commercial need to insure** – An initial distinction must be made between the contractual duty to insure and the commercial need to insure. Thus, under CIF and CIP Incoterms, the exporter has a contractual duty to the importer to provide a minimum level of insurance to cover the goods during international transit. Under all other Incoterms, there is no contractual duty for either side to provide insurance (although the parties may freely stipulate any additional insurance requirements in the sale contract).

However, the absence of a contractual duty to insure does not remove the obvious practical need to obtain insurance in most cases. The parties will normally obtain insurance coverage to protect themselves as a matter of ordinary commercial prudence. At a minimum, the parties will wish to be insured during that part of transit in which they are at risk. Each Incoterm fixes a point for the transfer of risk from seller to buyer; before that point, the seller is at risk and will wish to be insured; after that point, the buyer is at risk and will wish to be insured.

b. **Splitting of insurance cover according to division of risk** – It might therefore seem reasonable that parties would only wish to pay for insurance coverage for that part of the transit in which they were at risk. Thus, if we take the example of an FOB shipment, transfer of risk is at the ship's side. Since the seller is at risk up to that point, he might reasonably wish the cargo to be insured by himself up to the ship's rail, and no further. He has no contractual duty at all to insure the goods up to the ship's side, but he will normally do so out of self-interest. Likewise, the buyer might desire that his insurance coverage should begin at the ship's rail, and no earlier.

However, since insurance coverage is most often warehouse to warehouse, it is not a common practice to split insurance coverage at the transfer of risk point. Splitting insurance coverage, each side seeking only to insure its own interest for its leg of the transport, has several disadvantages. First of all, there is the risk that the two insurance covers will not match up exactly, leaving a gap – a portion of the transport chain where there is no insurance cover. Second, if loss or damage is only discovered upon arrival, it may be difficult to prove where the loss or damage occurred (and therefore, under which policy), with the result that both insurers may be able to avoid payment. Finally, two separate partial insurance covers are generally more expensive than a single warehouse-to-warehouse cover for the entire transit.

> **Example:** Consider an FOB or CFR seller on open account terms, who will only be paid *after* the goods are received by the buyer. Such a seller would be unwise to only insure the transit leg prior to the transfer of risk point (the ship's rail). If the goods are lost or damaged after the transfer point, the buyer may refuse to effect payment, leaving the seller without coverage. The seller would have to file a lawsuit rather than a somewhat simpler insurance claim.

It would therefore seem preferable that one of the parties obtain continuous coverage for the entire transit, warehouse to warehouse, from a single insurer. However, this is not always possible. Many countries require by law that their importers and exporters insure transport risks with domestic insurers. Also, many traders already have long term marine cargo insurance under a floating policy or open cover (discussed below). Moreover, some traders are reckless enough to wish to do without insurance cover for their leg of transport.

Even in those cases where the other party has taken out a warehouse to warehouse policy, the coverage may be for an insufficient amount, or may exclude certain likely risks. The trading partner in such a case may wish to take out supplementary *"difference in conditions"* or *"contingency"* insurance.

As can be seen from the foregoing, traders should consider carefully how much insurance coverage they need, and for what portion of the transit they need coverage. They should consider whether insurance coverage provided under minimum standard terms such as the Institute Cargo Clauses is sufficient for their purposes, and if not, they should consider amplifying or increasing the coverage. If the other party has procured insurance, they should also consider whether it is sufficient, or whether it should be complemented with contingency insurance.

They should review with their insurance agent or broker, as well as their trading partners, the various options for obtaining such coverage. Finally, they should stipulate precisely in the contract of sale the desired level of coverage and who must pay for it.

c. **Insurable interest** – Regardless of who takes out the insurance policy, a party can only recover under a claim on that policy if he has an "insurable interest" in the goods at the time they were damaged or lost. Roughly, this means that a party must have ownership or some other interest (including risk) in the goods in order to claim under the policy. Generally speaking, the seller will have an insurable interest in the goods up to the transfer of risk point, and the buyer will have an insurable interest thereafter. However, there are exceptions to this rule, and in some cases one of the parties will assign his rights under the policy to the other party.

d. **"Open" Cover or "Floating" Policies** – *"Open" cover* and *"floating"* policies are intended to cover multiple shipments over a period of time, and therefore only state the general conditions of the insurance contract. In each case, the insured party notifies the insurer of the specific voyages to be covered under the policy. Open cover may also be taken out by forwarders or carriers, who then use it to cover specific consignments for their clients.

Under a *floating policy*, the value of the risk insured on each voyage is deducted from the total value of the insurance contracted. Under an open policy, the insurance limit is automatically renewed after each voyage.

In some cases, such as those involving payment under a letter of credit, the shipper will need to have an insurance document included in the set of shipping documents. Under an open policy, this is accomplished by the use of "insurance certificates", which are issued by the insurers at the instruction of the insured party. Traders should take care, because a letter of credit which explicitly requires submission of an insurance policy will not allow an insurance certificate as a substitute.

e. Cost of insurance – Insurance premiums vary widely according to the mode of transport and the nature of the goods. Premiums for air shipment are generally the lowest, in the area of 0.3% of the value of the goods, while the highest are for long road or rail transport legs (especially in developing countries), which in exceptional cases may be up to 2%. Sea transport premiums are commonly in the range of .6% − .7%.

f. Incoterms and insurance – Only two Incoterms, CIF and CIP, specifically require insurance. Under these terms, the seller must take out an insurance policy for the buyer. The minimum amount of coverage is set at 110% of the value of the goods, and the conditions of the coverage are specifically those set out in the Institute of London Underwriters Cargo Clauses. The Institute of London Underwriters is a professional association of insurance companies; there are three standard clauses, known respectively as Institute Cargo Clauses A, B and C. These clauses define the risks covered by the insurance policy, and were intended to replace and improve the previously common clauses known as "all risks", "with average" (WA), and "free of particular average" (FPA).

Institute Cargo Clause A provides the broadest coverage and is therefore sometimes considered to provide "all risks" cover. However, such terminology is deceptive, because several important risks are not covered by Clause A, notably the risks of strikes or war, as well as damage resulting from insufficient packing, delay, ordinary wear and tear of transport, or the insolvency of the carrier, amongst others.

Clauses B and C are even more restrictive, covering only risks which are specifically referred to.

Under Incoterms, the seller may choose Clause C, which provides the least coverage. Importers should therefore be forewarned that in cases where such minimum coverage is insufficient, they will need to specify in the contract the level of additional insurance they require. For example, if the importer expects to earn a high profit margin on the goods, coverage of 110% of the value of the goods may be insufficient; 120% or 130% may be advisable (although this will obviously raise the cost of the premium).

One solution is to provide a specific clause in the contract of sale setting out the scope, time and extent of insurance coverage, and particularly whether coverage will extend to risks of strikes, riots and civil commotion (called "SRCC" coverage; an example of such a clause is set out in the Chapter 4 on Incoterms.)

9.13 Customs

International trade transactions always involve at least two customs clearances, one upon export and one upon import. Upon export, an export license may or may not be required. Export licenses are most commonly required in the case of sales of politically or strategically sensitive goods, such as exports of arms or weaponry, chemicals or high-technology goods.

Upon import, duties and taxes will be payable. The choice of Incoterm will determine who, as between exporter and importer, has the responsibility of export or import clearance. The clearance responsibility has 3 components:

- the responsibility to obtain necessary *licenses* and fill out *forms* and *declarations*;

- the responsibility to pay official *duties* and *taxes*; and

- assumption of the *risk* that customs clearance may be physically or legally impossible.

The World Customs Organisation (WCO), an intergovernmental organisation based in Brussels, promotes the standardisation of customs procedures; it has 98 member countries. The ICC has issued a series of Guidelines for efficient customs services, which are intended to help customs authorities set clear goals and benchmarks for measuring service performance.

Traders generally rely on *customs brokers* to clear goods through customs. Brokers act as the agents of the exporter or importer in their dealings with customs authorities. It is therefore important that traders carefully instruct their brokers as to the nature of the goods and the taxes and duties they expect – and are willing – to pay. Traders may explicitly require that the broker contact them for assistance in the event of difficulties arising during clearance, because the trader will frequently be better placed to answer questions or resolve disputes concerning the technical, quality or price details of the cargo.

a. **Amount of Duty – Valuation, Origin and Customs Classification** – The amount of duty varies widely, depending on the value of the goods, tariff schedules of the importing country, customs classification of the goods and in some cases, the origin of the goods. Customs officers will strictly verify the declared value of the goods, since duty is often calculated as an ad valorem percentage. Customs valuation is covered by an international treaty, the *GATT Customs Valuation Code*[1], which sets forth the basic rule that the customs value of the goods is the value agreed between exporter and importer in the invoice. Clearly, the invoice value will in turn depend on the amount of transport services included in the price under the chosen Incoterm; for the same goods, a CIF value will always be higher than an FOB value. In some countries duties are calculated on an FOB basis, in other countries on a CIF basis. This may generate confusion when customs officers refuse to accept values based on invoice prices calculated under other Incoterms.

The easiest solution is to convert the invoice value to a customs value for the purposes of the customs declaration.

In some cases customs officers will consider that the invoice value is suspect. This may be because the transaction contains some element of fraud (as in an attempt to circumvent foreign-exchange control by paying inflated prices to a co-conspiring exporter), or because the exporter is "dumping" goods into the import market at prices below the production cost in order to capture market share. In these cases, the invoice value may have to adjusted upward to arrive at a value acceptable to the customs officials. If traders have any reason to anticipate problems in this area, they should consult with customs in advance.

In most countries, goods are classified into various categories under the *Harmonised Commodity Description and Coding System* (Harmonised System) promulgated by the World Customs Organisations. Under the Harmonised System, goods are classified into more than 5000 separate categories, each of which is identified by a specific code. It is not unusual for a particular piece of merchandise to fall between two official customs designations. Understandably, the traders will wish to have applied whichever designation is assigned the lower duty. In the event of disputes, the trader will commonly have the right to appeal the customs ruling to a specialised legal tribunal.

b. **Country of origin – Generalised System of Preferences** – The amount of the duty assessed will often depend on the country of origin. Thus, certain European or Mediterranean countries have customs agreements with the European Union such that imports and exports are imposed duty at preferential rates. More importantly, under the United Nations' *Generalised System of Preferences (GSP)*, many developed countries have granted preferential or free entry to imports from developing countries.[2]

This leads to the important question of the *origin* of export goods. Generally, this origin is determined and documented by a *certificate of origin* which is procured from, and stamped by, a chamber of commerce or other official export agency. Origin is a simple matter in the case of agricultural products or raw commodities, or even in the case of manufactured products the components of which come from the same country.

The question becomes more complex in the case of manufactured products, the components of which may not come from countries accorded preferential status. The two criteria for deciding whether a particular product meets the origin requirement for preferential status are a *process criterion* and a *percentage criterion*. Under the process criterion, the finished product will generally be accepted for preferential rates if it falls into a different product category than the components. Under the percentage criterion, a minimum of from 35% to 50% (depending on the importing country) of the content of the final product must come from the country accorded preferential status.

c. **Bonded Warehouses** – A bonded warehouse is authorised to store imported goods without payment of duties for a given period of time. The proprietor of the warehouse must provide a bond to the customs authorities in order to cover any potential liability for duties. The utility of these warehouses is that the importer can inspect the goods, or have her customers inspect them, before paying the duty. In the event that the goods are unsatisfactory, the importer can either reject them, or if she has already purchased them, seek to have them sold or re-exported to a third party. Another advantage is that for goods assessed high duties (i.e., tobacco and alcohol products), payment of the duty can be delayed, thereby enabling the importer to save the interest value on the amount of the duty throughout the period of storage.

Notes

[1] For full list of signatory countries, contact the *World Customs Organisation* in Brussels.

[2] For a full list of currently participating countries, contact the UNCTAD Secretariat in Geneva.

Chapter Ten

International Electronic Commerce

The basics: The convergence of computers and telecommunications is opening up new ways of doing business with a potentially vast impact on trade. International computer networks have provided new ways of finding information, new marketing channels and techniques, and new ways of making contracts and exchanging legal documents. To gain access to the world electronic business community, exporters may begin by subscribing to a commercial "online service", preferably one which will allow them access to the Internet. Firms with many branches may wish to communicate internally via electronic mail (e-mail). Exporters and importers should investigate whether local transporters and customs officials accept EDI (electronic data interchange) communications.

The firm may wish to create a commercial presence on Internet by establishing a "home page" on the World Wide Web, a substandard of the Internet which allows companies to present information in a visual and highly-interactive mode. The firm may offer its goods on one of numerous electronic "bulletin boards" which function as international electronic bazaars.

0.1 Overview

Exporters need to have access to a wide range of information, and therefore usually have libraries with directories of companies and industry magazines and so forth. However, when new or unusual information is needed, it can take a good deal of time and effort to acquire. This explains the great value and popularity of *commercial electronic networks*, which now provide a multitude of databases at ones' fingertips. An exporter may need information to prepare a business visit to several countries. Profiles of the countries, their economic statistics, their top companies, and other pertinent information, can be accessed easily and instantly over the Internet.

As we have seen in previous chapters, international trade is highly dependent on documents. As the number of documents increases, so does the cost of handling them, and the risk that there will be an inconsistency between the information on one document and another. If documents such as purchase orders, bills of lading, and documentary credit applications could be sent electronically, the documentary credit system could benefit from potentially dramatic gains in speed and reliability.

Electronic messaging capabilities have long been part of the payment and shipping infrastructure of international trade, and this trend is still on the increase. Banks rely on the SWIFT protocol for electronic interbank transfers, permitting the speeding of international payments, and many shipping companies are now equipped with electronic booking and tracking services. Customs services in various countries allow for electronic submissions of documents, and ports and harbours have installed electronic management systems as well. SWIFT has also embarked on a joint venture called BOLERO to develop a standard platform for the transmission of electronic trade messages (see below).

10.1.1 The range of products and services

a. Networks – A group of computers linked together, allowing them to share and transmit information. A network can be a small one within a company (*"LAN"* for "local area network"), or it can be a large international one with open or commercial access. Currently gaining many converts is the *Intranet*, a type of closed or proprietary network which allows its members to communicate over the Internet (generally, such systems are based on passwords or digital keys which restrict access). Intranets allow international companies or markets to link all of their members over a secure electronic network.

b. "E-mail" – Electronic messages sent from one computer to another, the simplest and broadest use of new messaging technology. The advantage over fax is not only that there is no need for paper, but that replying is so much easier. When you reply to an e-mail message, you do not have to re-address it; the return message is automatically routed. This ease of response is a spur to instantaneous reply, so that e-mail tends to be a quick and lively way to receive information from, and distribute it to, an international group of correspondents.

E-mail messages do not have to be structured in any particular way – they are basically like expandable envelopes, allowing the sender to prepare a message of any type or length. That is the difference between e-mail and EDI – EDI must always adhere to standards regulating the structure of the commercial message.

E-mail greatly facilitates international communications across time-zones, where telephoning becomes impractical. As a result, *e-mail is probably the best form of communication for teams of people spread out across several continents.* E-mail messages can be sent to a pre-programmed list of individuals, permitting a sort of "direct mail" capability. Also, "reflector" systems can be used, which allow a user to take all or part of some information she has received and «reflect» it to a select group of interlocutors.

c. Electronic Data Interchange (EDI) – EDI, (explained in greater depth below), is the electronic transmission of structured business messages such as purchase orders and invoices. An EDI message must conform to a standard format so that the receiving computer can automatically process it. The power of EDI becomes apparent with regard to companies transmitting high volumes of standard messages. Supermarkets, for example, must send out tens of thousands of invoices per week. With EDI, the messages are received instantly and errors *cannot* subsequently be introduced into the information (assuming the initial data entry is correct).

d. Online Services – The online service is a private commercial entity which provides access to a large computer network, and which is interconnected to the Internet, allowing for exchange of e-mail even with people who subscribe to different online services. The most successful in the United States have been *Compuserve, America Online* and the *Microsoft Network.*

Online services provide a relatively cheap and easy introduction to the world of electronic networks. They tend to provide both an internal network (including the e-mail addresses of other subscribers, databases, newsgroups and bulletin boards) as well as a connection to the Internet, which allows for communication with thousands of other networks.

Even without using the Internet "gateway" of the online service – that is, simply by staying within the commercial services directly offered by the online service – the international trader can access much valuable information. For example, Compuserve provides access to several business databases consisting of thousands of articles on a great variety of business issues, including several on the payment, legal and shipping aspects of international trade. Compuserve also devotes one of its numerous "forums" – which are basically electronic conversation areas – to international trade. The user can choose from a menu of conversation topics, including international banking, shipment, etc. The user can enter into an ongoing conversation, in which case he can review the "string" of e-mail exchanges made before he arrived.

In addition, Compuserve offers a sort of international bazaar for exporters and importers, with products offered for sale or requested for purchase, in its ProTrade Forum. There are many other commercial services also offering this sort of "bulletin board" for the export trade, such as the Export Hotline or the IBCC-Net initiative of the ICC (described below).

e. **Internet** – The Internet is a worldwide amalgamation of computer networks that allow for communication according to certain standards. Anyone on the Internet can contact anyone else on the Internet, instantly. The amount of information available over the Internet is vast, and the volume of electronic traffic over the Internet is enormous and growing. Accurate estimates as to the total population connected to the Internet are of uncertain accuracy, and in any event, go rapidly out of date. As of the publication date of this book, there are probably somewhere between 50 and 100 million individuals connected to the Internet, with new users joining at a rate of several per minute. Since the commercial online services are virtually all connected to the Internet, anyone who is a member of one of these services can send e-mail to any member of another service (provided it offers Internet access).

f. **World Wide Web** – The World Wide Web ("WWW" or "the Web") is a sort of subset of the Internet. The Web is basically a computer standard that allows individuals to: 1) Attach attractive graphics to files, and 2) Link articles and databases via a device called *hypertext*. With hypertext, certain words in the text of an article are underlined or highlighted; when the user clicks on them, he or she is instantly connected to another document or database. This function allows people to browse through many interconnected or related documents.

The Web is thus the locus of most commercial activity over the Internet, because the attractive graphics can be used to support advertising or marketing messages. The Web has become the most popular way for people to browse, or "surf" the Net.

10.2 Export "cybermarkets" – electronic marketplaces for international trade

10.2.1 Introductory

Much of this book has been devoted to a discussion of the documentary complexity which can underlie even simple export transactions. We have seen that many of the problems and misunderstandings in international trade arise from, or are aggravated by, the following factors:

- traders are unable, or do not seek, to obtain sufficient credit information on their counterparties;

- essential paper documents, like bills of lading and bills of exchange, are transmitted via the mails and private courier services; this is extremely slow relative to the speed of telecommunications;

- although paper documents have certain evidentiary advantages (forgeries and alterations may in some cases be detectable), the advent of low-cost sophisticated printing has made paper-based systems increasingly susceptible to forgery and trade fraud;

- international commodities markets are able to effectuate large trades in a matter of seconds, but the underlying export transactions require weeks and months to complete, largely owing to the inherent slowness of paper-based systems;

- international payments often transit through two or more banks; bank charges may be high; the risks for banks associated with documentary credit procedures makes this a high-cost alternative.

The above problems have led much of the international business community to hope that solutions can be found by transacting trade over secure, international electronic networks. Such networks, it is expected, will eventually function as export-import "cybermarkets" – markets where real transactions, with legally binding effect, could be negotiated, signed, in some cases even performed and paid, with each of the constituent steps taking place in a matter of seconds. Moreover, security features built into electronic systems could render the cybermarket a much more secure and fraud-free environment than the traditional markets.

However, the theoretical attractiveness of new electronic products has not always been an accurate predictor of market success in the past. As this book went to press there were a good number of private and public electronic markets in embryonic phases. It is not possible to state at this time whether we will see one universal standard electronic market in the near future, or whether there will be a much greater number of regional and sectoral markets.

10.2.2 Trade Point / ETO (Electronic Trading Opportunity) System

The Trade Point system developed by a specialised unit of the United Nations Commission for Trade and Development (UNCTAD) provided, as this text went to press, more than 60 electronic sites known as Trade Points, which has allowed traders to exchange trade information using standard EDIFACT messages. More information can be obtained from the UNCTAD Trade Development Centre, Palais des Nations, CH 1211 Geneva 10 Switzerland, Fax (41 22) 907 0052.

0.2.3 IBCC Net

A comprehensive trade-lead and information network serving the international community of chamber of commerce, set up by a special branch of the ICC, the International Bureau of Chambers of Commerce (IBCC). Amongst the key services to be offered by IBCC Net is that of matching exporters with importers, or manufacturers with distributors/agents. Since these services are offered through the trusted intermediary of chambers of commerce, it is expected that the reliability of resulting agreements or transactions will be very high.

0.2.4 Commercial markets

Amongst the commercial electronic markets are the following (please note, neither the author nor the ICC makes any recommendation as to the reliability of these services; we cannot even assure that they will be in commercial existence by the time this book reaches the reader; readers are therefore cautioned to seek up-to-date information and references):

a. **IBEX** – IBEX is a joint effort based on software and a trading system developed by Global Business Alliance, a private company. A consortium of major international corporations have in principle agreed to support the IBEX trading system (amongst them AT&T and General Electric Information Systems). In its own terms, IBEX facilitates encounters between prospective business partners, enables them to buy and sell goods and services, or to negotiate investment deals. All of this is accomplished by a user sitting at a computer terminal and interacting with a simple menu-driven software programme. Users will pay a flat amount for the software and a certain amount per transaction.

b. **GINS/World Business Network (@WBN)** – @WBN defines itself as a value-added network that enables companies to manage the business processes of international trade on a single client-server online platform. @WBN has formed an alliance with IBM which allows to @WBN to be accessed from more than 850 cities in over 100 countries. @WBN is divided into different sections providing 1) interactive trade facilitation, 2) market development, 3) information and education, and 4) technical support. Via @WBN it is possible to access the services of various sub-providers, such as Dun & Bradstreet (which offers credit reporting services).

d. **Trade Compass** – (http://www.tradecompass.com) describes itself as a "one-stop shop" for international commerce. Trade Compass consists of five categories: 1) News, 2) Library, 3) Marketplace, 4) Trade Forum, and 5) Search. Trade Compass also offers a service for American exporters allowing them to file customs forms with US Customs. Trade Compass also offers the service of creating home pages for traders. In addition, Trade Compass provides a logistics management system, consisting of a wide range of proprietary logistics services.

d. Compuserve ProTRADE Forum – This is a special service provided by Compuserve for an extra monthly fee. Not only are users provided with a variety of information sources about international trade, they are permitted to post expressions of interest in commercial deals. Other online services can be expected to have similar international trade sections, but it would not be possible to review them all here.

e. World Trade Center TRADE CARD – The World Trade Center Association has created an export trade payment mechanism for its members based on the concept of a stored-value card.

10.3 EDI – electronic data interchange

The basics: EDI (Electronic Data Interchange) involves sending *standardised* commercial messages (e.g., purchase orders and invoices) between the computers of two companies, via telecommunications. The power of EDI is that the transmission is instantaneous and error-free. EDI-capability is a must for any large firm with substantial distribution and logistics needs. EDI is especially valuable for firms which have to transmit large volumes of similar types of information (e.g., supermarkets, because they must repeatedly transmit purchase requests to many suppliers), or for firms who need the greater accuracy provided by computer to computer transmissions (e.g., banks and insurance companies, because they are dealing with very high-value transactions).

a. Definitions: What is EDI? – In essence, EDI allows one company's computer system to be connected to those of its trading partners via public or private networks. The difference between EDI and electronic mail (E-mail) and private computer networks is that EDI involves standardised messages, like purchase orders and invoices. Since message structures conform to an agreed standard, a company can use a single software program to dialogue with hundreds of different clients or suppliers.

EDI is thus the computer-to-computer transmission of electronic messages according to an agreed standard, often in substitution for traditional paper documents that were previously mailed or sent by telefax. In an era of increased global competition, many companies are using EDI, which enables instantaneous transmission of business data, to help them cope with mountains of information, and ever-tighter deadlines. "Just-in-time" manufacturing, for example, with its premium on quick delivery, depends on EDI.

EDI has also been a key to the recent growth of electronic banking services, port and transport management, and commercial invoicing. Since an EDI message is transmitted instantly, it allows for goods to be ordered and shipped much more quickly, allowing companies to save money on the maintenance of warehouses and inventory. Although the United Nations' EDIFACT standard for EDI is rapidly gaining ascendancy over other regional and industry-specific standards, the American ANSI X12 standard remains important, as do various proprietary standards.

One of the innovations of the ICC's Incoterms 1990 was to provide for the validity of electronic messages, in recognition of the arrival of EDI business practices. Thus, in section A8 of Incoterms, "Proof of delivery, transport document or equivalent electronic message", it is provided that: "Where the seller and the buyer have agreed to communicate electronically, the [usual document] may be replaced by an equivalent electronic data interchange (EDI) message." This mention of EDI avoids any incompatibility between Incoterms and "electronic bill of lading" systems, such as the one set out in the CMI Rules Electronic Bills of Lading or in the BOLERO project (see below).

In some countries, EDI evidence and EDI documents are not formally acceptable. Companies wishing to enter into EDI networks should carefully consider the relevant legal issues, as set out in the *ICC Guide to EDI Interchange Agreements*.

b. **Objectives: Why use EDI?** – When companies using EDI are asked why they use it, they generally list "time savings" and "speed of response", along with "increased order speed" as the most common reasons. The next most important reasons include "cost savings", "greater accuracy", "better customer relations", "better access to data", and "better control of stocks". Interestingly, only 2% of respondents in one European survey listed "reduction of staff" as a reason for EDI. Although many people express a fear that advanced technologies such as EDI will lead to widespread unemployment and a situation where "one black box is talking to another black box", in reality firms that increase efficiency with EDI may end up re-assigning their personnel from boring computer-entry jobs to more challenging positions in sales and customer service.

Many companies have initially adopted EDI in their purchasing, order-taking and invoicing departments because of EDI's ability to reduce costs there. Electronically handled, these business tasks are performed faster, with virtually zero mistakes, and with a neat, computerised record.

It has been estimated that without EDI up to 70% of all computer output produced by a computer is manually re-keyed in elsewhere, with resultant loss of time and multiplication of costly error. To illustrate the type of business problem solved by EDI, consider the case of a supermarket chain that prior to adopting EDI had received 30,000 paper invoices a week, employing 19 people just to key them in to its computer system; a stable percentage of the data entries contained errors, generating disputes and litigation. The inefficiency of these paper-based systems is reflected in studies showing that up to 10% of the cost of goods stems from the manipulation of paper documents alone. This may also explain why reports of rapid returns on EDI investment are fairly common.

EDI specialists contend that EDI is much more than just a cost-cutting tool. In their view, EDI confers essential strategic and competitive advantages. While rudimentary forms of EDI have been around for many years (as in computerised airline reservation systems), two recent developments allowed EDI to make a quantum leap forward in terms of business acceptance. First, evolved standards made EDI more reliable, and secondly, an explosion in the variety of EDI services offered by commercial networks (often called VANs, for Value Added Networks) gave users a wide choice of business tools.

c. **What are the EDI standards?** – With respect to the complex world of standards, in essence, there are two international multi-sectoral standards which have gradually achieved predominance, the official North American standard, ANSI X12, and the United Nations' EDIFACT (EDI for Administration, Commerce and Trade), which has also been endorsed by the International Standards Organisation. Message standards are necessary because of the tremendous diversity of incompatible computer systems in use around the world.

The idea behind EDIFACT was to create a universal structure which allows information elements to pass directly from one computer to another, even if the computer hardware and software are completely different and incompatible. An EDI standard can be compared to a spoken language, in that it is composed of "messages", "message units" and "syntax" in the same way that a language is composed of words, sentences and grammar. The purpose of an EDI standard is for a trading company to send a document, such as an invoice, to any other trading company in such a fashion that the other company's computer will instantly recognise the document as a specific and unique type of document. Because of the central importance of the commercial invoice in international trade, the standard invoice message was one of the first messages approved by the EDIFACT board.

Although EDIFACT continually grows in importance, many proprietary or sectoral standards remain, such as ODETTE for the European automotive industry and TRADACOMS for the UK retailing industry. Most of the proprietary standards have promised to eventually consolidate with EDIFACT. Currently, however, it appears that ANSI X12 and EDIFACT may co-exist for some time, with X12 dominant in the North American and in some Pacific Rim countries, and EDIFACT dominant in Europe. Some experts are not even convinced that the arrival of a single standard is practicable or desirable. They argue that the desire to standardise EDI at all costs runs contrary to commercial realities. It is likely that several major norms will co-exist, although EDIFACT may well become the lingua franca for those sectors that are typically international, such as customs and sea transport. In any event, translation software will make it possible to work with several different norms in a way which is completely transparent for the user.

d. **What EDI standards are used in transport and port management?** – Under the EDIFACT standards a set of messages have been developed specifically for the transport area. These are known as the International Forwarding and Transport Message Group (IFTM). The purpose of these messages is to provide a tool by which service can be improved between the customer and the transport company. EDIFACT Customs messages also enable customs declarations to be made electronically from one's office. It is now possible for a company to keep track of its merchandise throughout the entire transport process, even if the merchandise is in transport several thousand miles away. Many standard messages have been approved for all of the most important transport communications, such as provisional and firm bookings, shipping instructions, contract status (similar to the non-negotiable waybill), and arrival notices.

In terms of port community systems, advanced electronic networks have been in place in many ports for some time, such as at Hamburg, Bremen, Felixstowe, Rotterdam, Marseilles and Singapore. These systems go far towards creating a "paperless" environment with respect to import and export procedures within the port, but international links between ports are still quite rare. The very strong competition between ports may explain why neighbouring ports are not rapidly connecting to each other. However, distant ports such as Singapore and Antwerp have formed electronic linkages.

e. How much EDI is international? – International EDI is still in a rudimentary phase. Europe is likely to be the spawning ground for future international networks, because of expanding intra-European Union trade.

Because of the voluminous red tape and paper documentation required in international trade, EDI could provide great benefits. International trade operates on the basis of a continual exchange of information between trading partners and their transporters, insurers, banks, and other parties.

At the present time, these exchanges of information are evidenced by a paper trail that may involve, in a single international sale, dozens of different documents. In the air cargo industry, one shipment can require several different airway bills. Whenever the shipment changes airlines or passes through customs, somebody has to sit at a keyboard and type in more data, producing more redundant paper, and very often producing several mistakes. It is not surprising that more than 50% of letters of credit are initially rejected because of errors in the documents, and up to 30% of customs documents also contain errors. Yet all of these different documents are based on the same pieces of information. Ideally, an exporter should only have to type the information into his computer once, and the computer would do the rest. Various commercial networks are currently seeking to provide this kind of "end-to-end" electronic international marketplace (see above section), and it is a certainty that a increasingly significant portion of international trade in the future will be conducted entirely over electronic networks.

10.4 The "electronic bill of lading"; Bolero Project

One of the problems commonly encountered in international commodities trade is that shipments arrive before their respective bills of lading. This is because the bill of lading can be traded many times while the ship is in transit, and each time the merchandise is sold the bill of lading must be legally transferred. Since the ship's captain is legally bound to deliver the goods only into the hands of the holder of the bill of lading, a problem can arise if that bill of lading has not yet reached the receiver of the goods. The ship's captain may accept to deliver the goods as against a letter of indemnity from the receiver's bank. However, in this case, the receiver cannot rely on the security of a clean bill of lading.

One of the solutions proposed to the above problem is that of the "electronic bill of lading" system. The basic idea here is to replace the traditional paper bill of lading with an electronic message. An example can be found in the CMI Rules for Electronic Bills of Lading. The CMI Rules revolve around the use of a "private key", which would be unique to each successive "holder", or owner, of the bill of lading. A transfer message from the holder to the carrier, confirmed by the new holder, effectively transfers ownership of the bill of lading, simultaneously generating a new private key.

The BOLERO project began as a large-scale consortium attack on the problem of the electronic bill of lading and was initially supported by the European

Commission. BOLERO has now entered into a cooperative programme with SWIFT, the electronic funds transfer system of the international banking network, to expand the electronic bill of lading concept to include all of the standard documents involved in an international trade transaction.

10.5 The "paperless credit" – electronic letters of credit/trade payments

There is continued interest and activity in international circles as regards transformation or integration of the documentary credit process into an electronic equivalent. Gains in speed and reliability are potentially great, but only if all of the various parties and document-providers in the process (i.e., insurance companies, forwarders, chambers of commerce, inspection agencies, etc.) could be persuaded to adhere to the same standards or become members of the same system. Here, the BOLERO platform may prove to be an essential catalyst.

A typical problem associated with the documentary credit procedure arises when discrepant documents are received so late before the deadline that the beneficiary may be unable to make a corrective submission before the expiry date of the credit. These types of problems could often be avoided if the documents were submitted to the bank electronically. If the electronic "documents" were inexact or insufficient, the bank could notify the parties immediately, and receive immediate corrections or updates. Nobody would have to bring a bundle of papers down to a bank.

Obviously, for such a system to work perfectly, all the relevant documents to a documentary credit transaction would have to be available in electronic form. Of the essential documents required, perhaps the hardest one to transform into an electronic equivalent is the bill of lading, in part because of its legal significance as a document of title. The title to goods is transferred with the bill of lading, so that any electronic system would have to provide for a system which would transfer a single electronic "original" from one holder to the next, without any possibility of duplication or forgery. It would also be necessary, of course, that a great number of transporters, traders and bankers agree to connect via secure lines according to a particular standard. The amount of cross-industry co-operation is daunting, and perhaps explains why the electronic bill of lading, and consequently the paperless credit, have been so long in coming (the United Nations as well as the ICC were already holding intensive discussions on the electronic credit in the mid-1980's; EDIFACT has already prepared standard messages for the various communications underlying credits).

The ICC has created a multi-industry task force called *the Electronic Commerce Project,* with the brief of investigating the most likely scenarios for the introduction of *world-wide electronic trade transactions.* This group is currently exploring, inter alia, guidelines for the registration and certification of digital signatures and the establishment of a global database for electronic legal documents and standard instruments (to be called the "E-terms" Repository). As this book went to press, the ICC was holding discussions with SWIFT, BOLERO and other institutions with a view to finally achieving a breakthrough to the long-awaited implementation of electronic trade practices.

Export–Import Glossary

A.A.A. – *see* American Arbitration Association. **A**

aar – against all risks

acceptance (also, acc.) – The agreement written on a draft and signed by the drawee – who becomes the acceptor – to pay the specified amount on the due date. The term is also applied to the accepted time draft itself. *See* bill of exchange.

acceptance credit – A documentary credit which requires, amongst the documents stipulated, provision of a term bill of exchange. The bill is then generally accepted by by the bank on which it is drawn or discounted. The practical result is that the beneficiary is paid promptly at a discount.

act.wt. – Actual weight.

A/d – *See* After date.

ad valorem duty – A duty assessed as a percentage rate of the value of the imported merchandise. *See* customs duty.

advance payment guarantee/bond – A guarantee that advance payments will be returned if the party having received such payments does not perform its part of the contract.

advising bank – The bank that notifies the exporter of the opening of a letter of credit in his or her favor. The advising bank, usually located in the exporter's country, fully informs the exporter of the conditions of the letter of credit without itself making a payment commitment. *See* generally letter of credit.

ADR – *See* alternative dispute resolution.

after date – Payment on a negotiable instrument, such as a bank draft, becomes due a specified number of days after presentation of the draft.

agent/agency agreement – An agent is an independent person or legal entity which acts on behalf of another (the "principal"). In international transactions, generally refers to a sales representative who prospects on behalf of a foreign principal, earning commission on sales eventually concluded between the principal and the ultimate client; see Foreign sales agent. To be distinguished from sales through employees and subsidiaires – who are not independent, or through distributorship relations, which involve the distributor's buying and re-selling in his own name. Sales agents should also be distinguished from buying or purchasing agents, as the respective rights and obligations are quite different.

agio – The extra amount over and above the market price which is paid in countertrade transactions and results from the particular costs of countertrade.

air waybill (airbill) (AWB) – A non-negotiable shipping document used by the airlines for air freight. It is a contract for carriage that includes carrier conditions, such as limits of liability and claims procedures. In addition, it contains shipping instructions to airlines, a description of the commodity and applicable transportation charges. It performs the functions of a bill of lading in land surface transport. *See* bill of lading.

A **all risks (AR)** – A type of insurance coverage providing somewhat more than the minimum coverage, at a premium above the base amount paid under a particular policy. Unfortunately, «all risks « coverage does not in fact cover *all risks* – thus, for example, coverage of war, riots and strikes is not usually included; moreover, there is no standard nomenclature for all risks coverage. Traders should understand what exactly is covered in all risks coverage, and decide whether or not they need additional coverage, before agreeing to such a term.

alternative dispute resolution (ADR) – A general term for a variety of dispute-resolution mechanisms which may be used as alternatives to traditional litigation before governmental courts or tribunals. May be said to include such techniques as conciliation, mediation, arbitration, re-negotiation, and mini-trial.

American Arbitration Association (A.A.A.) – Perhaps the world's largest arbitration forum and institution; the great bulk of cases handled under its rules and procedures are domestic US cases, although the AAA does have specific rules for international cases.

AN – Arrival notice.

applicant – In the documentary credit process, normally the buyer or importer, who applies (thus, the applicant) for a letter of credit in favour of the beneficiary, the seller.

AQ – Any quantity.

arbitration – A process of dispute resolution in which a neutral third party (arbitrator) renders a decision after a hearing at which both parties have an opportunity to be heard. Arbitration may be voluntary or contractually required. The advantages of arbitration – compared to litigation – are neutrality, confidentiality, reduced costs, faster procedures and the arbitrator's expertise. Internationally, the main arbitration body is the International Chamber of Commerce, other arbitration institutions include the London Court of International Arbitration, the Stockholm Court of Arbitration, and the American Arbitration Association (AAA).

ATA Carnet – "Admission Temporaire/Temporary Admission". An international customs document for the temporary duty-free admission of goods into a country for display, demonstration or similar purposes. ATA Carnets are issued by National chambers of commerce, which guarantee the payment of duties to local customs authorities should the goods not be ultimately re-exported.

Av. – Average

aval – A bank's guarantee to a pay a bill of exchange. An irrevocable, unconditional promise to pay on the due date. The use of avals is common in the practice of forfaiting.

AWB – *See* Air waybill.

banker's acceptance – A bill of exchange accepted by a bank usually for the **B** purpose of financing a sale of goods to or by the bank's customer. The bill may be drawn, for example, by an exporter on the importer's bank and be sold on the open market at a discount. *See* bill of exchange.

back-to-back credit – A commercial device under which a middleman uses a documentary credit to open a second credit in favour of a supplier. Should be distinguished from a transferable credit. *See* letters of credit, also Chapter 6.

BAF – *See* Bunker adjustment factor.

bank guarantee – Contract between a bank as *guarantor* and a *beneficiary* in which the bank commits itself to pay a certain sum under certain, specified conditions. Thus, a *demand* guarantee is one in which the bank agrees to pay against the simple written demand of the beneficiary.

barter – The direct exchange of goods and/or services for other goods and/or services without the use of money and without the involvement of a third party. Barter is an important means of trade with countries using currency that is not readily convertible. *See* countertrade.

basis points – One thousandths; 1/100 of 1%; i.e., 100 basis points is equal to 1 %.

B/B – Breakbulk (cargo).

B/D – Bank draft.

beneficiary – Documentary credit context: generally, the exporter-seller; the one on whose behalf the documentary credit is opened by the applicant (the importer-buyer). Guarantee/bond context: the one who will receive payment under the bond should the specified documents or contingencies be produced.

Berne Union – International Union of Credit and Investment Insurers.

B/G – Bonded goods; *see* Bonded warehouse.

bill of exchange (B/E) – A draft. An unconditional order addressed by the exporter to the importer for the payment of a specific sum. A sight draft requires immmediate payment, while usance or term drafts indicate payment at a specified future date.

bill of lading (B/L) – A document issued when goods are entrusted to a shipping company for carriage. It can serve as a formal *receipt* for the goods by the shipowner, a memorandum of the *contract of carriage*, and documentary evidence of *control over the goods*. The holder or consignee of the bill has the right to claim delivery of the goods from the shipping company when they arrive at the port of destination. Bills of lading may be negotiable (*order B/L*) or non-negotiable (*straight B/L*). Bills of lading may also be distinguished by the mode of transport used for the shipment. *See marine bill of lading, multimodal transport bill of lading, air waybill, railway consignment note and sea waybill.*

B/L terminology:

• *ocean/marine* – the classic B/L, a negotiable instrument used for goods shipped on board oceangoing vessels.

• *on board/shipped* – a B/L evidencing the loading on board of cargo in good condition.

- *received for shipment* – a B/L which only evidences that goods have been received, not that they have been loaded on board; common with container shipments delivered to port terminal; must be converted by subsequent «on board» notation if shipper needs an «on board» or «shipped» document for payment under a letter of credit.

- *clean* – a B/L/ which contains no notation indicating that the goods have been wholly or partially lost/damaged.

- *dirty/foul/claused* – a B/L with a notation to the effect that the goods have been partially/wholly lost or damaged.

- *straight* – a non-negotiable B/L; consignee only needs to identify himself to pick up the goods.

- *order* – a negotiable B/L, issued "to the order" of a particular party, commonly the shipper

- *through* – a B/L used when shipment will involve successive transport stages with different carriers.

- *direct* – a B/L for direct transport between loading and discharging ports.

- *multimodal/combined transport* – a B/L issued to cover transport involving successive stages via different transport modes, e.g., road transport followed by sea followed again by road transport.

- *FIATA FBL (FBL)* – a standard-form B/L issued by a freight forwarder; considered under the UCP 500 – along with other forwarder bills in which the agents accepts full responsibility as a carrier – as acceptable as a clean on board B/L issued by a carrier.

- *house* – a B/L issued by a forwarder in its own name («house») covering grouped consignments.

- *freight pre-paid* – a B/L indicating on it that the freight has been paid.

- *liner* – a B/L issued subject to the terms and conditions of a shipping line.

- *short-form* – a B/L which does not contain the full terms and conditions of the contract of carriage; instead, it contains an abbreviated version of the carrier's condition, with a reference to the full set of conditions.

- *stale* – a B/L which is presented late (for documentary credit purposes, a B/L must be presented within a certain number of days after shipment).

- *full set of originals* – for documentary credit or collection purposes, the buyer may require the seller to produce a full set (commonly up to three) of signed originals – that is, B/L's which bear the original signature of the ship's master or agent.

- *waybill* – a non-negotiable transport document.

B   BOLERO – Originally a system for transmission of electronic bills of lading. In the process of being expanded by SWIFT into an electronic platform for transmission of all trade documents.

bonded warehouse – A warehouse authorised by customs authorities for storage of goods on which payment of duties is deferred until the goods are removed for domestic consumption. If the goods are re-exported, no duty has to be paid at all. *See* foreign trade zone.

breakbulk (BB) – Non-containerised cargo which is grouped or consolidated **B** for shipment, and then is later broken down, sub-divided or distributed at a further destination point. Breakbulk cargo is often unitized cargo on pallets or packed in boxes; specialised *breakbulk vessels* tend to carry their own loading/ unloading machinery.

bunker adjustment factor (also, BAF) – A surcharge charged by ocean carriers to account for fluctuations in the cost of shipping fuel, which is known as *bunker fuel.*

buy-back (compensation) – A form of countertrade under which exporters of, e.g., heavy equipment, technology, or plant facilities agree to purchase a certain percentage of the output of the new facility once it is in production. *See* countertrade.

CAD – Cash against documents. **C**

call – A demand for payment under a loan or guarantee. In the case of demand guarantees, the abusive resort to the guarantee (i.e., in the absence of non-compliance by the principal) is sometime referred to as an *unfair call.*

CBD – Cash before delivery.

certificate of inspection (also, certificate of quality) – A document certifying the quality, quantity and/or price of a given shipment of goods. The inspection certificate is often required by buyers, especially those paying via documentary credit, from sellers, in order to assure that the goods are of contract quality. Generally, the buyer will designate a neutral, independent inspection company.

certificate of origin – A document certifying the country of origin of specified goods. It is often required by the customs authorities of a country as part of the entry process, for instance to grant preferential tariff treatment on imports of goods originating in a particular country. Such certificates are usually obtained through a semi-official organization in the country of origin, such as a local chamber of commerce or a consular office.

c & f (C&F) – Warning: common but non-standard version of Cost and Freight – CFR Incoterms 1990 (Cost and Freight); see Incoterms 1990.

CFR – Cost and Freight. *See* Incoterms 1990.

charter party – A contract under which a *charterer* agrees to rent/hire the use of a ship or part of a ship from a *shipowner.* The charterer in some cases will be empowered to issue his own bills of lading, known as *charter party bills* of lading, subject to the conditions of the original charter party contract. Note that the charter party itself is not a bill of lading, but rather a contract between the shipowner and charterer under which the shipowner hires out all or part of his ship for a given period to the charterer.

CIA – Cash in Advance.

CIF (also, c.i.f.) – Cost, Insurance and Freight. *See* Incoterms 1990.

C **CIF & C** – Cost, insurance, freight and commission. (also, CIF & I – Cost, insurance, freight and interest); and CIF & CI (Cost, insurance, freight, commission and interest). *Warning*: these are variants on the standard Incoterms 1990 term, so the additional abbreviations are not covered by international standard definitions. Traders may, therefore, wish to inquire and expressly stipulate as to the precise requirements implied by the additional "C" or "CI".

CIP – Carriage and Insurance Paid To...(named point). *See* Incoterms 1990.

claused bill of lading – A *claused*, or *foul* bill of lading contains notations or remarks as to defects in the goods and/or packaging. *See* Bill of lading and Clean bill of lading.

cld. – Cleared (through customs).

clean bill of lading – A bill of lading indicating that the goods were received in apparent good order and condition. A clean bill is one which contains no notatins of defect, damage or loss, and is signed by the carrier or its authorised representative. Note that a clean bill does not have to have any positive affirmation or mention to the effect, e.g., "clean bill" or "merchandise in good order". If a bill does contain a notation of damaged or missing merchandise, the bill of lading is called "claused", "foul" or "dirty". *See* bill of lading and claused bill of lading.

CMR – International road transport convention.

collecting bank – In a documentary collection, the bank acting as an agent for the seller's bank in collecting payment or acceptance of a time draft from the buyer to be forwarded to the seller's bank (the remitting bank). *See* documentary collection.

commercial invoice – A document containing a record of the transaction between a seller (exporter) and a buyer (importer), containing information such as a complete listing and description of the goods including prices, discounts and quantities, and the delivery and payment terms. A commercial invoice is often used by governments to determine the true value of goods for the assessment of customs duties, and must therefore conform to the regulations of the importing country.

commission agent – A foreign sales representative who is paid a percentage of the sales he or she generates. See also Agent and Foreign sales agent.

common carrier – In some jurisdictions, a legal term referring to carriers who offer transport services to the general consumer or business public. In contrast, for example, to carriers who may work as employees, sub-contractors or agents of the manufacturer/shipper.

compound duty – A combination of both a specific rate of duty and an ad valorem rate of duty. Whereas specific duties are based on factors such as weight or quantity, ad valorem duties are based on the value of the goods. *See* customs duty.

conference – (also, steamship conference, shipping conference) A group of steamship companies or shipping *lines* which have associated to offer regular service on specific routes at publicly-announced prices. Conferences generally offer specific rebates for regular or high-volume shipments. Shipment by conference lines is sometimes referred to as *liner* shipping and the freight rates are referred to as "*liner terms*". Shipping lines which are not members of a conference for a particular route are known as *outsiders, independent lines,* or *non-conference liners. See also* Liner terms.

confirmed letter of credit – A documentary credit issued by a foreign bank **C** which has been confirmed by another bank (usually a local bank or an international leading bank), the *confirmation* consisting in: an additional irrevocable undertaking to pay according to the terms of the credit.

confirming bank – In letter of credit transactions, the bank which adds its own irrevocable undertaking for payment in addition to that given by the issuing bank. The confirming bank is usually located in the exporter's country. *See* letter of credit.

consignee – In international export transactions: the intended receiver of a cargo shipment. The named person or legal entity having the right to claim the merchandise from the carrier at destination, and generally recognised as the legal owner for customs purposes.

In international representation or distributorship relations (viz., *consignment sales*): the holder and re-seller of merchandise, who receives payment in the form of commission or a discount as and when sales are made but does not have to purchase the goods in advance.

consular declaration – A description of goods to be shipped, made in official form to a consulate.

consular invoice – An invoice covering a shipment of goods certified by the consul of the country for which the merchandise is destined. The invoice is used by customs officials of the country to verify the value, quantity, and nature of the merchandise imported to determine the import duty. In addition, the export price may be examined in the light of the current market price in the exporter's country to ensure that dumping is not taking place.

counterpurchase – Counterpurchase is the agreement of an exporter to purchase a quantity of unrelated goods or services from a country in exchange for and approximate in value to the goods exported.

countertrade – All foreign trade transactions resulting from exporters' commitments to take products from the importers or from their respective countries in full or part payment for their exports. Countertrade is typical of trade with East European and less developed countries, which often suffer from a lack of foreign exchange and/or credit facilities. Countertrade transactions include barter, buy-back or compensation, counterpurchase, offset requirements, and swap. *See* respective terms.

contingency insurance (or "difference in conditions") – Insurance coverage taken out by one party to an international transaction to complement and fill in any gaps in the coverage taken out by the counterparty. Thus, the open account exporter on FOB Incoterms does not have an obligation to insure the goods during the main international transport, but may wish in any event to take out contingency insurance so that if the goods are lost or damaged there will be no loss to the buyer (such a loss might lead to disagreements or disruption of commercial relations with the buyer, even if the seller was not legally at fault).

C **correspondent bank** – A bank which performs certain operations on behalf of another bank, usually in a different country. Correspondent banks hold deposits with each other, and accept and collect items on a reciprocal basis. It is through networks of correspondent banks that trade banks are able to service and support international business transactions.

courtage (French) – Brokerage; brokerage fee.

cover note (also, broker's cover note) – An insurance document indicating coverage of a particular shipment under an open cover policy. To be distinguished, particularly as regards presentation under a documentary credit, from an insurance *policy* or an insurance *certificate*.

CPT – Carriage Paid To...(named point). *See* Incoterms.

credit risk insurance – An exporter's insurance against nonpayment by the importer.

c/s – Case(s).

CSC – Container service charge.

currency future – A contract for the future delivery of a commodity, currency or security on a specific date. In contrast to forward contracts, futures contracts are for standard quantities and for standard periods of time and are primarily traded on an exchanges. Forward transactions enable importers and exporters who will have to make, or will receive, payment in a foreign currency at a future time to protect themselves against the risk of fluctuations in the spot rate.

currency option – The contractually-agreed right to buy (call option) or to sell (put option) a specific amount of a foreign currency at a predetermined price on a specific date (European option) or up to a future date (American option).

customs broker – Licensed agent or broker whose function is to handle the process of clearing goods through customs for importers.

customs duty – Tax levied by the government on goods crossing the customs border, usually a tax imposed on imports. Duties, or tariffs, are either based on the value of the goods (ad valorem duties), some other factors such as weight or quantity (specific duties), or a combination of value and other factors (compound duties).

customs union – An association between two or more countries whereby they eliminate tariffs and other import restrictions on each other's goods and establish a common tariff on the goods from all other countries. The European Community is the best known example of a customs union.

cw – Commercial weight.

CWO – Cash with order.

cwt – hundredweight; unit of measurement.

D **date draft** – A draft which matures a specified number of days after issuance.

DAF – Delivered at Frontier. *See* Incoterms.

D/D – Delivered.

ddc (also D.D.C.) – Sometimes said to be "delivered destination charges", **D** referring to various miscellaneous charges in the port of destination; alternatively said to refer to dispatch money at discharge; *see* Dispatch money.

DDP – Delivered Duty Paid. *See* Incoterms.

DDU – Delivered Duty Unpaid. *See* Incoterms.

deadfreight – Freight charge to paid even when shipment was not made, owing to failure by shipper or charterer to actually ship goods in the shipping space for which a reservation was made.

deadweight – Total carrying capacity of a vessel.

deck cargo – Goods shipped on the deck of a ship rather than in its holds. Since deck cargo is more exposed to the elements, traders may wish to stipulate that goods not be carried on deck (except in such cases as transport of hazardous materials, in which case carriage on deck may be mandatory).

deferred air freight – Air freight offered at cheaper rates for non-urgent shipments.

del credere – As relates to international commercial agency relationships: a *del credere agent* is one who guarantees the ability to pay of prospective clients he has brought to the principal; in exchange, the del credere agent is usually accorded a higher percentage commision than is a regular agent.

As relates to risk in general: del crcdcrc risk is the risk that a party will be unable to meet its financial obligations.

del. – Delivery.

delivery order – An order, commonly addressed to a terminal superintendent or warehouse manager, directing the release of specified cargo to a particular receiver. The order may in some cases be issued by seller, shipper or consignee, while in other contexts the order will be issued by the shipping line or carrier. Commonly, a delivery order directs delivery of part of a larger consignment, which is itself covered by a single bill of lading; i.e., the issuance of several delivery orders «splits up» the cargo covered by the bill of lading. In any event, delivery orders should be clearly distinguished from bills of lading: the delivery order is not a negotiable document, nor does it evidence receipt of the goods, nor does it contain the provisions of the transport contract under which the goods were shipped.

demand guarantee – A guarantee usually issued by a bank, under which the beneficiary is only required to make a *demand* in order to receive payment. In contrast to the *conditional* or *suretyship* guarantee – which require the beneficiary to provide proof of the principal's default, a demand guarantee only requires that the beneficiary make a simple demand, and therefore this latter type of guarantee is relatively risky in terms of exposure to an unjustified demand on the part of the beneficiary. Some protection against such an unfair demand can be obtained by making the guarantee subject to the Uniform Rules for Demand Guarantees (URDG 458).

demurrage – The extra charges paid to a shipowner or carrier when a specified period for loading/unloading is exceeded. The demurrage may, depending on the context, be paid by the charterer or shipper.

D **DEQ** – Delivered Ex Quai. *See* Incoterms.

DES – Delivered Ex Ship. *See* Incoterms.

destuffing – Unloading goods from a container; *see also* Stripping, Devanning.

devanning – Unloading goods from a container; *see also* Stripping, De-stuffing.

discrepancy – Documentary credit context: a discrepancy arises when documents presented under a documentary credit do not conform to the terms of the credit; generally, an error, contradiction or omission related to the documents constitutes the discrepancy. The bank will refuse to pay against the documents unless the applicant (buyer) agrees to amend the credit or otherwise waive objections to payment under the credit.

discount – The purchase by a bank or finance house of a bill of exchange at face value less interest. It is used as a financing tool, should the holder of an accepted bill of exchange require the money before the bill matures. *See* bill of exchange.

dispatch money (also, despatch) – An incentive payment offered by a shipowner to a charterer in exchange for completing loading or unloading in less time than is specified in the charter party contract (this time is often calculated as a number of "lay days"). *See also* Charter party, Demurrage.

distributor – An independent person or legal entity which sells goods locally on behalf of a foreign principal. Distributors can be distinguished from agents because distributors buy the goods in their own name, then re-sell them at prices which they have some liberty to set. Distributorship is frequently based on a contract which grants the distributor exclusivity for a specific territory. *See* for comparison, foreign sales agent.

Dk. – Dock.

D/O – *See* Delivery order.

dock receipt – A document certifying receipt of goods by the international carrier at the port of departure.

documentary collection – A method of payment under which the shipping documents relating to a particular cargo are released to the importer on payment (documents against payment: "D/P") or acceptance (documents against acceptance: "D/A") of a documentary draft drawn on him by the exporter. Under collections, the exporter presents a draft together with shipping documents to a bank (the remitting bank) in his country, which then forwards the documents and draft to the collecting bank in the buyer's country. The documents enabling the buyer to take possession of the goods will only be released by the collecting bank when the buyer either pays or accepts the draft.

documents against acceptance (D/A) – The documents transferring title to goods are delivered to the buyer (drawee) only upon the buyer's acceptance of the attached draft guaranteeing payment at a later date. *See* documentary collection.

documents against payment (D/P) – In the case of a sight draft, the documents transferring title to goods are released to the buyer/importer only against cash payment. *See* documentary collection.

documentary credit (D/C) – *See* Letter of credit.

door to door – A transport service covering carriage from the seller's premises to the buyer''s premises.. Note that this term refers to a *freight charge* in a *carriage contract* between a *carrier* and a *shipper,* and thus is distinct from the issue of the Incoterm chosen in the contract of sale (an agreement between seller and buyer). Depending on the circumstances of the transaction, it could be possible to quote prices on either EXW, FCA, CPT, CIP, DDU, or DDP Incoterms in conjunction with so-called "house to house" transport services. Attention should be given to the inclusion of loading/unloading charges in the "house to house" rate, especially in comparison with the responsibility under the respective Incoterm for loading or unloading. The shipper should make sure that the transport service corresponds to the contractual obligations under Incoterms. It is sometimes said that "door to door" services imply that loading and unloading are *not* included in the freight charge, but this is not a standard rule and traders should inquire in each particular case. Door to door is sometimes used synonymously with *house to house,* but it is claimed by some that there is a distinction between the two, namely that "house to house" only refers to rental rates for containers from container yard to container yard; *see* house to house.

draft (*see also* Bills of Exchange) – An unconditional order in writing, signed by a person (drawer) such as a buyer, and addressed to another person (drawee), typically a bank, ordering the drawee to pay a stated sum of money to yet another person (payee), often a seller. A draft, also called a bill of exchange, may be payable to a named person or his order (order draft), or to bearer (bearer draft).

　　The most common versions of a draft are the *sight draft,* which is payable on presentation or demand, and the *time (or usance) draft,* which is payable at a future fixed (specific) or determinable (30, 60, 90 days etc.) date. Should the beneficiary under a time draft require the money before the bill matures, he may *discount* his claim for immediate payment with his bank.

drawee – The individual or firm on whom a draft is drawn. The drawee is instructed by the drawer to pay a specified sum of money to, or to the order of, the payee, or to bearer. In a documentary collection, the drawee is generally the buyer. *See* bill of exchange.

drawer – The individual or firm that issues or signs a draft, instructing the drawee to pay a specified sum of money to, or to the order of, a named person (payee), or to bearer. In the case of a draft to one's own order, the drawer is also the payee. Like the indorser(s), the drawer is secondarily liable on the draft. In a documentary collection, the drawer is the seller. *See* bill of exchange.

D/S – Days after sight (payment term often used in conjunction with bank drafts and documentary credits).

dumping – The practice of selling a product in a foreign market at an unfairly low price (a price which is lower than the cost in the home market, or which is lower than the cost of production) in order to gain a competitive advantage over other suppliers. Dumping is considered an unfair trade practice under the GATT and World Trade Organisation agreements; it is regulated by national governments through the imposition of anti-dumping duties, in some cases calculated to equal the difference between the product's price in the importing and the exporting country.

E **ECU** – European Currency Unit.

EDI (edi) – *See* Electronic data interchange.

Electronic data interchange (EDI) – the computer-to-computer transmission of business messages (such as purchase orders, invoices, booking instructions, etc.) according to an agreed standard (such as EDIFACT).

EMC – See export management company.

est. – Estimated.

E.T.A. – Estimated time of arrival.

E.T.D. – Estimated time of departure.

E.T.S. – Estimated time of sailing.

EU – European Union.

Eurocurrency – A currency being used or traded outside the country which issued the currency. The most widely used Eurocurrency is the Eurodollar.

European Currency Unit (ECU) – The ECU is the European Union's accounting unit and is a popular private financial instrument. It is expected that the ECU will give way to the EURO in the 1999–2002 period.

export credit insurance – Special insurance coverage for exporters to protect against commercial and political risks of making an international sale. Export credit insurance is available from insurance underwriters as well as from government agencies. Examples of well known public export credit agencies include the U.S. Eximbank, the U.K. Export Credits Guarantee Department, and France's COFACE.

export broker – An individual or firm that brings together buyers and sellers for a fee without taking part in actual sales transactions.

export credit insurance – Exporter's insurance, provided either by a private supplier or government agency, against non-payment by importer and certain other risks depending on the type of policy.

export license – A government document granting the "Licensee" the right to export a specified quantity of a commodity to a specified country. This license may be required in some countries for most or all exports and in other countries only under special circumstances.

export management company (EMC) – A private firm serving as the export department for several manufacturers, soliciting and transacting export business on behalf of its clients in return for a commission, salary, or retainer plus commission.

E&OE – Errors and Omissions Excepted: when appended to a signature on a shipping document, indicates a disclaimer of responsibility for spelling, typographical or clerical errors.

Ex factory – Warning: this is a non-standard trade term, a variation of the preferred formulation: *EXW Incoterms 1990.*

EXW – *See* Ex Works. *See* Incoterms.

Ex Works – *See* Incoterms.

factoring – In the export trade: the financial service consisting in the granting of **F**
a cash advance against accounts receivable from foreign customers. More generally,
a range of financing and risk management services offered by specialised firms,
called *factors*, to sellers/exporters, particularly those who deal with a stream of
low-value, short-term foreign accounts receivable. The exporter transfers title to
its foreign accounts receivable to a factoring house in exchange for cash at a *discount*
from the face value. Other basic services offered by factors include: foreign credit
risk assessment, collection of overdue foreign accounts, and administration of
accounting ledgers.

FAS – Free Alongside Ship. *See* Incoterms

FAK – *See* Freight all kinds.

FB – Freight bill.

F& D. – Freight and demurrage.

FCA – Free Carrier. *See* Incoterms.

FCL – Full container load.

FO – Free out; see Free in and out.

FOB – Free on Board. *See* Incoterms.

fob airport – Warning: no longer a valid Incoterm, see FCA, Incoterms 1990.
Free on board airport; a trade or delivery term used when delivery is effected at
an airport. It was withdrawn from use as a valid Incoterm because it was felt that
the term was the source of much potential disagreement, especially as regards
allocation of customs clearance and export handling charges.

f.o.c. – Free of charge.

f.o.d. – Free of damage.

FOR – Free on rail. Warning: no longer a valid Incoterm, but still used by some
traders. The problem is that there is on occasion confusion as to whether it only
applies to rail shipments. The suitable term from Incoterms 1990 is FCA; *see*
Incoterms.

FOT – Free on truck. Warning: no longer a valid Incoterm, but still used by some
traders. The problem is that there is on occasion confusion as to whether it applies
to motor vehicle or to rail shipments. The suitable term from Incoterms 1990 is
FCA; *see* Incoterms.

force majeure – A clause which protects the parties to a contract in the event
that a part of the contract cannot be performed due to causes which are outside
the control of the parties and could not be avoided by exercise of due care.
These causes may be earthquakes, floods, storms, or war.

foreign sales agent – An individual or firm that serves as the foreign
representative of a domestic supplier and seeks sales abroad for the supplier.

foreign trade zone (FTZ) – Special commercial and industrial areas in or near
ports of entry where foreign and domestic merchandise may be brought in without
being subject to payment of customs duties. Merchandise, including raw materials,
components, and finished goods, may be stored, sold, exhibited, repacked,
assembled, sorted, graded, cleaned or otherwise manipulated prior to reexport
or entry into the national customs authority. Duties are imposed on the

merchandise (or items manufactured from the merchandise) only when the goods pass from the zone into an area of the country subject to the Customs Authority. Foreign trade zones are also called free trade zones, free zones, free ports or bonded warehouses.

F forfaiting – The purchase by the forfaiter of an exporter's accounts receivable which are based on negotiable instruments such as bills of exchange and promissory notes. In contrast to factoring, forfaiting involves a series of independent, medium to longer term obligations of higher value. Since the forfaiter purchases the bills on a non-recourse basis, he assumes both commercial and political risk.

forward rate – The price of a foreign currency which is bought or sold for delivery and payment at a fixed future time, usually 30, 60 or 90 days. Forward transactions enable importers and exporters who will have to make, or will receive, payment in a foreign currency at a future time to protect themselves against the risk of fluctuations in the spot rate.

franchising – A system based on the licensing of the right to duplicate a successful business format or industrial process. The franchisor (licensor) permits the franchisee (licensee) to employ its business processes, trademarks, trade secrets and knowhow in a contractually-specified manner for the marketing of goods or services. The franchisor usually supports the operation of the franchisee's business through the provision of advertising, accounting, training, and related services and in many instances also supplies products required by the franchisee for the operation of the franchise. The franchisee, in return, pays certain moneys to the franchisor (in terms of fees and percentage commissions) and agrees to respect contractual provisions dealing, inter alia, with quality of performance. The two principal kinds of franchise contracts are *master franchise* agreements, under which the franchisor grants another party the right to sub-franchise within a given territory, and *direct* or *unit franchise* agreements, which are direct contracts between the franchisor or sub-franchisor and the operator of the franchise unit.

franco (French; European shipping) – "Free delivered": Shipper pays all charges to a particular point. <u>Warning</u>: non-standard term; for preferred formulation, see *Incoterms 1990*.

Free in and out (F.I.O.) – A transport or freight term which indicates that loading/discharging costs are not included in the freight; in the charter party context this means that loading/discharging are not the shipowner's responsibility – the charterer is responsible for loading/discharging. Also possible to use either *Free in (FI)* or *Free out (FO)* independently. Also used with additioned of *stowed* and/or *trimmed*: e.g., *FIOS*, or *FIOST*.

free trade area – A group of countries which agree to eliminate tariffs and other import restrictions on each other's goods, while each participating country applies its own independent schedule of tariffs to imports from countries that are not members. Well known examples are the North American Free Trade Association (NAFTA), the European Free Trade Association (EFTA), and Mercosur.

freight all kinds (FAK) – Freight rate applicable to all types of goods.

freight forwarder – Assembles and consolidates small shipments into a single lot and assumes, in some cases, full responsibility for transportation of such property from point of receipt to point of destination.

Hague Rules – International Convention for the Unification of Certain Rules **H** relating to Bills of Lading – Brussels Convention of 1924 – A set of rules for international transport contained in an international treaty first published in 1924 and subsequently implemented by the greater part of world trading nations. The Hague Rules were revised and updated in the so-called Hague Visby Rules, published in 1968, which have not received so universal an implementation as their predecessors.

Hague-Visby Rules – Set of rules amending the Hague rules, published in 1968, which have not been implemented by as many countries as the predecessor Hague Rules.

house air waybill (house AWB; or, HAWB) – A transport document issued by an air freight consolidator.

house bill of lading (house B/L) – A bill of lading issued by a freight forwarder. Often covers a consignment of parcels from various shippers that has been grouped or consolidated by the forwarder. The forwarder may, for example, receive a single groupage bill of lading from the carrier, then issue a series of *house B/L's* to the respective shippers.

house to house – This term generally refers to a container yard to container yard (CY/CY) shipment (in which case it may be used merely to quote the rental rate for the container itself), but is also used in some cases synonymously with «door to door», a term which more generally refers to overall transport services from seller's premises to buyer's premises. *See* door to door.

IATA – International Air Transport Association, air transport industry association **I** and issuer of standard air waybill form.

IBCC – International Bureau of Chambers of Commerce; an ICC-administered network of national, local and municipal chambers of commerce. Administrator of *ATA Carnet* system for temporary duty-free admission of industrial/commercial samples.

IBCC-Net – An international data bank for the posting of commercial offers, including the purchase and sale of consumer goods and commodities; operates through networks of chambers of commerce.

ICC – International Chamber of Commerce, the world business organisation, headquartered in Paris, with approximately 7000 members in more than 140 countries.

ICC Arbitration – Refers either to *ICC Rules for Conciliation and Arbitration* or the process of submittting an arbitral complaint to the *ICC Court of International Arbitration*.

ICPO – Irrevocable Corporate Purchase Order; an offer to buyer stated goods under specified terms and conditions; for example of misuse.

Incoterms 1990 – A set of 13 internationally-standard *trade terms* (also known as *delivery terms*) Incoterms 1990 allows the parties to designate a point at which the costs and risks of transport are precisely divided between the seller and the buyer. Incoterms also allocate responsibility for customs clearance/duties between the parties. Since Incoterms are not law but are contractual standard terms, they do not apply to a given transaction unless the parties specifically *incorporate* them as by referring to Incoterms, e.g.: "100£/tonne Liverpool Incoterms 1990" (in exceptional cases, Incoterms apply regardless of explicit mention in the contract, if there is a custom of trade or prior course of dealing which indicates reliance on Incoterms, or if the local jurisprudence creates a presumption in favour of applicability of Incoterms). Incoterms are elements of the contract of sale, which may be derived from the seller's tender or pro forma invoice. Thus, Incoterms only apply to the seller and buyer, one of whom will assume the role of shipper and enter into a contract of carriage. The contract of carriage should dovetail with the Incoterm in terms of allocation of transport costs and risks, but this will depend on the shipper giving precise directions to the carrier to ship according to the constraints of the given Incoterm. For a definition of the 13 currently valid Incoterms, their standard abbreviations, see Chapter 4 of text.

I **Inland clearance depot (inland dry port)** – A combination transport terminal and customs clearance center.

Institute clauses – Standard international transport insurance clauses, published by the Institute of London Underwriters. The *Institute Cargo Clauses* are 3 sets of clauses providing different levels of protection: the "A" Clauses correspond to the general notion which is commonly referred to in the trade as "all risks" coverage, while clauses "B" and "C" indicate a lower level of coverage and a greater number of exclusions.

inv. – Invoice.

ISO 9000 – International production quality standards established by ISO (International Standards Organisation). Certification that an exporter meets ISO 9000 manufacturing standards, for example, may be a minimum requirement for competing in certain markets or for certain tenders.

issuing bank – The buyer's bank which establishes a letter of credit at the request of the buyer, in favor of the beneficiary (seller/exporter). It is also called the buyer's bank or opening bank. *See* letter of credit.

L **laydays/laytime** – The time allowed by the shipowner to the charterer or shipper in which to load or discharge the cargo. May be expressed in days or hours, or tonnes per day. Laydays may be set in *running days* (every calendar day), *working days* (excludes Sundays and holidays observed by the port), or *weather working days* (excludes in addition days where operations are prevented by bad weather). It may be contractually provided that if the charterer or shipper loads/unloads more quickly than is necessary, he will be eligible for payment of an incentive called *dispatch* money; if the loading/unloading time is excessive, however, the charterer or shipper may have to pay a penalty known as *demurrage*.

LCL – Less than container load. Refers to shipments of goods which will have to be packed together with other consignments in order to fill up a container.

LCL/FCL – A way of quoting container freight rates in which the carrier agrees to pack the container at the outset (LCL) but the unpacking at destination must be carried out by the receiver or consignee. A common approach for buyers who wish to consolidate small purchases from multiple suppliers in a foreign market into container shipments.

LCL/LCL – A way of quoting container freight rates in which the carrier agrees to pack the container on departure as well as unpack the container at destination.

ldg. – Loading.

letter of credit (L/C; also, documentary credit, D/C) – A document issued by the importer's bank stating its commitment to honour a draft, or otherwise pay, on presentation of specific documents by the exporter within a stated period of time. The documents the importer requires in the credit usually include, at a minimum, a commercial invoice and clean bill of lading, but may also comprise a certificate of origin, consular invoice, inspection certificate, and other documents. The most widely used type of credit in international trade is the *irrevocable* credit, which cannot be changed or canceled without the consent of both the importer and the exporter. In a *confirmed* irrevocable credit, the *confirming bank* adds its irrevocable commitment to pay the beneficiary (the confirmation is an additional guarantee of payment).

Types of L/C:

• *irrevocable* – a credit which cannot be retracted or revoked once the beneficiary has been notified; there is a presumption under the UCP 500 that a credit is irrevocable.

• *advised* – a credit the opening of which the beneficiary has been informed by a local bank.

• *confirmed* – a credit which has received an additional guarantee of payment by a local or highly reputable bank.

• *back-to-back* – a system utilised by middlemen/intermediaries to finance a single transaction through the use of two L/C's opened in succession (e.g.,"back-to-back") in order to permit the middleman/broker to use the proceeds from the first credit to pay off his supplier under the second credit.

• *transferable* – an L/C which allows the beneficiary to make part or all of his credit payable to another supplier; used in middleman/brokerage contexts; distinguishable from back-to-back L/C's because the transferable credit requires the knowledge and authorization of the importer (applicant/principal).

• *revolving* – a credit which can be drawn against repeatedly by the beneficiary; can take a variety of different forms, depending on whether the credit is limited in terms of time, number of possible drafts, maximum quantity per draft, or maximum total quantity.

• *cumulative revolving L/C* – revolving L/C under which unused amounts can be carried forward and become available under the next draft.

• *red clause* – an L/C allowing payments of advances to the beneficiary (originating in the wool trade in Australia, these clauses used to printed in red ink).

• *deferred* – an L/C under which payment by the importer is to take place a specified time after his receipt of the shipping documents.

• *sight* – an L/C under which the beneficiary is entitled to present a *sight draft* or *sight bill of exchange,* which is a call for immediate payment upon acceptance of shipping documents.

- *import* – an L/C used to finance importation of goods.

- *standby* – akin to a *demand guarantee* or bank guarantee, the standby L/C is generally used to assure performance or payment by the counterparty.

L letter of indemnity (LOI) – A document commonly used in international trade to allow a carrier to release goods to a receiver who is not yet in possession of the bill of lading (exceedingly common in the oil trade, for example). The letter of indemnity is, in essence, a guarantee which the receiver provides to the carrier, assuring the carrier that he will not suffer any financial loss by having released the goods in the absence of a bill of lading. Also referred to as a steamer guarantee.

lex mercatoria – internationally accepted general trade practices; the international, informal law of merchants.

licensing – A contractual arrangement in which the licensor's patents, trademarks, service marks, copyrights, or know-how may be sold or otherwise made available to a licensee for compensation negotiated in advance between the parties. Such compensation may consist of a lump sum royalty, a «running» royalty (based on volume of production), or a combination of both. Licensing enables a firm to enter a foreign market quickly and poses fewer risks than setting up a foreign manufacturing facility. Furthermore, it allows parties to overcome tariff and non-tariff barriers of trade.

l.i.f.o. – In international trade: *liner in free out*, referring to a freight charge which includes the cost of loading in the port of departure but does not include unloading costs in the port of destination. In accounting practice: last in first out.

lighters – Barges used for unloading sea vessels when normal harbour facilities are non-existent or unavailable.

liner shipping – Services provided by a steamship company or shipping line, under which cargo vessels operate according to a fixed schedule and publicly-advertised freight rates.

liner terms – Freight rates which include loading/unloading charges according to the *custom of the respective ports* – which unfortunately varies widely. "Liner terms" is, thus, not yet a standard designation, and *may or may not include* cargo handling charges or the costs of moving cargo between the ship's hold and the quay; traders are therefore well advised to require full details in advance from carriers. The ICC is currently working on establishing a standard liner term.

Lkg. & Bkg. – Leakage and breakage.

LOI – *See* Letter of indemnity.

LTL – Less than truck load.

M marine bill of lading (also, ocean bill of lading) – The classic document of the traditional export trade, it plays three potential roles: 1) as a receipt for the cargo and evidence that the goods have been received in apparent good order, 2) evidence of the terms of the contract of carriage between the shipper and the ocean carrier, and 3) an instrument enabling transfer of control over delivery of the goods ("negotiability"), which allows the holder of the bill to trade the goods in transit by simple endorsement and physical transfer of the bill. *See* Bill of lading, B/L.

marine insurance – Generic term for insurance covering international transport of export transactions; used even in cases where ocean transport is not a predominant leg in the transport chain. Marine insurance can be provided either in terms of a specific *policy* or *ceritificate* (exporters should pay attention to which of the two is required under a documentary credit), or by *open cover,* under which the insurer covers an indefinite number of future shipments; the shipper declares each shipment to the insurer as they are made.

Policy terms:

* *Average* – loss or damage.

* *General average* – loss occurring when extraordinary measures are taken to preserve the safety of the vessel.

* *Particular average* – partial loss or damage; loss to an individual cargo interest rather than entire vessel.

* *With average (WA) or With Particular Average (WPA)* – coverage of partial loss provided the claim amounts to at least 3% of the cargo's insured value.

* *Free of Particular Average (FPA)* – coverage does not include partial loss; a very restrictive form of policy.

* *Free of Particular Average American Conditions (FPAAC)* – coverage only of losses resulting from vessel's sinking, collision, stranding or fire.

* *Free of Particular Average English Conditions (FPAEC)* – coverage only of losses resulting from or connected to a vessel's sinking, collission, stranding or fire.

master document/form – central document in export administrative systems under which all necessary information is entered into a single master document or computer file, which is then used to generate all shipping and export documents. See also Chapter 15 on export software systems; also known *as aligned export documentation systems.*

mate's receipt – A document issued by the carrier to the shipper, indicating receipt of the goods, but not loading on board. Like a B/L, a mate's receipt can be either clean or claused/dirty/foul, depending on whether or not the goods have been received in apparent good condition. The mate's receipt can later be exchanged for the bill of lading.

MO – Money order.

MTO – *see* Multimodal transport operator.

multimodal transport bill of lading – Bill of lading used for carriage whenever there are at least two different forms of transport, such as shipping by rail and by sea. *See* bill of lading.

multimodal transport operator (MTO) – A carrier who concludes multimodal transport contracts; i.e., contracts involving transport by more than one mode of carriage, and for which the MTO accepts liability as a carrier.

M/V – motor vessel

N N/A – Not applicable.

NCND – *See* Non-circumvention non-disclosure agreement; Warning: often contains a false reference to non-existent ICC standard rules.

NCV – No commercial value.

NE (ne) – Not exceeding.

negotiable instrument – A written document that can be used to transfer the rights embodied in it by mere delivery (in the case of instruments made out to bearer) or by indorsement and delivery (in the case of instruments made out to order). Some instruments, such as the bill of exchange and the cheque, are negotiable unless their negotiability is explicitly excluded, while the bill of lading is negotiable only if made negotiable by the shipper.

N/F – No funds

non-circumvention non-disclosure agreements (NCND's) – A type of contract frequently requested by international brokers or middlemen in order to prevent buyers from trying to go around the broker to deal directly with suppliers. Warning: *these agreements are sometimes ERRONEOUSLY said to be issued pursant to ICC Rules – such ICC Rules are NON-EXISTENT: There is no connection between the ICC and these documents.* While the ICC is in fact studying the possibility of issuing a model international brokerage agreement, it will certainly not include the term "non-circumvention non-disclosure" in its title.

non-vessel-operating common carrier (NVOCC) – A company providing point-to-point international transport of goods although it does not necessarily operate or own transport vehicles or equipment. NVOCC's will commonly contract with a shipper to move goods from exporter's premises to importer's premises and will issue their own door-to-door transport document, although they will in fact sub-contract the different stages of the transport chain to various road hauliers and ocean carriers.

nostro account – A bank account held by a bank with its foreign correspondent bank, in the currency of that foreign country.

N/S/F – Not sufficient funds

NVOCC – see Non-vessel-operating common carrier.

O ocean bill of lading – Marine bill of lading.

offset – A type of countertrade transaction. In an offset contract, which may be required by importers' governments as a condition for approval of major sales agreements, the exporter makes an additional agreement to buy goods and services from the importer's country. In a "direct offset" transaction, an exporter may be required to establish manufacturing facilities in the importing country or to use a specified percentage of the components in the product sold from the importer's country. In an indirect offset, an exporter may be obliged to buy goods or services from the importing country without any link to the product sold. *See* countertrade.

O/N – Order notify.

O/o – Order of.

OP – *See* Open policy.

open account trading – The exporter allows the buyer to pay a specified time after receiving the shipment.

open policy (OP) – A type of insurance policy intended to cover an indefinite number of future individual shipments. The insurance contract remains in force until cancelled. Under the open policy, individual successive shipments are periodically reported or declared to the insurer and automatically covered on or after the inception date. Open policies can provide efficiency and savings for all parties concerned, especially when the insured conducts a significant volume of highly-similar transactions.

order bill of lading – A negotiable bill of lading, which is made out to, or to the order of, a particular person and can be transferred by indorsement and delivery of the bill. In practice, the bill is made out either to the shipper's order or to the consignee or his order. *See* bill of lading.

Owner's risk (OR). Also: *O.R.B.* – Owner's risk of breakage; *O.R.F.* – Owner's risk of fire; *O.R.L.* – Owner's risk of loss (or leakage).

pallet – Flat support of wood or steel on which goods can be stacked and which can be easily moved by forklift trucks.

paramount clause – The clause in a bill of lading or charter party invoking coverage by the Hague Rules, Hague-Visby Rules, or by the particular enactment of these rules in the country with jurisdiction over the contract.

P/A – Power of attorney.

PA – Particular average.

PD – Port dues.

PU & D. – *See* Pick up and delivery.

performance bond (guarantee) – A bond or guarantee which has been issued as security for one party's performance: if that party (the principal) fails to perform the beneficiary under the bond/guarantee may obtain payment. A performance bond may be of either the demand or conditional variety, which means that the beneficiary may or may not be required to prove default by the principal in order to obtain payment.

P & I Club (Protection and Indemnity Club) – A shipowners' insurance association.

pick up and delivery (PU & D) – Freight quote includes service of picking cargo up at shipper's premises and delivering it at consignee's premises.

pier-to-pier (quay to quay) – Freight quote which only covers from export pier to import pier (that is, which excludes handling charges to bring cargo to and from piers).

P/N – *see* Promissory note.

POD – Pay on delivery.

ppd. (or P.P.) – Pre-paid.

P **pre-shipment inspection (PSI)** – An inspection of contract goods prior to shipment to ascertain their quality, quantity or price. Importers may insist on PSI, requiring the exporter to furnish a certificate of inspection (commonly, issued by neutral, internationally-respected firms such as SGS or Bureau Veritas), so that the importer is assured of receiving goods of contract quality/quantity. Government agencies may require inspection certificates as regards price, so as to prevent parties from under- or over-invoicing in an attempt to pay lower customs duties or evade foreign-exchange restrictions.

pro forma invoice – A sample invoice provided by an exporter *prior* to a sale or shipment of merchandise, informing the buyer of the price, kinds and quantities of goods to be sent, and important specifications (weight, size, and similar characteristics). The pro forma invoice not only acts as the contractual *offer* (which may be accepted by the importer's transmission of a purchase order), it is intended to be exactly replicated in the final *commercial invoice*, so that the buyer receives no surprises as regards either the goods or the price. Importers may need a pro forma invoice to be able to apply for an import licence or a foreign exchange permit. In the case of a letter of credit, the pro forma invoice is frequently used to inform the importer of the amount for which the letter of credit has to be opened.

promissory note – An unconditional written promise to pay a specified sum of money on demand or at a specified date to, or to the order of, a specified person, or to bearer. Promissory notes are negotiable instruments and perform more or less the same function as an accepted bill of exchange.

PSI – *See* Pre-shipment inspection.

PSV – post-shipment verification; *see* Pre-shipment inspection.

purchasing agent – An agent who purchases goods on behalf of foreign buyers.

R **r & c.c.** – Insurance clause: riots and civil commotion; also: *s.r.c.*c. – strikes, riots and civil commotion.

railway consignment note – A freight document indicating that goods have been received for shipment by rail. *See* bill of lading.

red clause L/C – A letter of credit provision allowing the beneficiary to draw partial advance payments under the credit. This provision used to be set out in red ink, therefore the "red clause" designation. Generally, the beneficiary is only required, in order to receive payment of the authorised advances, to present drafts along with a statement that shipping documents will be provided in due time.

reefer box/container/ship – A refrigerated container or ship. Refrigeration may either be *mechanical*, which means involving an external power supply, or by *expendable refrigerant* (dry ice, liquefied gases, etc.), which requires no external power supply.

remitting bank – In a documentary collection, the bank forwarding the exporter's documents and the draft to, and receiving payments from, the buyer's bank (collecting bank). *See* documentary collection.

retention of title (reservation of title) clause – A contract clause whereby a **R** seller declares his intention to retain title or ownership over the contract goods until payment by the buyer is complete.

roll-on/roll-off (RoRo) –A combination of road and sea transport, where loaded road vehicles are driven on to a ferry or ship (roll-on/roll-off ship) and off at the port of destination. Major benefits of RoRo are reduced handling of the actual goods and packages, competitive costs for unit loads and scheduled services.

ROT – see Retention of title.

S.A. – abbreviation after names of corporations in French and Spanish-speaking **S** countries: Société Anonyme (Fr.); Sociedad Anonima (Sp.).

SAD – Single Administrative Document; European administrative document for intra-European trade.

Surcharge –Charges added to ocean freight, variously, for bunker (fuel), currency fluctuation, congestion, port detention, or extra risk insurance.

SD – *See* Short delivery.

sea waybill – A transport document for maritime shipment, which serves as evidence of the contract of carriage and as a receipt for the goods, but is not a document of title. To take delivery of the goods, presentation of the sea waybill is not required; generally, the receiver is only required to identify himself, which can speed up processing at the port of destination. *See* bill of lading.

shipper – Export trade: The party (as between exporter and importer) who enters into a contract of carriage for the international transport of goods. The party receiving the goods (the importer or buyer) may be called the receiver or the *consignee*. Depending on the Incoterm chosen, either the exporter or importer (or a middleman) can be the shipper.

shipper's load and count (S & C) – A carrier's notation disclaiming responsibility for the quantity of the cargo's contents; the quantity declared is thus purely the shipper's statement. If there is a dispute because less than contract quantity is delivered, the carrier wishes to be free from liability and that the receiver will have to claim directly against the shipper or insurer.

short delivery (SD) also, short-landed cargo – Non-delivery of cargo at the intended port. When reported, will result in ship's agent sending a *cargo tracer* to see if the cargo has been mis-delivered in another port.

short-form bill of lading (B/L) – A simplified B/L which contains a reference to or an abbreviation of the carrier's full B/L or carriage conditions.

sight draft (sight bill) – A financial instrument payable upon presentation or demand. It must be presented for payment by its holder (payee, indorsee, or bearer) within reasonable time. *See* draft.

S & C. – See Shipper's load and count.

S & T. – Shipper's load and tally; *see* Shipper's load and count.

S/N – *See* Shipping note.

S **specific duty** – A duty based on some measure of quantity, such as weight, length, or number of units. *See* customs duty.

spot rate – Rate of exchange quoted for purchases and sales of a foreign currency for immediate delivery and payment.

standby credit (also, standby letter of credit, standby L/C) – A form of guarantee, usually indistinguishable from the demand guarantee. Origin lies in the fact that American legislation prevented American banks from directly issuing guarantees, so they resorted to the device of the "standby credit". In function the standby is usually used more as a security device, like a bank guarantee, than as a payment device, like a documentary credit. Under a standby credit the beneficiary usually obtains payment by presentation to a bank of a draft and some form of written demand, which may include a statement that the principal is in breach of his contractual obligations. Standby credits may be issued so as to be governed by either the UCP 500 or the URDG 458 (to the extent permitted by national law). A standby credit can be used to back up a payment commitment – thus, an exporter may agree to sell on open account terms, granting the importer 90-day credit terms, on the condition that the importer open a standby credit in the exporter's favour; if the importer fails to honour the exporter's invoices, the exporter simply draws against the standby.

steamer guarantee – *See* letter of indemnity.

STC (said to contain) / **STW** (said to weigh) – Notations on transport documents by which carriers give notice that they do not wish to accept responsibility for the accuracy of a shipper's declarations as to the content, weight or quantity of a particular shipment. see also, Shipper's load and count.

straight bill of lading – A non-negotiable bill of lading, which specifies the consignee to whom the goods are to be delivered. The carrier is contractually obliged to to deliver the goods to that person only. It is often used when payment for the goods has been made in advance. *See* bill of lading.

stripping – Unloading goods from a container; *see* also Devanning, Destuffing

stowage – The placing of cargo in a ship's hold in such a fashion as to assure safe and stable transport.

stuffing – Loading goods inside a container.

surety/surety-ship bond/guarantee – A surety bond is a guarantee, usually issued by an insurance or surety company, that a particular company will perform according to a contract. In order to collect payment under such a bond, the beneficiary normally must *prove* actual default on the part of the counterparty, as by furnishing a court judgement, arbitral award or official certificate. Suretyship bonds may be issued subject to the *ICC Uniform Rules for Contract Bonds.*

swap – The trading of almost identical products (such as oil) from different locations to save transportation costs. *See* countertrade.

SWIFT payment – International electronic funds transfer via the system known as SWIFT (Society for Worldwide Inter-bank Financial Telecommunications), offered by most major banks.

tare – Weight of packaging/container, without merchandise.

tender bond/guarantee – A guarantee provided by a company responding to an international invitation to submit bids or tenders (as for a large construction project); the tender bond is submitted along with the tender; the tender bond is required with the purpose of discouraging frivolous bids and ensuring that the winning bidder will actually sign and execute the contract.

Terminal handling charge (THC) – Handling charges assessed for services rendered within container terminals or with respect to containers which will be processed through terminals. When delivery or pickup of the goods is expected to be at a container terminal, traders are well-advised to stipulate precisely which party will pay for all or part of the terminal handling charges.

TEU – Twenty-foot equivalent units; a means of measuring the carrying capacity of container ships; e.g., a ship can be said to be capable of 3000 TEU's, which is roughly equivalent to saying it could carry 3000 standard containers.

THC – *See* Terminal handling charge.

through bill of lading – A B/L issued to cover transport by at least two successive modes of transport.

time draft (time bill) – A financial instrument demanding payment at a future fixed date, or a specified period of time after sight (30, 60, 90 days etc.), or after the date of issue. It is also called a usance draft (usance bill). *See* Draft.

TIR – *TIR Carnets* are transport documents used to cover international transport shipments on road vehicles such as trucks/lorries. TIR Carnets, issued pursuant to the 1949 *TIR Convention*, allow the truck or other vehicle to pass through all TIR-member countries without having to go through customs inspection until reaching the country of destination.

T/L – Total loss.

trade acceptance – A bill of exchange drawn by the seller/exporter on the purchaser/importer of goods sold, and accepted by such purchaser. *See* bill of exchange.

tramp vessel – A "freelance" seagoing cargo vessel, available on a contract basis to carry cargoes to any given port. To be distinguished from liner ships, operating according to advertised routes, schedules and rates.

trimming – The operation of shovelling and spreading, within the ship's hold, dry bulk cargoes such as cement, ore or grains, so as to avoid weight imbalances which might hinder the ship's handling or unloading.

UCC – (US) Uniform Commercial Code, the codification of American commercial law, followed in substantially uniform fashion by the US states. Article 5 of the UCC deals with letters of credit.

UCP 500 – *Uniform Customs and Practice for Documentary Credits*, ICC Publication N°500, the set of rules which govern international documentary credit practice. UCP 500 are generally considered contractually incorporated into the documentary credit transaction by virtue of a mention in the credit application form; the UCP 500 may also have additional force as a trade custom, and in some countries UCP are even recognised as having legal effect generally. In other countries, the UCP 500 is complementary to national law and jurisprudence on documentary credits.

U **UNCITRAL** – United Nations Commission on International Trade Law – UN Agency based in Vienna, specializing in the development of model legal instruments and conventions in the area of international trade law. Most notable success is perhaps the so-called 1980 *Vienna Convention, the Convention on the International Sale of Goods ("CISG")*. Also, *UNCITRAL Rules for Arbitration*, which provide a procedural framework for international commercial arbitration but which, unlike the ICC Rules, do not provide direct administrative supervision of the arbitral process.

UNCTAD – United Nations Commission for Trade and Development – UN Agency based in Geneva, which has developed numerous international instruments as regards trade with developing or transition economies. Notably, UNCTAD houses the ITC (International Trade Centre), a developer of useful guides and manuals for small to medium-sized exporters.

Unfair calling insurance – Insurance coverage to protect principals who have issued demand guarantees or bonds against an unfair or abusive call of the bond/ guarantee (i.e., one which is not truly based on non-performance by the principal).

Unidroit – Institute for the Unification of Private Law – International governmental organisation headquartered in Rome. Administrative organisation of treaties, conventions, model instruments, and legal guides and research.

usance draft (usance bill) – Time draft; a written demand for payment which comes due at a specified future date.

V **VAT** – Value-added tax.

Vienna Convention – *1980 Vienna Convention on the International Sale of Goods*. International treaty signed by approximately 45 nations, including most leading trading nations. Amounts to a virtual commercial code for international sales transactions, but excludes contracts for services, securities, electricity, and some others; parties may be able to "opt out" of coverage by the Vienna Convention by explicitly stating so in the contract of sale.

vostro account – An account held by a bank with its foreign correspondent bank, in the currency of the bank's domestic country.

W **W** – tonne of one thousand kilogrammes.

WA – *See* With average.

waybill (WB) – A non-negotiable transport document, issued for either ocean transport (sea waybill) or air transport (air waybill).

warehouse-to-warehouse clause – Insurance coverage of international cargo from export warehouse to import warehouse; coverage may also be substantially extended or limited according to time.

wharfage (WFG) – Charge for the use of docks.

wharfinger – (also Wharf inspector, Wharf superintendent, Dock superintendent) **W**
Personnel in charge of receiving and registering goods in a port on behalf of the
carrier. Wharfinger's signature of the *shipping note* assures the shipper that it
can proceed to draw up bills of lading pursuant to the terms of the note.

With Average (WA) – Marine insurance term meaning that coverage includes
partial loss (and not just total loss) of the cargo. *See* marine insurance.

WP (w/o p) – Without prejudice.

WPA – With particular average; see marine insurance.

Warehouse receipt (WR) – A document issued by a warehouse operator
acknowledging receipt of goods; also referred to as a *dock warrant* or shed
receipt. A *warehouse warrant*, in contrast, generally connotes a document of
ownership/control over goods stored in a particular warehouse.

Worldscale – A scale for quoting freight rates for oil tankers.

World Wide Web (WWW; the Web) – A graphics standard which has become
a virtual subset of the Internet; organisations, universities and companies maintain
presences on the Web via "home pages", which are much like animated telephone-
book advertisements; the information on the home page may be highlighted
(hypertext) in which case the viewer may click on the particular text to obtain
access to another data base, home page, or further information.

WTDR – A US government credit report on a foreign firm.

References

general / introductory

A BASIC GUIDE TO EXPORTING compiled by US Department of Commerce, 1991 NTC Business Books, 4255 West Touhy Avenue, Lincolnwood, Illinois 60645, USA

BUILD UP YOUR EXPORTS – MAURICE WRIGHT, 1995 Tate Publishing Ltd., Waybill House, 1 Fitzhamon Court, Wolverton Mill, Milton Keynes MK12 6BA, UK

THE DO'S AND TABOOS OF INTERNATIONAL TRADE: SMALL BUSINESS PRIMER – ROGER E. AXTELL, 1989 John Wiley & Sons, 7222 Commerce Center Drive, Suite 240, Colorado Springs, CO 80919, USA

DICTIONARY OF INTERNATIONAL TRADE 4,071 INTERNATIONAL TRADE, ECONOMIC, BANKING, LEGAL & SHIPPING TERMS – EDWARD G. HINKELMAN, Copyright 1994 World Trade Press, 1505 Fifth Avenue San Rafael, California 94901 USA

ELEMENTS OF EXPORT MARKETING AND MANAGEMENT – ALAN E. BRANCH, 1984 Chapman and Hall Ltd 11 New Fetter Lane, London EC4P 4EE / Chapman and Hall 733 Third Avenue, New York NY10017, USA

EXPORT DOCUMENTATION, PROCEDURES AND TERMS OF SALE – FRANK REYNOLDS, 1996 2nd edition, Unz & Co., Inc., 700 Central Avenue, New Providence, NJ 07974 USA

THE EXPORT HANDBOOK, A COMPLETE GUIDE & REFERENCE SOURCE FOR INTERNATIONAL TRADERS – LONDON CHAMBER OF COMMERCE & INDUSTRY, 1996, Kogan Page Ltd, 120 Pentonville Road, London N1 9JN, UK

IMPORT/EXPORT, HOW TO GET STARTED IN INTERNATIONAL TRADE, SECOND EDITION – CARL A. NELSON, McGraw Hill, Inc.

IMPORTING FOR THE SMALL BUSINESS – MAG MORRIS, Rvd. 2nd edition 1991 Kogan Page Ltd 120 Pentonville Road London N1 9JN, UK

INTERNATIONAL BUSINESS INTRODUCTION AND ESSENTIALS – DONALD A. BALL & WENDELL H. McCULLOCH JR., 1985 2nd edition Business Publications Inc. Plano, Texas 75075 USA*

RECOMMENDATIONS AND GUIDELINES FOR TRADE EFFICIENCY – United Nations International Symposium on Trade Efficiency, 1994 United Nations New York & Geneva

SMALL AND MEDIUM-SIZED TRANSNATIONAL CORPORATIONS: ROLE, IMPACT AND POLICY IMPLICATIONS – 1993 United Nations, New York, USA

INTERNATIONAL BUSINESS TRANSACTIONS IN A NUTSHELL – DONALD WILSON, 1983 Nutshell Series West Publishing Company, P.O. Box 3526 St. Paul, Minnesota 55165 USA

French:

COMMENT NÉGOCIER LES ACHATS ET LES VENTES À L'ETRANGER 2ÈME EDITION – NICOLE FERRY, 1988 Editions du Moniteur, Paris, France

COMMERCE INTERNATIONAL – ANDRÉ GUYOMAR & ETIENNE MORIN, seconde édition 1995 Editions Dalloz, 11, rue Soufflot, 75240 Paris Cedex 05, France

EXPORTER, PRATIQUE DU COMMERCE INTERNATIONAL 9EME EDITION – BARRELIER, DUBOIN, DUPHIL, CONTAL, GRATALOUP, KUHN, LEVY, PAVEAU, SARHAN, 1992 Editions Foucher, France

marketing and management

ELEMENTS OF EXPORT MARKETING AND MANAGEMENT – ALAN E. BRANCH, 1984 Chapman & Hall, 733 Third Ave., NY, NY 10017, USA

EXPORT MARKETING STRATEGIES AND PLANS, A CASE BOOK FOR TRAINERS – 1992 International Trade Centre UNCTAD/GATT, Geneva, Switzerland

THE ESSENCE OF INTERNATIONAL MARKETING – STANLEY PALIWODA, Prentice Hall, Englewood Cliffs, New Jersey 07632, USA

FUNDAMENTALS OF INTERNATIONAL BUSINESS MANAGEMENT – STEVEN GLOBERMAN, 1986 Prentice Hall, Englewood Cliffs, New Jersey 07632, USA

Spanish:

PROYECTOS DE EXPORTACION Y ESTRATEGIAS DE MARKETING INTERNACIONAL – OEA, CICOM, 1993 Ediciones MACCHI, Buenos Aires, Argentina

legal aspects

COMMERCIAL LAW, SECOND EDITION – ROY GOODE, 1995 Penguin Books, 27 Wrights Lane, London W8 5TZ, UK

ELEMENTS OF EXPORT LAW – GEOFFREY WHITEHEAD, "Elements of Overseas Trade Series", 1983 Woodhead Faulkner Ltd., 17 Market Street, Cambridge CB2 3PA, UK

INTERNATIONAL BUSINESS LAW – TEXT, CASES, AND READINGS – RAY AUGUST, 1993 Prentice Hall, Inc. Englewood Cliffs, NJ 07632, USA

INTERNATIONAL BUSINESS TRANSACTIONS – D. CAMPBELL, REINHARD PROKSCH, Kluwer, Farrington Loose Leaf, Co. NY, NY 10016, USA

INTERNATIONAL COMMERCIAL AGREEMENTS : A PRIMER ON DRAFTING, NEGOTIATING AND RESOLVING DISPUTES – WILLIAM F. FOX, 2nd Editions 1992 Kluwer Law International, Carnegieplein 5D, 2508CN The Hague, Netherlands

INTERNATIONAL CONTRACT MANUAL – EDITED BY ALBERT H. KRITZER, Kluwer, Farrington Loose Leaf, Co. New York, NY 10016, USA

INTERNATIONAL EXPORTING AGREEMENTS – SHAUL I. EZER, Matthew Bender Times Mirror Books 1992

INTERNATIONAL PRIVATE TRADE – ANDREAS F. LOWENFELD, 1981 Second Edition, Matthew Bender, 235 E. 45th Street, New York, NY 10017, USA

INTERNATIONAL SALES: THE UNITED NATIONS CONVENTIONS ON CONTRACTS FOR THE INTERNATIONAL SALES OF GOODS – NINA M. GALSTON & HANS SMIT, Matthew Bender, 235 E. 45th St., NY, NY 10017, USA

I. Mech. E./I.E.E. Conditions of Contracts – Andrew Pike, 1984 London Sweet & Maxwell, 100 Avenue Road, London NW3 3PF, UK

Law of International Trade – Hans Van Houtte, 1995 London Sweet & Maxwell, 100 Avenue Road, London NW3 3PF, UK

Sale of Goods Carried by Sea – Charles Debattista, 1990 Butterworths, Halsbury House, 35 Chancery Lane, London WC2A 1EL, UK

Schmitthoff's Export Trade The Law & Practice of International Trade – Clive M. Schmitthoff, 9th edition 1990 Stevens & Sons Ltd part of Sweet & Maxwell Ltd, 100 Avenue Road, London NW3 3PF, UK

Principles of International Commercial Contracts – UNIDROIT 1994 International Institute for the Unification of Private Law, Via Panisperna 28, Rome 00184, Italy

French:

Les Ventes Internationales et Les Transports – Jacques Putzeys, Les Nouveaux Incoterms, 1992 Maison du Droit de Louvain, France

Spanish:

Negociacion y Contratacion Internacional – Juan Luis Colaiacovo, OEA, CICOM, 1992 Ediciones MACCHI, Buenos Aires, Argentina

arbitration

International Chamber of Commerce Arbitration – Laurence W. Craig, William Park, Jan Paulsson 2nd edition 1990 Oceana Publications Inc. New York, London & ICC Publishing S.A. Paris, 38 Cours Albert 1er, 75008, Paris, France

agency, distributorship, franchising, licensing

Commercial Agency and Distribution Agreements: Law and Practice in the Member States of the European Community and the European Free Trade Association – Geert Bogaert & Ulrich Lohmann, 2nd edition AIJA Law Library 1993 Graham & Trotman Ltd, Sterling House, 66 Wilton Road, London SW1V 1DE, UK

The ICC Agency Model Contract, A Commentary – F. Bortolotti, D. Ferrier, O. Lando, D. MAtray, K.M. Swantee, V. Roberts, 1993 Kluwer Law International, Carnegieplein 5D, 2508CN The Hague, Netherlands

International Agency, Distribution and Licensing Agreements Third Edition – Richard Christou, 1996 FT Law & Tax, 21-27 Lamb's Conduit Street, London WC1N 3NJ, UK

Establishing a Transnational Franchise, International Business Portfolios – Joseph Pattison, 1988 Edited by Matthew Bender

International Franchising: an In-depth Treatment of Business and Legal Techniques – Edited by Yanos Gramatidis & Dennis Campbell, 1991 Kluwer Law International, Carnegieplein 5D, 2508CN The Hague, Netherlands

LICENSING, A STRATEGY FOR PROFITS – EDWARD P. WHITE, 1990 KEW Licensing Press, 907 Linden Rd., Chapel Hill, NC 27514-9162, USA

trade finance / documentary credits

BILLS OF EXCHANGE AND OTHER NEGOTIABLE INSTRUMENTS: A HANDBOOK OF EFFECTIVE PRACTICE – PAUL H. SHOVLIN, Woodhead-Faulkner Ltd 1988, Cambridge, UK

BILLS OF EXCHANGE: A GUIDE TO LEGISLATION IN EUROPEAN COUNTRIES – UWE JAHN, First Edition ICC Publication No 476 1990, Second Edition ICC Publication N°531 1995, ICC Publishing S.A., 38 Cours Albert 1er, 75008 Paris, France

BILLS OF LADING AND BANKERS' DOCUMENTARY CREDITS – PAUL TODD, 1990 Lloyds of London Press, Sheepen Place, Colchester, Essex CO3 3LP, UK

CURRENT PROBLEMS OF INTERNATIONAL TRADE FINANCING – EDITED BY PENG KEE HO & CHAN HELENA HM, 2nd edition Singapore Conferences on International Business Law, Faculty of Law National University of Singapore 1990, Butterworths, Halsbury House, 35 Chancery Lane, London WC2A 1EL, UK

FINANCE OF INTERNATIONAL TRADE, 5TH EDITION – ALASDAIR WATSON, 1994 Bankers Books Limited, c/o The Chartered Institute of Bankers, 10 Lombard Street, London EC3V 9AS, UK

FINANCE OF INTERNATIONAL TRADE – 6th edition 1990 written by technical officers of International Banking Division, National Australia Bank Ltd

THE FUNDAMENTALS OF TRADE FINANCE, THE INS AND OUTS OF IMPORT-EXPORT FINANCING – JANE KINGMAN-BRUNDAGE & SUSAN A. SCHULZ, 1986 John Wiley & Sons Inc., 7222 Commerce Center Drive, Colorado Springs, CO 80919, USA

GUIDE TO INTERNATIONAL TRADE FINANCE SERVICES, 1995 Deutsche Bank AG London, 6–8 Bishopsgate, London EC29 2AT, UK

THE HANDBOOK OF INTERNATIONAL TRADE FINANCE – EDITED BY CAMPBELL DUNFORD, 1991 Woodhead-Faulkner Ltd, Cambridge, UK

THE LAW OF INTERNATIONAL TRADE FINANCE VOL. 6 – EDITED BY HORN NORBERT, Studies in Transnational Economic Law 1989 Kluwer Law International, Carnegieplein 5D, 2508CN The Hague, Netherlands

THE LAW OF LETTERS OF CREDIT, COMMERCIAL AND STANDBY CREDITS – JOHN F. DOLAN, Second Edition 1991 Warren Gorham & Lamont, Inc., 210 South Street, Boston, MA 02111, USA

A PRACTICAL GUIDE TO LETTERS OF CREDIT – CHARLES E. ASTER & KATHERYN C. PATTERSON, 1990 Executive Enterprises Publications Co. Inc.

PROJECT AND TRADE FINANCE 1995 HANDBOOK – West Merchant Bank, Euromoney Publications plc, Nestor House, Playhouse Yard, London EC4V 5EX, UK

THE TIMES GUIDE TO INTERNATIONAL FINANCE, HOW THE WORLD MONEY SYSTEM WORKS – MARGARET ALLEN, Times Books, 1991 HarperCollins Publishers, 77-85 Fulham Palace Road, Hammersmith, London W6 8JB, UK

TRADE AND PROJECT FINANCE IN EMERGING MARKETS – MICHAEL ROWE, Euromoney Publications, Nestor House, Playhouse Yard, London ECV4 5EX, UK

UCP 500: GUIDE – ABDUL LATIFF ABDUL RAHIM, 1994 Institute of Bankers Malaysia, 5 Jalan Semantan, Damansara Heights PO Box 11857, 50760 Kuala Lumpur, Malaysia

UNDERSTANDING DOCUMENTARY BILLS AND CREDITS, A PRACTICAL GUIDE FOR EXPORTERS, IMPORTERS, FORWARDERS AND BANKERS – Frank Dow, 1990 Croner Publications Ltd, Croner House, London Rd, Kingston Upon Thames, Surrey KT2 6SR, UK

French:

GESTION DU CREDIT COMMERCIAL À L'EXPORTATION – JACQUES LARDINOIS, 1993 Formatick, TED & DOC Lavoisier, 11 rue Lavoisier, Paris, France

LE CRÉDIT DOCUMENTAIRE ET AUTRES SECURITES DE PAIEMENT – DENIS CHEVALIER, Collection Defi Export, Editions Foucher, France

countertrade

COUNTERTRADE – MICHAEL ROWE, Euromoney Books 1989, Nestor House, Playhouse Yard, London EC4V 5EX, UK

THE COUNTERTRADE HANDBOOK, A PRACTICAL GUIDE TO TECHNIQUES AND OPPORTUNITIES IN WORLD MARKETS – DICK FRANCIS, Woodhead Faulkner Ltd, Cambridge, UK

PRACTICAL GUIDE TO COUNTERTRADE – Edited by Peter Harben & Thierry Cooke, Metal Bulletin Inc. Publications, 708 3rd Ave., NY, NY 10017, USA

guarantees, bonds and standby credits

BANK GUARANTEES IN INTERNATIONAL TRADE, FIRST EDITION – BERTRAMS R.I.V.F. Kluwer Law International 1990, Carnegieplein 5D, 2508CN The Hague, Netherlands

BANK GUARANTEES IN INTERNATIONAL TRADE, SECOND EDITION – BERTRAMS R.I.V.F. Kluwer Law International/ICC Publishing S.A. 1995

DEMAND GUARANTEES IN INTERNATIONAL TRADE – ANTHONY PIERCE, 1993 London Sweet & Maxwell, 100 Avenue Road, London NW3 3PF, UK

STANDBY LETTERS OF CREDIT – BROOKE & DIANE WUNNICKE, 1989 John Wiley & Sons, 7222 Commerce Center Drive, Suite 240, Colorado Springs, CO 80919, USA

STANDBY AND COMMERCIAL LETTERS OF CREDIT, SECOND EDITION – BROOKE WUNNICKE, DIANE WUNNICKE & PAUL. S. TURNER, 1996 John Wiley & Sons, 7222 Commerce Center Drive, Suite 240, Colorado Springs, CO 80919, USA

Incoterms

C.I.F. & F.O.B. CONTRACTS– DAVID M. SASOON, 1995 Fourth Edition, London Sweet & Maxwell, 100 Avenue Road, London NW3 3PF, UK

INCOTERMS FOR AMERICANS: SIMPLIFIES AND ANSWERS QUESTIONS ABOUT INCOTERMS, FOR U.S. FOREIGN TRADERS – FRANK REYNOLDS, 1993 International Projects, Inc.

TRADE TERMS AND MARINE CARGO INSURANCE – DR. GERHARD LUTTMER & KLAUS WINKLER, 2nd edition 1991, Gerling-Konzern

shipping and transport

CARRIAGE OF GOODS BY SEA, 13TH EDITION – E R HARDY IVAMY, 1989 Butterworths, Halsbury House, 35 Chancery Lane, London WC2A 1AL, UK

INTERMODALITY: CONCEPT AND PRACTICE – HAYUTH YEHUDA, 1987 Lloyd's of London Press Ltd, Sheepen Place, Colchester, Essex, CO3 3LP, UK

THE LAW OF FREIGHT FORWARDING AND THE 1992 FIATA MULTIMODAL TRANSPORT BILL OF LADING – JAN RAMBERG, International Federation of Freight Forwarders Association (FIATA)

LEGAL HANDBOOK ON FORWARDING – PETER JONES, 2nd edition 1993, Co-published by International Federation of Freight Forwarders Associations (FIATA)

MANUAL ON THE PHYSICAL DISTRIBUTION OF EXPORT GOODS VOLUME II – 1988 International Trade Centre UNCTAD/GATT Geneva

MARITIME JOINT VENTURES – EDITED BY ABHYANKAR JAYANT & S.I. BIJWADIA, ICC Publication No 527 – 1994 ICC Publishing, 38, Cours Albert 1er 75008, Paris, France

PROFESSIONAL EDUCATION COURSE VOLUME 1 – 1991 Canadian International Freight Forwarders Association

CUSTOMS CLEARANCE MANUAL (FCCM) – FIATA, Baumackerstrasse 24, PO Box 177, Zürich CH8050, Switzerland

French:

LE TRANSPORT – D. CHEVALIER & F. DUPHIL, CFCE, 1991 Les Editions Foucher, 128 rue de Rivoli, 75038 Paris Cedex 1, France

export forms

EXPORT FORMS, SITPRO, 2a Glasshouse Street, London W1R 5RG, UK

EXPORT FORMS, Unz & Co., Inc., 700 Central Avenue, New Providence, New Jersey USA, fax +1 (908) 665 7866

electronic commerce

MARKETING ON THE INTERNET, MULTIMEDIA STRATEGIES FOR THE WORLDWIDE WEB – JILL & MATTHEW ELLSWORTH, 1995 John Wiley & Sons, Inc., 7222 Commerce Center Drive, Suite 240, Colorado Springs, CO 80919, USA

INTERNATIONAL ORGANISATIONS

BIC – International Containers Bureau
14 rue jean Rey
75015 Paris
France
tel   +33 (1) 42 73 01 40

BIMCO – Baltic and International Maritime Council
19 Krtianiagade
DK 2100 Copenahagen
Denmark
tel   +45 (1) 26 30 00
fax   +45 (1) 26 33 35

FIATA – International Federation of Freight Forwarders Associations
Baumackerstrasse 24, PO Box 177
CH 8050 Zurich
Switzerland
tel   +41 (1) 311 65 11

Hague Conference on Private International Law
6 Scheveningsweg
2517 KT The Hague
Netherlands
tel   +31 (70) 363 33 03
fax   +31 (70) 360 48 67

IAPH – International Association of Ports and Harbours
Kotokira, Kaikain Building, 2-8 Toranomon
1 Chome, Minato-ku
Tokyo 105, Japan
tel   +81 (35) 91 42 61
fax   +81 (35) 80 03 64

International Air Transport Association (I.A.T.A.)
I.A.T.A. Centre
Route de l'Aéroport 33, PO Box 672
CH1215 Genève 15 Airport
Switzerland
tel   +41 (22) 799 2953
fax   +41 (22) 799 2685

International Bar Association
2 Harewood Place
Hanover Square
London W1R 9HB, UK
tel   +44 (171) 629 1206
fax   +44 (171) 409 0456

(ICS) International Chamber of Shipping
30-32 St. Mary Axe.,
London EC3A 8ET, UK
tel   +44 (171) 283 29 22

International Civil Aviation Organization (I.C.A.O.)
999 University Street
Montréal, Québec
Canada H3C 5H7
tel   +1 (514) 954 8036
fax   +1 -514) 954 6077

International Financial Statistics
International Monetary Fund
Publications Unit
700 19th Street, NW
Washington, DC 20431

IMO (International Maritime Organisation)
4, Albert Embankment
London SE1 7SR, UK
tel   +44 (171) 735 76 11

International Trade Centre
UNCTAD (UN Commission on Trade and Development)
Palais des Nations
1211 Geneva 10
Switzerland

(IRU) International Road Union
Centre international, BP 44
3, rue de Varembé
CH 1211 Geneva 20, Switzerland
tel   +41 (22) 34 13 30

UNCITRAL (UN Commission on International Trade Law)
Vienna International Centre
PO Box 500
A 1400 Vienna, Austria
tel   +43 (1) 26 31 40 60

UNIDROIT
28 Via Panisperna
Rome, Italy 00184 - tel   +39 (6) 684 1372

World Customs Organisation
Rue de l'Industrie, 26-38
B-1040 Brussels, Belgium
tel   +32 (2) 508 4211

The ICC at a glance

The ICC is the world business organisation. It is the only representative body that speaks with authority on behalf of enterprises from all sectors in every part of the world.

The ICC's purpose is to promote an open international trade and investment system and the market economy worldwide. It makes rules that govern the conduct of business across borders. It provides essential services, foremost among them the ICC International Court of Arbitration, the world's leading institution of its kind.

Within a year of the creation of the United Nations, the ICC was granted consultative status at the highest level with the UN and its specialized agencies. Today the ICC is the preferred partner of international and regional organizations, such as the World Trade Organization, whenever decisions have to be made on global issues of importance to business.

Business leaders and experts drawn from the ICC membership establish the business stance on broad issues of trade and investment policy as well as on vital technical or sectorial subjects. These include competition law, the environment, financial services, information technologies, intellectual property, marketing ethics, taxation, telecommunications and transportation, among others.

The ICC was founded in 1919 by a handful of far-sighted business leaders. Today it groups thousands of member companies and associations from over 130 countries. National committees in all major capitals coordinate with their membership to address the concerns of the business community and to put across to their governments the business views formulated by the ICC.

Some ICC Services

The ICC International Court of Arbitration (Paris)

The ICC International Centre for Expertise (Paris)

The ICC International Bureau of Chambers of Commerce - IBCC (Paris)

The ICC Institute of International Business Law and Practice (Paris)

The ICC Centre for Maritime Co-operation (London)

ICC Commercial Crime Services (London), grouping:

The ICC Counterfeiting Intelligence Bureau

The ICC Commercial Crime Bureau

The ICC International Maritime Bureau

Selected ICC Publications

NEW INCOTERMS 1990 SOFTWARE

An electronic guide to *Incoterms 1990* geared to give the user instant access to Incoterms through easy-to-understand graphical and textual presentations. The interactive Incoterms 1990 offers you features you will not find in any written publication: quick access, a simultaneous look at several related questions concerning Incoterms, and an ability to evaluate your performance as you go along. It is particularly suited to anyone who needs a detailed knowledge of *Incoterms 1990*: students of international trade, import-export professionals, lawyers and university lecturers.

E   ISBN 92-842-1229-4   N°470

MANAGING FOREIGN EXCHANGE RISKS

This book sets out a simple model showing the stages that a company needs to work through to establish a foreign exchange policy; it emphasises the need for rigour and discipline in the management of exchange rates and the importance of identifying the company's exposures properly and comprehensively; it examines a number of hedging techniques critically but fairly.

E   ISBN 92-842-1202-3   N° 549

ICC GUIDE TO COLLECTION OPERATIONS

The essential guide to the URC 522's 1995 revision, this publication provides a basic introduction to the operation of collections as part of international trade. It explains the part played by banks in collection operations, provides a background to the changes made in the revision and examines some of the issues relating to collections. An accessible guide for bankers, traders and all beginners in the collections process.

E   ISBN 92-842-1214-6   N° 561

THE ICC AGENCY MODEL CONTRACT: A COMMENTARY

A co-publication ICC Publishing/Kluwer International

A clause-by-clause commentary by the experts who wrote the *ICC Model Commercial Agency Contract* (N°496). It provides extensive illustrations of the clauses of the contract and gives lawyers and businesspeople a comprehensive explanation of the problems encountered by those who negotiate commercial agency agreements. The Commentary enriches the original text and provides new insights into the drafting process. In addition, it also includes two disks (Apple and MS DOS) with English, French, German and Italian versions of the Contract. This added feature is a useful tool for drafting agency agreements in several languages.

E   ISBN 92-842-1146-8   N° 512

THE ICC MODEL DISTRIBUTORSHIP CONTRACT (SOLE IMPORTER-DISTRIBUTOR)

In this model form, the ICC provides a set of uniform contractual rules for those distributorship agreements where distributors act as buyers-resellers and as importers who organise distribution in the country for which they are responsible. Containing flexible and general rules, the contract can also be employed on its own as a ready-to-use balanced model form if the parties are not in a position to prepare a specific contract.

E-F   ISBN 92-842-1153-0   N°518

INCOTERMS 1990

When drafting their contracts, buyers and sellers can be sure of defining their responsibilities simply and safely by referring to one of the ICC *Incoterms*. In so doing they eliminate any possibility of misunderstanding and subsequent dispute. Traders, lawyers, insurers and bankers will all find *Incoterms 1990* both easy to use and easy to understand.

EF   214 pages   ISBN 92-842-0087-3   N° 460

GUIDE TO INCOTERMS 1990

Organised with the user in mind, the *Guide to Incoterms* takes the basic text of *Incoterms 1990* and explains how each of the terms is used in practice. It has an expanded introduction placing *Incoterms 1990* in the context of previous versions of Incoterms. Subsequent chapters take the user through Incoterms and the contract of sale; the elements of E-, F-, C- and D-terms; an overview of the buyer's and seller's obligations and a section-by-section analysis of each of the 13 Incoterms.

Crisply written, coherent and easy to follow, this is the only official guide to *Incoterms 1990*, developed under the auspices of the ICC.

E-F   152 pages   ISBN 92-842-1088-7   N° 461/90

INCOTERMS IN PRACTICE

This useful complement to *Incoterms 1990* and the *Guide to Incoterms 1990* contains ten highly useful chapters drafted by experts and professionals in the field examining the impact of technology and changing market practices on the commercial application of Incoterms. The book covers the topics of Incoterms and the contract of carriage, Incoterms, EDI and electronic messaging, Incoterms and insurance and Incoterms and the UCP 500. A must for all players in international trade.

E   184 pages   ISBN 92-842-1186-7   N°505

ICC GUIDE TO DOCUMENTARY CREDIT OPERATIONS UNDER UCP500

by Charles del Busto

A unique combination of charts and sample documents which illustrate the Documentary Credit process from the time of the Credit application through the issuing process and concluding with the means of settlement. Using concrete examples of how the Documentary Credit process works in practice with specific references to the *Uniform Customs and Practice for Documentary Credits* (UCP 500), this guide provides an indispensable tool for import/export traders, bankers, training services, and anyone involved in day-to-day credit operations.

E-F   112 pages   ISBN 92-842-1159-X   N° 515

HOW TO OBTAIN ICC PUBLICATIONS

ICC Publications are available from ICC National Committees or Councils which exist in some 60 countries or from:

ICC PUBLISHING S.A.
38, Cours Albert 1er
75008 Paris (France)
Customer Service:
 +33 (1) 49.53.29.23/56
Fax: +33 (1) 49.53.29.02
E-mail: pub@iccwbo.org

ICC PUBLISHING, INC.
156 Fifth Avenue, Suite 308
New York, N.Y. 10010
USA
 +1 (212) 206 1150
Telefax +1 (212) 633 6025
E-mail: iccpub@interport.net